Please remember that this is a library book,
and that it belongs only temporarily to each
person who uses it. Be considerate. Do
not write in this, or any, library book.

THE STONES OF TIME

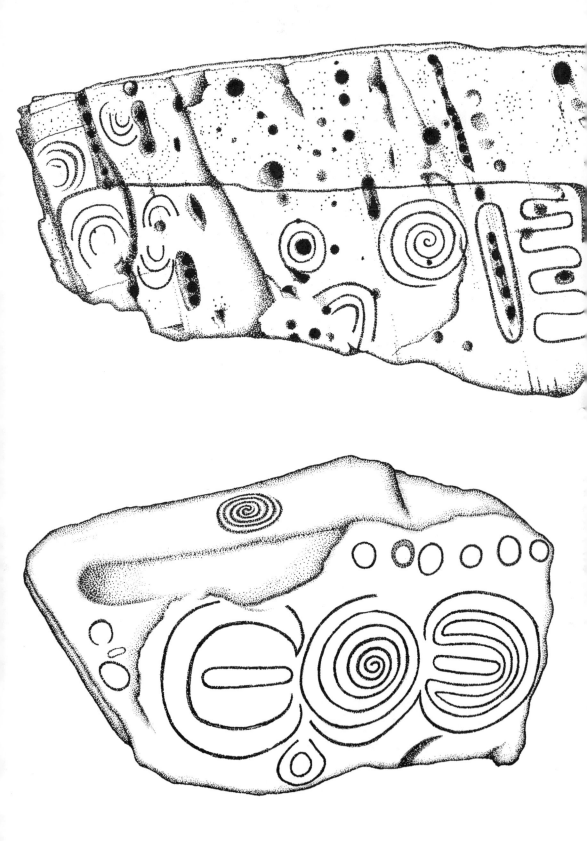

THE STONES OF TIME

Calendars, Sundials, and Stone Chambers of Ancient Ireland

MARTIN BRENNAN

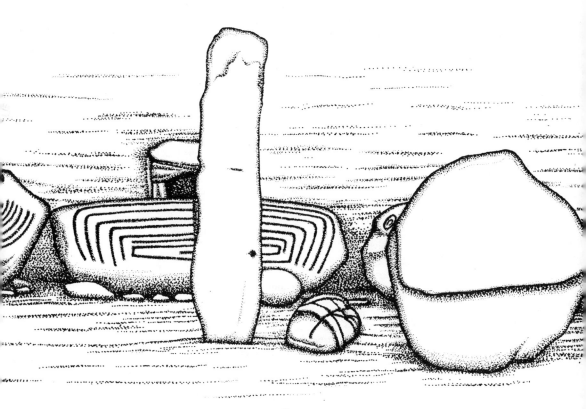

Inner Traditions International
Rochester, Vermont

Inner Traditions International
One Park Street
Rochester, Vermont 05767

First U.S. edition published in 1994 by Inner Traditions International

First published in Great Britain under the title *The Stars and the Stones: Ancient Art and Astronomy in Ireland* by Thames and Hudson, 1983

Library of Congress Cataloging-in-Publication Data
Brennan, Martin.
[Stars and the stones]
The stones of time : calendars, sundials, and stone chambers
of ancient Ireland/ Martin Brennan.
p.   cm.
Originally published: The stars and the stones. New York : Thames
and Hudson. 1994. With new epilogue.
Includes bibliographical references and index.
ISBN 0-89281-509-4
1. Astronomy, Prehistoric—Ireland. 2. Megalithic monuments—Ireland.
3. Art. Prehistoric—Ireland. 4. Ireland—Antiquities. I. Title.
GN806.5.B74   1994
936.1'5—dc20   94-4016
CIP

Printed and bound in the United States

10 9 8 7 6 5 4 3 2 1

Distributed to the book trade in Canada by
Publishers Group West (PGW), Toronto, Ontario

Distributed to the book trade in the United Kingdom
by Deep Books, London

Distributed to the book trade in Australia by
Millennium Books, Newtown, N. S. W.

Distributed to the book trade in New Zealand
by Tandem Press, Auckland

Contents

Acknowledgments 6

Note on the illustrations 6

Part I *INTRODUCTION* 7

The lords of light 10
MEGALITHIC MOUNDS IN ANCIENT
IRELAND

The caves of the sun 18
MEGALITHIC MOUNDS IN
EIGHTEENTH-CENTURY ANTIQUARIAN
LITERATURE

The coming of the light 25
MEGALITHIC MOUNDS IN THE
NINETEENTH CENTURY

To catch a sunbeam 32
NEOLITHIC ASTRONOMY AND
TWENTIETH-CENTURY ARCHAEOLOGY

The shadow artists 37
BASIC FUNDAMENTALS OF NEOLITHIC
SUNDIALING

Movements in the mountains 46
THE FIRST FORAY AT LOUGHCREW

The second light 51
LUNAR OBSERVATIONS DURING THE SUMMER OF
1980

The realms of light 55
SOLAR OBSERVATIONS DURING THE
SUMMER OF 1980 AND THE AUTUMNAL
EQUINOX AT KNOWTH

The triumph of the light 60
SOLAR OBSERVATIONS DURING THE
WINTER OF 1980

Part II *MEGALITHIC
OBSERVATORIES* 67

The Loughcrew complex 68

The Boyne Valley complex 71

The solstice 72
NEWGRANGE 72 DOWTH 82
LOUGHCREW 87 SESS KILGREEN 89

The equinox 90
CAIRN T, LOUGHCREW 90
KNOWTH 101

Between equinox and solstice 109
CAIRN I, LOUGHCREW 109 CAIRN L,
LOUGHCREW 110 CAIRNS H AND F,
LOUGHCREW 114 CAIRNS S AND U,
LOUGHCREW 116 NEWGRANGE 119
TARA 121

North and south alignments 122
MOUND K, NEWGRANGE 122 CAIRN W
AND KNOCKMANY 124

Part III *MEGALITHIC ART* 127

Rock engraving techniques 128

The essential elements of
megalithic art 130

The moon in megalithic art 135
THE CRESCENT AND WAVY LINE 137
CALENDRICAL ENGRAVINGS 144

The sun in megalithic art 158

Megalithic art and cosmology 179
THE CIRCLE 180 THE
QUADRANGLE 182 THE SPIRAL 189

Conclusions 204

Epilogue 206

Select bibliography 214

Index of sites and stones 215

Acknowledgments

I am deeply indebted to my colleague Jack Roberts and to the other members of the field research teams who helped me collect the essential data for this book. At various times the groups included Mitsutake Chimura, John Curran, Owen Duffy, Archibald Gibson, Toby Hall, Hank Harrison, Dierdre Hefernan, Siobhan Hefernan, Sheila Lindsay, Cecily Macnamara, Paddy McNamee, Denis McCarthy, Brian Martin, Paula Miller, John Merron, Al Morrison, Helen O'Clery, David O'Hehir, Joan O'Sullivan, David Patrick, Lynn Patrick, Beth Ridgell, Julie Roberts, Pauline Solan, Robert Stoney, Garreth Williams and David Wollner.

I thank Kimitaro Kitamura and Kinji Matsue for helping to initiate the project. I am especially grateful to Alexander Marshack of the Peabody Museum of Archaeology and Ethnology for advice and encouragement. It was Roger Parisious who first introduced me to the work of Charles Vallancey.

Considerable advice and encouragement – which I gladly acknowledge – were given by the astronomers at the Dunsink Observatory, Dublin, Derek McNally, Department of Physics and Astronomy, University of London Observatory and Dr Susan McKenna-Lalor, Department of Physics, St Patrick's College, Maynooth.

I am very much obliged to the Meteorological Service, Central Analysis and Forecast Office, Glasnevin for their assistance, and to the Commissioners of Public Works in Ireland for facilitating entry into Cairn L, Cairn T, Dowth and Newgrange.

Photographs produced during field research are by Hank Harrison, Siobahn Hefernan, Paula Miller, David O'Hehir, David Patrick, Beth Ridgell (pp. 93, 96, 99) and Jack Roberts. The photographs of winter solstice at Newgrange on pp. 11, 73, 74 (above), 79, 81 are by Mike Bunn, and the photographs on pp. 17, 29, 33, 71, 120, 121, 129, 167, 176 are from the Commissioners of Public Works in Ireland.

I thank Thomas Birrane and Dierdre McGuirk for their work on the manuscript and finally, I would particularly like to acknowledge Jane and Louise Randolph, John Michell and the publishers, Thames and Hudson Ltd, for contributing to the completion of this book.

Dublin 1982   M.B.

Note on the illustrations

The great majority of the drawings in this book have been rendered at a standard scale, viz:

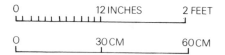

In some instances, a smaller scale has been used (indicated by the symbol ••):

The symbol (•) indicates that the drawing is not rendered to scale.

Emphasis has been placed on an accurate rendering of the engravings on the stones. The intention is to produce a documentation of the actual signs and symbols carved by the artists. I have usually shown an outline of the stone and used shading to indicate its shape and form, but primary consideration is directed towards depicting the engraved art.

The renditions are based on rubbings, photographs and drawings taken at the actual sites and then compared in the studio to produce a final drawing. For the most part, the engravings are remarkably well preserved considering that they were done about 5,000 years ago.

At the Loughcrew sites there are special problems in rendering the stones, because the engravings appear to be older than those in the Boyne Valley, inferior techniques are used on an inferior quality stone, and they have suffered far more from weathering. Cairns T and L, as the focal mounds in the Loughcrew complex, contain the most engravings, and fortunately both these sites are roofed. The satellite mounds are completely exposed, and it is here that discrepancies are likely to arise. I have rendered the art at these subsidiary sites by consulting the early illustrations done by Du Noyer and early photographs, as well as the present archaeological evidence. Nevertheless, these drawings must be treated with caution, and the details are not always reliable. I have drawn conclusions from these stones only in cases where the existing evidence is substantial, or where my own renderings agree with documentation done by other researchers.

Part I

INTRODUCTION

The River Boyne takes a spiral course as it meanders up from the plains of Kildare, winds its way through Meath and takes a curious bend before emptying into the Irish Sea. The bend in the river encloses a picturesque area dominated by three large stone structures known as megalithic mounds and named Newgrange, Knowth and Dowth. These are strategically positioned on ridges, appearing above a landscape dotted with smaller mounds, earthworks and standing stones.

The Boyne Valley complex continues to be an imposing and impressive feature of the landscape today, as it was when erected over five thousand years ago during the age of stone. It belongs to the Neolithic period and its major structures were completed sometime between 3200 and 3700 BC according to radiocarbon dating. This places the mounds among the world's oldest remaining buildings. Another striking feature has only recently become known. One of the mounds in the complex, Newgrange, was found to be aligned to the position of the rising sun at winter solstice, the shortest day of the year. The earliest reports of this event were not taken seriously, but in time the evidence proved overwhelming – Newgrange was a large-scale solar construct, intentionally designed and of a type previously unknown.

The recognition that the long passage within the mound at Newgrange admitted a narrow beam of light illuminating the central chamber at midwinter added an entirely new dimension to Boyne Valley studies. There was no doubt that the light made its appearance every year in spectacular fashion, but how could this discovery be reconciled with conventional archaeological theories regarding the purpose of the mound? Newgrange was – and still is – considered to be a giant tomb, yet the new information tended to support the alternative theory that such megalithic structures were designed for astronomical purposes.

My own field of research involves yet another intriguing feature of the mounds. The complex of sites in the Boyne Valley contains, painstakingly engraved in the chambers and passages and on the kerbstones surrounding the mounds, perhaps the largest accumulation of Neolithic art in the world. My main long-term project was, if possible, to explain the meaning and purpose of this vast collection of enigmatic abstract art. By the end of 1979, after ten years of research, I had already come to some preliminary conclusions. The alignment of Newgrange to the midwinter sun was evidently a major feature, central to the concept of the mound. I also concluded that the art contained in the mound must directly or indirectly

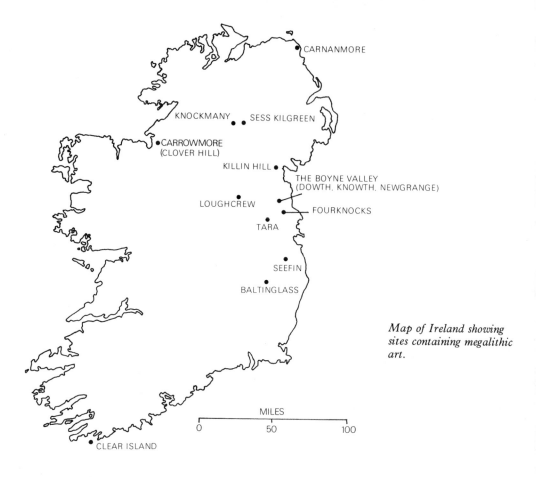

CARNANMORE

KNOCKMANY • • SESS KILGREEN

• CARROWMORE
(CLOVER HILL)

KILLIN HILL •

THE BOYNE VALLEY
(DOWTH, KNOWTH, NEWGRANGE)

LOUGHCREW

FOURKNOCKS

TARA

SEEFIN

BALTINGLASS

*Map of Ireland showing
sites containing megalithic
art.*

MILES

0   50   100

• CLEAR ISLAND

relate to this central feature. If this relationship between the mound and its art was correct, it would imply that similar mounds containing similar art would also feature astronomical alignments.

From the very beginning I could not regard Newgrange as a unique solar construct. Its size and use of complex techniques suggested that there must have been preliminary models upon which the scheme had been based. I was also aware that unless comparable Neolithic devices could be found elsewhere, very little could be determined about the precision with which Newgrange had been laid out, or whether or not it represented a systematic method of time reckoning.

The line of enquiry I was pursuing could be verified only by systematic field research embracing all the major mounds in the Boyne Valley. In order to help eliminate possibilities of coincidence, another large complex of mounds situated in the Loughcrew Mountains would also have to be investigated. The Loughcrew complex is second only to that of the Boyne Valley in its size and in the quantity of megalithic art it contains. Together the two complexes provide the great majority of all megalithic art in Ireland. Eventually the project would expand to include most of the Irish sites containing megalithic art.

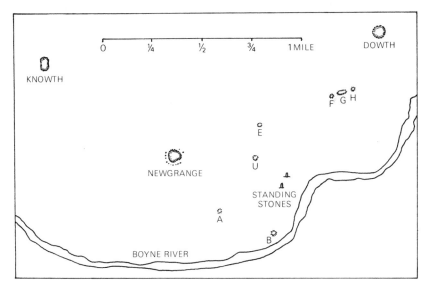

Map of the Boyne Valley complex of megalithic mounds.

The mysteries of the art could be explained only in terms of the mysteries of the mounds themselves, especially the way they interacted with light. The original art research project was therefore expanded to include an archaeo-astronomical investigation. Although I had failed to interest archaeologists in my ideas, a fellow artist and amateur astronomer, Jack Roberts, saw a certain logic in my reasoning and was keen to test my ideas in the field.

Our field research began in late 1979 at Newgrange, where we observed the midwinter sunrise, and ended one year later in the chamber of nearby Dowth, where the rays of the setting sun projected a beam of light at winter solstice. During 1980 we had made comparable solar observations at over thirteen megalithic sites. We gradually came to realize that the mounds were indeed accurate sun chronometers whose structures are a celebration of light and measurement. We also discovered a clear and distinct link between megalithic art and the astronomical events that animate megalithic structures, giving them meaning and function.

The story of our discoveries is the subject of this book. But many researchers before us had, in varying degrees, anticipated or at least suspected an astronomical significance, both in the alignments of the mounds and in the signs and symbols that make up megalithic art: their story should also be told. Even before these comparatively modern visitors, however, Celtic history and tradition alike echo the high prestige of the mounds. Locked away in Gaelic manuscript and lore are fragments of evidence which show that these mounds have captured the imagination and admiration of generations of peoples, extending down through ages of time.

The lords of light

Megalithic mounds in ancient Ireland

Newgrange casts its long shadows over a mist of legend and myth through which we can perceive only glimpses of a real place in the moving billows of fable and fantasy. The mound first appears in the very earliest Irish prose stories which belong to a group known as the Mythological Cycle. Although what survives of these tales is contained in a few large manuscripts written in medieval times, the origin of the cycle is far more ancient. The Mythological Cycle concerns the *Tuatha Dé Danann*, the earliest known native Irish gods disguised as a supernatural race of wizards and magicians, who descended from the sky and inhabited Ireland before the coming of the Celts. They have been referred to as 'The Lords of Light', and when Newgrange is first encountered in literature, it is they who dwell in the mound. The Newgrange of mythology is a magnificent otherworld palace or festive hall, existing in an eternal timeless realm of the supernatural and not as a place of human habitation. It is the domain of gods, a place of perpetual festivities and a wonderful 'land' where no one ever dies. Such a location is described as a *Brú* in the ancient literature, and the *Brú na Bóinne*, or Newgrange, is the most famous of these magical sites. It contained three fruit-trees which were always in fruit, and an inexhaustible cauldron from which no company went away unsatisfied. 'Three times fifty sons of Kings' dwelt there, in this mysterious world of the Celtic imagination.

Very little is known about the first occupant of the 'wonder-hill' except that his name was *Elcmar* and that he was married to *Boand*, the divinized personification of the river Boyne. In mythology the Boyne itself has magical and mystical attributes, and its source is described as being the well of *Segais*, an Otherworld Well regarded as the origin of all wisdom and occult knowledge. This well is surrounded by hazel trees whose nuts drop into its waters, forming *na bolcca immaiss* or 'bubbles of mystic inspiration'. Either once a year, or once in seven years, these pass into the river Boyne. The river is closely associated with the mound, which is sometimes called *Brú mná Elcmair*, or 'the *Brú* of the woman of Elcmar', who is known to be Boand or the Boyne.

A great deal is known about the next proprietor of the Brú, none other than the all-powerful and omniscient *Dagda*, the most prominent of the older native Irish gods. His name means 'the good god'. He is considered to be a god of wisdom and is also called *Ruad Ro-fhessa*, 'The Lord of Great Knowledge'. Some scholars see in him an atmospheric god, others regard him as a sky-god. In his book, *Early Irish History and Mythology*

The beam of light entering Newgrange on winter solstice sunrise.

(1946), T. F. O'Rahilly states that the question of the Dagda's identity is fully answered if we say that he was the god of the sun. There is a striking connection here between the mythological sun-god dwelling in a supernatural residence and an actual Neolithic archaeological site that was constructed to admit the rays of the rising sun annually.

The Dagda gains possession of Brú na Bóinne and achieves carnal union with Boand by the use of a magical trick which utilizes his mastery over time. He sends Elcmar on an errand for one day which really becomes a period of nine months. During this time *Óengus* is conceived and born. He is called *Mac ind Óc*, or 'the Youthful Son', by his mother who says: 'Young is the son who was begotten at break of day and born betwixt it and evening.' Óengus is regarded as a personification of the day, and it is curious that his birth takes place during a magical lengthening of the day at Newgrange. The entrance of the sun's rays into the chamber of Newgrange occurs at winter solstice and therefore marks the beginning of the actual lengthening of the days in the sun's yearly cycle.

The most widely used name for Newgrange in the ancient literature is *Brú Mac ind Óc*, or the *Brú of Óengus*. Óengus later approaches the Dagda requesting a mound of his own. When the Dagda says, 'I have none for thee', Óengus replies, 'Thou let me be granted a day and a night in thy own dwelling.' When the Dagda informs him, 'thou hast consumed thy time', Óengus says, 'It is clear that night and day are the whole world, and it is that which has been given to me.' From then on it is Óengus who has possession of the mound, and this association is retained down through the various cycles of the ancient literature.

Some poems invented by Christian scribes were evidently intended to remove from the popular mind the persistent belief that the Tuatha Dé Danann were immortal. The poems describe the death that befell each of the best-known gods, and the mounds are usually presented as their burial places. Thus, in a poem by Flann Mainistrech dated 1056, we find that Óengus met his end by drowning in the Boyne, yet an entry in Tigernach's Annals from the year 1084 assures us that Óengus is alive and well in his Brú.

In ancient Ireland the introduction of Christianity was directly opposed by the worship of Coll (or Goll), the great orb of the heavens. The earliest documentary allusion to the worship of the sun comes from fifth-century Ireland and occurs in St Patrick's *Confessio*, wherein he warns, 'The splendour of the material sun, which rises every day at the bidding of God, will pass away, and those who worship it will go into dire punishment.' It is easy to see from this and the above discrepancies that, even if the rising sun's triumphant entry into Newgrange was evident in ancient times, it would not have been in the interests of the Christian scribes, who recorded the literature, to make the event known. The two other major mounds in the Boyne Valley, Knowth and Dowth, appear in the ancient literature as *Cnogba* and *Dubad*. Here again, we can detect the presence of the sun, but only through a haze of magic and wizardry. References to Knowth and Dowth occur in the *Dindshenchas*, a collection of lore that attempts to explain the hills and other features of the Irish landscape including the mounds. The collection contains a great deal of artificial learning and pseudo-history as well as fragments of genuine traditional mythology.

Knowth is connected with *Englec* who is the daughter of Elcmar and the lover of Óengus Mac ind Óc and thereby associated with Newgrange. The Dowth legend has the Druid *Bresal* attempting to build a tower that would reach to heaven. This part is clearly based on a biblical motif, however the incidents which follow seem to relate to the Newgrange legend and reflect native Irish sources. For a single day, Bresal has contracted the men of Erin to work on the building. His sister works a druidic spell so that the sun might not set until the mound is built. Bresal commits incest with her, interrupting the magic and causing the sun to set. 'Night came upon them then', and Bresal's sister declares, '*Dubad* [or darkness] shall be the name of that place forever.' And so it is today, but stranger still, one of the two chambers inside Dowth is illuminated by the setting sun at winter solstice marking the longest night of the year. This association of light and darkness with the actual structure of the mound is still reflected in the place-name.

It is clear from the earliest mythology surrounding the mounds that they were never considered to be graves but, on the contrary, were regarded as abodes of living gods conceived and born there. The mounds were places of importance wherein resided the chief and prominent gods of the pantheon. In a later group of tales, known as the Ulster cycle, the Boyne Valley monuments make another appearance, and here again they are not graves and are regarded as places of considerable importance.

The *Táin Bó Cuailnge*, the centrepiece of the Ulster cycle, is the oldest vernacular epic in Western literature. It describes the exploits of the warrior hero *Cúchulainn* in the kind of culture that existed in Iron Age Ireland. In these tales the Brú on the Boyne again features in a wonder-birth of a hero. The setting is typically imaginative and magical. In the events immediately preceding the birth of Cúchulainn the nobles of Ireland with nine chariots chase a flock of wonderful birds, nine score of them, each couple linked by a silver chain. Toward nightfall three birds separate out from the rest. The men of Ulster press on until they reach the Brú on the Boyne where night overtakes them. These incidents open the tale called 'How Cúchulainn Was Begotten'. Later in the *Táin*, while Cúchulainn is on a kind of tour of the country connected with his initiation as a warrior, his charioteer, *Ibar*, points out all the places of Ulster around him. 'He pointed out the plains and strongholds and renowned places of the province. "Well now, Ibar," said Cúchulainn, "what plain is that to the south of us which is full of retreats and corners and nooks and glens?" "That is Mag Breg," said Ibar. "Show me the buildings and high places of that plain." The driver showed him Temair and Tailtiu, Cleitech and Cnogba and Brug Meic in Óc and the fortress of the sons of Nechta Scéne.' Some of these places can be identified as megalithic mounds. *Temair* is Tara, *Cnogba*, as we have seen, is Knowth, which is here clearly distinguished from *Brug Meic in Óc* (Newgrange). The term applied to these sites in the text is the *déntai ocus dindgnai*, which means 'the buildings and high places' and does not imply any idea of a burial place. Completely different terms are used for burial places in the *Táin*. In another tale, Cúchulainn journeys between Tara and the north, passing between Newgrange (described as 'the Hill of Síd in Broga, in which is Óengus') and Dowth (called 'Síd Bresail, the druid'). The term *Síd* has similar connotations as the term *Brú*, referring to the magical dwelling places of living gods.

Óengus reappears in connection with Newgrange in the Fenian cycle, which was the latest to take shape as a separate tradition in the literature. Finn, the warrior hero of these tales, describes the mound as the house of

Óengus of the Brú which cannot be burned or destroyed as long as Óengus is alive. This 'description' is in a tale called 'The Fort of the Rowan Tree'. Another tale in which Newgrange figures is the famous love story of Diarmaid and Grainne known in the tenth century. Upon Diarmaid's death, for which Finn is partly responsible, Finn says, 'Let us leave this tulach for fear that Óengus and the Tuatha Dé Danann may catch us.' Óengus then brings Diarmaid to Newgrange in order to 'put an aerial life into him so that he will talk to me every day'. However strange and mysterious these later tales may be, it is here at last that we finally have literary evidence of a possible burial site.

In the context of a tomb, Newgrange appears among the tales relating to the kings of Tara. Newgrange is referred to as a 'cemetery of idolators' and Cormac mac Airt, as a Christian king, refuses to be buried there. When the body is being taken across the Boyne the river swells up three times so that Cormac attains his wish and is buried south of the Boyne. There seems to be a tradition that the kings of Tara were buried at Newgrange, but this concept is absent from the earlier literature. Neither is it consistent in the later literature. In the 'Colloquy with the Ancients' from a fifteenth-century manuscript, one of the Tuatha Dé Danann resident at Newgrange is asked where he comes from. His reply is, 'Out of yonder Brú chequered with the many lights.' This is more in keeping with the mythological concept of Newgrange.

In ancient Irish literature and place-names there are a number of astronomical references concerning the site of Tara. In view of this, it is interesting that the remains of what was once the Hall of Tara seem to be in alignment with the megalithic mound north-south, marking the position of the midday sun. There is a very curious tale in one of the ancient Irish manuscripts concerning Conn, a High King, and the Rí Ráith (Royal Fortress) at Tara which encompasses the megalithic mound. The manuscript is entitled 'The Magical Stone of Tara', and it states: 'one evening Conn of the Hundred Battles repaired at sunrise to the *Rí Ráith* at Tara, accompanied by his three Druids, Mael, Bloc and Bluicné, and his three poets, Ethain, Corb and Cesare; for he was accustomed every day to repair to this place with the same company, for the purpose of watching the stars, that no hostile aerial beings should descend upon Ireland unknown to him. While standing in the usual place this morning, Conn happened to tread on a stone, and immediately the stone shrieked under his feet so as to be heard all over Tara and throughout all East Meath. Conn then asked the Druids why the stone had shrieked, what its name was, and what it said. The Druids took 53 days to consider, and returned the following answer: *Fal* [destiny] is the name of the stone; it came from the Island of Fal. . . .'

The story continues to describe the fantastic properties of this stone, which is called the *Lia Fal*, or 'Stone of Destiny'. What is startling about the story is that the stone remains within the enclosure of the *Rí Ráith* today, although it has been moved 400 feet from its original site beside the megalithic mound. Apparently Conn is visiting the megalithic mound at sunrise in order to make astronomical observations of some kind, even though his interest is in 'hostile aerial beings'. Although the story contains much of the marvellous and miraculous imagery typical of ancient Irish literature, as in all these tales, there is a real element of fact. Continuous sunrise observations at the megalithic mound would reveal that the chamber is brilliantly illuminated at the time of the two important Celtic festivals, *Samhain* in the early part of November and *Imbolc* in early February at the beginning of spring. Both of these festivals have in fact been associated with Tara, *Samhain* being the major one.

In ancient Celtic Ireland the year was divided into two periods of six months, a bright half and a dark half known as *Samh*, summer, and *Gamh*, winter. This is evident in the Brehon Laws, the ancient codes governing the country. The bright half began in early May on the feast of *Beltine* or 'the Sun's Fire'. Winter commenced early in November on the feast of *Samhain*, which probably means 'summer's end'. Other sources indicate that each of these periods was further subdivided by the feast of *Imbolc* or 'the budding' early in February, and by *Lugnasad* or 'the Feast of Lug', a solar god, early in August. It is remarkable that these feasts correspond closely to the solar alignments of megalithic mounds, where *Samhain*, the greatest feast of the Celtic calendar and probably a harvest festival, is of particular importance.

In another ancient Irish manuscript, the *Senchus Mor*, we learn that seven divisions of the firmament above the earth were recognized, consisting of the moon, Mercury, Venus, the sun, Mars, Jupiter and Saturn. About the stars they believed, 'as a shell is about an egg, the firmament is around the earth'. They believed that twelve constellations represented the year and that the sun 'runs through one each month'. In the ancient Welsh annals, the 'Triads of the Island of Britain' maintain that on the megalithic stones of Gwidden-Ganhebon, 'one could read the arts and sciences of the world'. They also tell us of 'the astronomer Gwydon -ap Don', who was buried 'under a Stone of Enigmas'. This Stone of Enigmas is no doubt an engraved stone. Ancient Irish festivals were known as an *Aonach*, a cycle of the sun numbering 365 days. Baal or Bel is another name for the sun and forms part of many place-names, including *Bel-ain*, which means 'Bel's ring' or 'the sun's circuit'. The festival of *Lucaid-Lamh-Fada* was known as a festival of love held in honour of the sun and moon. This was equivalent to *Lugnasad*, which marked the cross-quarter day early in August.

The connection between the sun and moon, place-names and megalithic sites was recognized very early. In 1811, the Reverend F. Leman spoke of an inscription upon a stone at Tory Hill, Kilkenny which was written in Old Irish characters and read *Sleigh-Grian* or 'the Hill of the Sun'. He said: 'Within view of this hill, towards the west, on the borders of Tipperary, rises the more elevated mountain of *Sleigh-Na-Man*, which from its name, was probably consecrated to the moon.' A contemporary, Dr Kenealy, stated, 'The Druidical temple called *Ana-Mor* was composed of 48 stones, denoting the numbers of the old constellations, with a kebla of nine stones near the circumference, on the inside, to represent the sun in its progress through the signs.' Many early antiquaries had in fact recognized connections between the megalithic monuments and astronomy, but they were never taken seriously. Nor did they themselves follow up the clues by making astronomical observations at the sites.

The poem called 'The Mystery of Amergin', although its date is unknown, has from ancient times been represented as the first poem made in Ireland. Amergin was a Druid, and his verses are considered incantations rather than poems. The structuring in the incantation is extremely archaic, and there has been much argument about the translation of many of the lines. The incantation consists of twenty lines, the first fourteen of which are a series of declarations,

> *I am wind on sea,*
> *I am ocean wave,*

by the sixth line he declares,

> *I am a beam of the sun.*

By the fifteenth line the incantation changes into a series of questions or riddles, which begin,

> *Who is he who announces the ages of the moon?*
> *Who teaches the place where falls the sunset?*

These references to the sun and moon are followed by two lines which refer to the stars. In the incantation the phrase for the stars used is *buar Tethrach*, which literally means 'the cattle of Tethrys', but is translated by R. A. S. Macalister as 'the stars rising out of the sea'. Macalister's translation of the incantation is generally recognized as the most authoritative. Literally the lines read,

> *Who calleth cattle from the House of Tethys?*
> *On whom do the cattle of Tethys smile?*

The end of the incantation follows this line and questions the first line and the incantation itself with,

> *Enchantments of wind?*

The entire set of questions which form the last part of the incantation in one way or another are concerned with the heavens. Although the incantation is referred to as a mystery, the identification with aspects of the sun and moon is explicit in the very earliest written documents. The incantation in its entirety is mysterious and bewildering, but there is running through it a number of interconnected lines expressing ideas that are related to megalithic mounds.

There is a wealth of information concerning Celtic sun symbolism in ancient Irish manuscripts, and it is possible that, although these symbols are natural and universal, they could have been derived directly from the Neolithic tradition of symbol usage. In his book, *Early Irish History and Mythology*, Thomas O'Rahilly deals with the emblem of the sun as a circle or ring. He explains that the Modern Irish term for dawn, *fainne an lae*, literally means 'the ring of light on the sky-line at day-break', and he traces the symbol back to the most ancient literature. He states that, 'One of the attributes of the sun-god was the healing of disease, and in this belief we have one of the reasons of the importance attached in ancient times to the wearing of rings or other solar emblems, which were primarily amulets and only secondarily ornaments. Sometimes the ring became a miniature wheel, and thus suggested not only the shape of the sun but also its motion. Hence we find the word *roth*, "wheel", applied to a kind of circular brooch. The sun itself was the great celestial wheel; compare *roth greine*, the sun, like Lucretius' *solis rota*. So we find God referred to not only as *ard-Ri grene*, "supreme King of the Sun", but also as *ard-Ruiri ind roith*, "supreme King of the wheel" which means just the same thing.'

Although it is possible to recognize a connection between Celtic symbols and decorative motifs, and symbolism developed by the megalith builders, the link is tenuous. The Celts never adopted a systematic use of the symbols and in all probability they were not aware of the depth of their meanings. The megalithic mounds were already very ancient when Celtic civilization emerged in Ireland. Nevertheless the frequent appearance and importance of the mounds in mythology, their continual presence throughout the various cycles of literature and the association of royal sites of the proto-historic and historic periods with the Neolithic mounds is a remarkable legacy, through which we can detect fleeting glimpses of the sun in a mysterious Celtic twilight.

Newgrange before reconstruction.

The caves of the sun

Megalithic mounds in eighteenth-century antiquarian literature

By the time the entrance to Newgrange was discovered in 1699, the mound had plunged from fame and splendour in the old Gaelic world into almost total obscurity. By 1142, the fabulous Brú na Bóinne had become part of outlying farmland in the possession of the Cistercian Abbey of Mellifont. These farms were known as 'granges', and by 1378 the mound had been completely stripped of its former identity and was called merely 'the new grange'. Complex historical circumstances leading to the Williamite confiscations brought a further change of ownership, and in 1688 Charles Campbell became the landowner of Newgrange as a grantee of estates forfeited. To Campbell the mound was a convenient source of stones that were ideal for use in roads and fences. During the summer of 1699 his servants were busy casting away stones from the base of the mound when they came across the engraved spirals of the entrance stone. Further digging revealed an opening to a long narrow passage which was still relatively intact and led to the large chamber. The landowner, who was apparently the second person to enter the chamber, notified Dublin of the strange curiosity found on his land. Soon after, Edward Lhuyd, the Welsh

General Charles Vallancey titled this print 'Section of the Contrum Mithrae' or Cave of the Sun at Newgrange. Vallancey is shown entering the passage in the eighteenth century.

antiquary, naturalist and philologist, came to investigate, and he is thus credited with the 'discovery' of Newgrange.

Lhuyd's visit was followed by a succession of visits by well-known antiquarians who tried to explain the origins of the 'barbarous monument' on the Boyne. Two basic ideas predominated. For the most part the very earliest megalithic researchers could not conceive that the monuments were indigenous constructions of the native Irish. They considered all the large engineering projects in Ireland to have been the work of Danes or other colonists. Secondly, the supposed presence of two skeletons in the chamber of Newgrange led Lhuyd to conclude that 'it must certainly have been the Sepulchre or burying of some person of note who had his wife interred with him'. Similar finds in other mounds reinforced the tomb theory, although there was no evidence to show that these deposits were contemporary with the original construction. Both these ideas, although modified and elaborated upon considerably, were to form the basis of archaeological thought right up to our own time.

One of Lhuyd's most interesting observations was made by interviewing a local man named Cormac O'Neil about the folklore concerning the mounds. Lhuyd states that he was told a 'vulgar legend about some strange operation that took place in the time of Heathenism'. The legend was later identified by Roderick O'Flaherty as being none other than the expulsion of Elcmar from Brú na Bóinne and the wonder tales of Aonghus. This means that, regardless of the tremendous social and political upheavals of the previous centuries, the people had preserved some of the old traditions and enshrined them in local folklore. If local tradition had been taken more

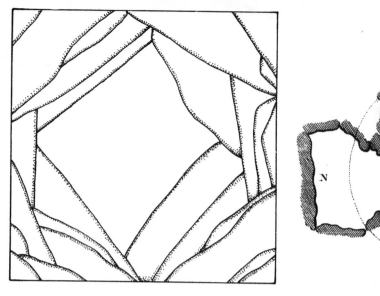

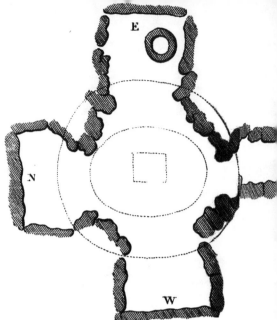

seriously the mound could have been linked with the fabulous Brú of ancient mythology. Instead, it was going to take over a hundred years before this was fully realized.

It was not only the tomb theory and the idea that the mounds were built by invading colonists that had their origins with the early antiquarians; the foundations for an astronomical explanation of the mounds were also established at this period. Although the astronomical explanation was quickly dismissed and long ridiculed, it has recently been found applicable to other megalithic sites in Europe. However, when Jack Roberts and I first became interested in the astronomical features of the Irish mounds, we found that very little research had been done. We had to start from the beginning, almost as pioneers; and thus we became attracted to the works of the real pioneer of our subject, the originator of the astronomical interpretation of Newgrange, General Charles Vallancey.

Vallancey came to Ireland in 1750 as a British army officer of the Engineers in the Tenth Regiment of Foot. He was a professional surveyor, and made notable contributions to the science and art of military mapping. His maps of Ireland are recognized as noteworthy achievements, but Vallancey was energetic in all things. Cartography, engineering and

Vallancey's drawings and ground plans of Newgrange are vastly superior to anything else done in the eighteenth century. It is intriguing that the standing stones depicted surrounding the mound can all be identified except for the triangular stone in front of the entrance.

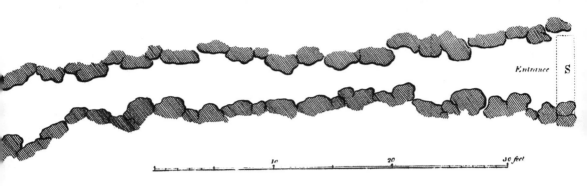

(Left) The capstone of the corbelled roof of Newgrange. In the ground plan (above) Vallancey indicates the position of the capstone and roofing with dotted lines. According to Vallancey's plan it appears that the capstone is in line with the beam of light entering the chamber.

physical geography were some of his many scientific interests. As a linguist his attempts to derive the Irish language from Phoenician and other Oriental sources were a failure, but modern scholars have given him the sympathy due to an amateur of Celtic studies living in a time of general indifference towards the subject. He studied ancient Irish astronomical tracts and was able to comment intelligently in the Irish language on manuscripts dating from the fourteenth century. He sometimes signed his comments with his name in Irish, *Cathal Uabhallansi.*

Vallancey's astronomical explanations of the megalithic mounds were very soon forgotten and, if he is mentioned at all by modern archaeologists, he is invariably ridiculed. A favourite target for criticism is his interpretation of Newgrange and other sites as *Antra Mithrae* or 'Caves of the Sun'. He observed that 'Several of these *Antra Mithrae* exist in Ireland and Britain at this day: They are of wonderful construction.' He also considered Stonehenge to be a temple of the sun, and a number of Irish standing stones and stone circles were explained as sun stones or stones set up to mark the cycles of the sun, moon and planets. *Antra* is taken by Vallancey to mean a cave, and he derives *Mithrae* from an Irish name for the sun or rays of the sun. Regardless of how these interpretations were

114 feet

Entrance

View of (New) Grange

arrived at, Vallancey anticipated the modern realization that Newgrange is orientated with reference to the rays of the sun. This is one of the reasons why I consider Vallancey to be the most important of the Irish antiquarians. Many of his insights are now being substantiated by current research.

Vallancey came so close to penetrating the facts about the astronomical features of Newgrange that it would be interesting to know his exact sources. By the early 1770s he was spending most of his time in Dublin, devoting himself to the problem of the megalithic mounds and other antiquarian pursuits. He had already begun 'to publish every thing of this kind he had notic'd in Ireland', and his researches came out over the years 1782–1806 in his monumental work, *Collectanea de Rebus Hibernicus*. In the pages of these volumes he appealed for information from his readers in questionnaires called 'Queries recommended to the curious'. A typical enquiry is, 'Are there any Raths, *Irish* or *Danish* or other pieces of antiquity remaining in your parish; what are they, and what traditions are there, or historical accounts of them? add a drawing if you can.'

Vallancey is today criticized for attributing the construction of the mounds to the Druids. Although we now know that Newgrange was built thousands of years before Druids were heard of in Ireland, it is not appreciated that Vallancey's ideas were much closer to the truth than those of his fellow antiquaries, who still thought the mounds to be of foreign origin. Vallancey believed that 'The engravings are certain proof of the purpose for which it [Newgrange] was constructed, and that it was not designed for a granary, or a Danish sepulchre, as has been asserted by a great pretender to a knowledge in Irish antiquities.' Vallancey and his informants, whoever they were, did not realize that the passage was constructed to admit rays of the sun. Vallancey stated that the Druids 'directed their worship to Saman [the sun] in caves and darkness. Such I take to be the cave of Newgrange.' He explained Saman, 'By *Samh*, our Druids understood the sun', and further elaborated, 'heat and light is the producer and preserver of life; therefore Sol was the god of nativity'. Elsewhere he informs us, 'We also frequently find subterraneous buildings in Ireland, which are evidently of Druidical workmanship, such as that of New Grange near Drogheda, which may probably have been the place of sacrificing to Samman.' It is unlikely that Vallancey could have created these associations entirely from his own imagination. It seems probable that his researches were tapping some elements of genuine oral tradition. His knowledge of the Irish language would have put him in touch with sources that would have been inaccessible to other antiquarians. He further anticipated later findings about Newgrange by successfully identifying it as Cairn Aongus. He correctly claimed, 'it was constantly distinguished by the name Oengus. We find it mentioned in the Chronicon Scotorum, with the grove which surrounded it, by the name *Fiodh Aongusa*, or the grove of Aongus, though several persons have imagined that a chief of the name of Aongus or Oengus was interred here.' He also correctly associated *Ruad-a-Daghdae* with an 'epithet of the sun', a

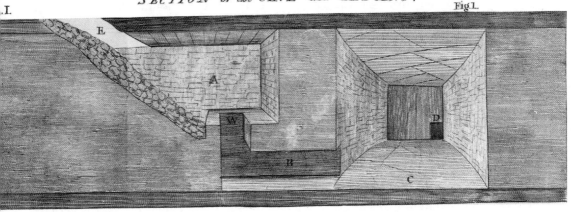

In 1790 John Whittley Boswell wrote a satire on Vallancey's Irish antiquarian researcher. The above print was used to lampoon the difficulties Vallancey supposedly encountered upon entering the passage especially at the point marked E, 'This I mention lest I should be thought guilty of disrespect, in putting my most unworthy parts foremost into the venerable remains of antiquity.' Boswell has Vallancey describing Newgrange as an inverted Egyptian pyramid (right).

Section of the inverted Pyramid.

'poetical name of Aurora, signifying the expander of the light of Dagh or Dagon'. This of course is none other than the mythological Dagda, lord of Brú na Bóinne.

Vallancey was among the very first to point out the importance of the cross-quarter days, which fall between the solstices and equinoxes in the ancient Irish calendar. Here he was very clear about his sources: 'The names of some of the ancient festivals are handed down to us by the mouths of the common people.' He also cited manuscripts, 'Thus Cormac, in his glossary, says the four great fires of the Druids were in the beginning of February, May, August and November.' According to Vallancey, 'The fire of the Druids lighted on the *Neomenia* [new moon] of the four quarter months', and 'high mountains were assigned for their astronomical observations'. 'Their festivals were generally governed by the motion of the heavenly bodies, was it not necessary that the people should be warned of their approach?' In his essay, 'A Vindication of the Ancient History of Ireland', Vallancey set forth a view of prehistory that was revolutionary for its time: 'Astronomy took its use in the latitude of 49° or 50°; here the arts had their birth, and from thence spread towards the South'. It is only in the past decade or so that we have begun to realize that megalithic structures demonstrate considerable astronomical skill on the part of their builders during the late Stone Age, and that the monuments in Ireland and northern Europe, some dating from the fourth millennium BC, are the earliest of their kind, predating those of the Mediterranean.

Vallancey could not have known that the mounds were constructed in remote ages long before the emergence of Druids. It is quite possible, however, that the Celtic Druids inherited some remnants of a much earlier system of astronomy. Vallancey described Druids as 'the revolution-prophets or the observers of time'. In *Druidism Revived* he claimed that 'the highest degree of Druidic order studied astronomy and divined by the aspect of the sun, moon and stars'. These comments correspond very closely with historical accounts of the Druids related by Roman and Greek writers, and they are also supported by references to Druids in ancient Irish literature.

Matching his interpretation of the mounds, Vallancey was the very first to advance an astronomical explanation of the rock engravings. Where other antiquarians could see only 'rude scribblings' and 'barbarous carvings', Vallancey saw the stars in the stones. These he aptly described as 'the most ancient inscriptions now remaining in Ireland, if not in these parts of Europe'. To him they were 'Hibernian Druidic Symbols', representing the cycles of the sun, moon and stars, 'the chief if not the only deities of the heathen Irish'. By 1804 he had identified symbols of the sun and moon and had already pointed out the numerical significance of some of the engravings and their relationship to astronomy. Had Vallancey been taken more seriously the great error of modern archaeology, in trying to imagine the human form in the engravings, could have been avoided. Instead, after his death in 1812, Vallancey's ideas were quickly abandoned as 'mystical speculation' and replaced by a wide range of theories that have proved to be much less convincing in the light of recent research. Referring to the followers of General Vallancey, William Wilde was relieved to be able to report a few years later that 'that school has now become nearly extinct'. To modern archaeologists, the only worthwhile contribution made by Vallancey was the entertainment provided by a crude satire on his work written by John Boswell and entitled *The Antiquities of Killmackumpshaugh in the County of Roscommon and Kingdom of Ireland, in which it is clearly proved that Ireland was originally peopled by AEGYPTIANS* (1790). Ironically, it is probable that impartial posterity will acknowledge that Vallancey's explanation of the mounds as 'Caves of the Sun' was the most realistic and perceptive interpretation of his time, and that his insights will eventually prove to be of far more significance than all other antiquarian contributions. Developments during the nineteenth century were already setting the stage for the eventual vindication of one of Newgrange's greatest illustrators and interpreters.

The coming of the light

Megalithic mounds in the nineteenth century

During the early part of the nineteenth century at least one researcher continued to take seriously the concepts first advanced by Vallancey, though with certain modifications. Miss L. C. Beaufort referred at this time to the mounds as 'Cairns of the Sun and Altars of the Sun'. In 'An Essay upon the state of Architecture and Antiquities, previous to the landing of the Anglo-Normans in Ireland' she remarked that 'Such artificial high places are generally situated in an eminence, frequently upon the tops of hills and mountains; and these stations were so chosen as to form a chain of connexion with each other in such a manner, that on the festival days, the first of May and the first of November most especially, the fires of Bel (the sun), were seen from one to the other over the whole country.' Regarding stone circles she related that 'it is thought that they expressed periods of time or astronomical epochs'. She believed that all megalithic structures were connected with the worship of the sun, arriving at this conclusion 'from the knowledge gleaned out of pagan authors'. As with Vallancey, current research lends considerable support to these conclusions, especially in connection with the Loughcrew Mountains, some 33 miles west of the Boyne Valley, where there is a large complex of mounds.

Beaufort herself was the first to point out the existence of the mysterious mounds at Loughcrew in an address to the Royal Irish Academy in 1827. 'In the County of Westmeath in one of the hills of Loughcrew, which are called by the peasants the Witches Hops, is an extensive excavation, consisting of three large chambers with a narrow passage leading to them. In one of these rooms is a flat altar-stone of considerable size; near to this artificial cave stand two lofty pillar stones known among the people by the names of "the speaking stones" and "the whisperers".' Beaufort is probably referring to two standing stones outside the entrance, as at Knowth. There are other stones a few miles away in Farranaglogh Townland which were known as the 'Speaking Stones', but these are too far away to be the ones that Beaufort is referring to. There is a holed standing stone in a field on a nearby farm which was removed from the area immediately in front of Cairn T, and this is probably one of the old 'speaking stones'.

It has been claimed that nothing was known of the character or contents of the Loughcrew cairns until 1858, when W. F. Wakeman measured and made plans of several of those remaining, and wrote a paper on the subject. The Ordnance Survey was working in this part of County Meath in 1836, and on their maps they marked Cairn T as a 'Fort' and Cairn V as 'Stones'. Unaccountably they omitted the mounds on the other two summits of the range, and even though they marked Cairn T with a Trigonometrical Station, apparently they were not aware of the vast complex of mounds in which Cairn T formed a central focal point. It was Eugene Alfred Conwell who was the first to publish an account that gave any idea of the full scope of the site. He was a local schoolmaster who, on 9 June 1863, was picnicking with his wife in these hills when 'to my great astonishment, I found this commanding site studded with the remains of a necropolis of pre-historic age . . . When I first stated that I had discovered a series of hitherto unnoticed and undescribed cairns, established for 2 miles along a range of hills, within 40 miles of the city of Dublin, I was laughed at, naturally enough. . . .'

Even in their present state of preservation, the mounds crowning the Loughcrew Mountains can be seen from points located over wide distances. As one travels by road from Dublin, the hills become clearly distinguishable just before Tara, and the prominent structures of Cairns D, L and T can be identified standing out against the horizon like beacons. Given that the mounds were designed to be clearly visible from so far off, it is extraordinary that no reference to them appears until 1827. Even today the full extent of what exactly is left of this extensive Neolithic landscape is not known, and new, unexpected discoveries are still being made.

By 1866 Conwell was able to communicate to the Royal Irish Academy the results of excavations, and a detailed, accurate description of thirteen cairns. A final description, entitled *The Discovery of the Tomb of Ollamh Fodhla*, was published in 1873. This contains ground-plans and illustrations of engraved stones by Herr Wilhelm Tomsohn. Conwell was partially aware that he had made an enormous discovery. Even though he evolved an elaborate and fanciful theory linking Loughcrew with the ancient Celtic cemetery of Taillten, he did realize that he had found a substantial corpus of prehistoric engravings. He regarded them as mystic symbols, and carefully recorded them with the idea of trying to decipher their meaning. In 1865 he reported to the Academy, 'In all – so far as the explorations have gone – I have laid bare 1,393 separate devices, which will be found to be many times more than had previously been supposed to exist in Ireland.' Conwell had unearthed a treasure house of megalithic art, which at that time had no known rivals.

Soon after these mounds were discovered, G. V. Du Noyer, an officer in the Irish Geological Survey, produced a remarkable set of drawings recording with considerable accuracy seventy-six of the engraved stones at Loughcrew. In many instances Du Noyer's drawings are the only remaining records of stones which are now either missing, or have entirely lost their incised markings through weathering. Du Noyer recorded the designs over a hundred years ago, when they had just been exposed, and as an illustrator of megalithic art he has been proved invariably accurate and highly perceptive. His approach was to record objectively exactly what was on the stones; he refrained from exaggerating or creating forms as he

Bone slips found at Cairn H, Loughcrew, showing Iron Age art.

thought they should be or might have been. Some of his drawings are remarkably precise, and his many sketches are still useful as reliable guides.

Only after the kerbstones at Knowth were uncovered during the 1940s did it become apparent that the engraved stones in the Boyne Valley exceeded those at Loughcrew in number. It is now known that there are at least 220 engraved stones in the Boyne Valley, which is double the number at Loughcrew. Together, the two districts contain the greatest collection of megalithic art in the world. All told, eleven of the passages leading into the mounds there still function as instruments of the lost art of Neolithic timekeeping, and many more await rediscovery or restoration. With those intact it is possible to view megalithic art in its intended context, and this allows for a new understanding that was never available to the earlier antiquarian investigators.

From the very beginning the mounds presented a confusing picture of prehistoric civilization. The engravings at Loughcrew were even more perplexing than those in the Boyne Valley, although sun and star signs were immediately recognized. Large deposits of undated bones, many of which represented the remains of animals, were taken to be indicative of extensive human burials. Excavations conducted later during the nineteenth century continued to unearth burials in most of the mounds. Even though these burials were haphazard and random, at no time was it ever questioned that the purpose of the mounds was to fulfil a burial function and that the complex was designed as a giant city of the dead. In 1943, at Cairn H, Joseph Raftery uncovered decorated bone combs of Celtic type and thousands of bone slips, some of which had Iron Age motifs. Included with this assemblage was an iron compass, which was presumably used to execute some of the patterns. On the basis of the stratigraphical position of the bone slips, Raftery was convinced that Cairn H was a tomb erected in the Early Iron Age and used exclusively as a burial place. Of course it is now realized that the bone slips belong to about the first century AD and that Cairn H is definitely a Neolithic structure, but the Loughcrew monuments in general are still considered to have been built later than those of the Boyne Valley, even though there is no real evidence for this assertion. Since the techniques of rock engraving at Loughcrew are at a much earlier stage of development than those employed in the Boyne Valley, it is quite probable that the Loughcrew monuments will be found to be the older of the two groups. When it is realized that most of the burial remains at Loughcrew are secondary, and have no relation to the original functions of the mounds, a less confusing picture of prehistoric civilization may emerge, and the Neolithic period will be seen in an entirely different light.

Identifying the Loughcrew complex in ancient Irish literature is still an unsolved problem. However, in 1845 George Petrie successfully identified the Boyne Valley monuments as being the Brú na Bóinne of folklore and legend, even though the argument he advanced in his book, *The Round Towers and Ancient Architecture of Ireland*, was not acknowledged by scholars of his time. George Coffey expanded Petrie's thesis in 1892, and now the identification is generally accepted. Yet by far the most significant discovery relating to megalithic mounds during the nineteenth century was that light entered the passage at Newgrange. It is not known when or by whom this was first noticed, but by 1897 it was a recurrent theme in the mystic poetry of George Russell, who wrote under the name 'A.E.'. The phenomenon was so far removed from the preconceptions of archaeologists that they refused even to consider investigating it until 1969, seventy-two years after it had first appeared in the visionary language of the key figure in the great Irish literary renaissance known as the Celtic Revival.

One may excuse archaeologists for not investigating an event portrayed in a clearly visionary style of literature, but the idea was also advanced by scholars in the early twentieth century and substantiated by numerous eye-witness accounts. In many ways this was one of the greatest blunders of modern Irish archaeology. If archaeologists had been more objective, not only could they have made a substantial contribution to knowledge of astronomical achievements in prehistory, but they could have prevented disastrous reconstructions of the mounds, which failed to take possible astronomical functions into account. Sadly, the observations of eye-witnesses were still being ignored at the time Jack Roberts and I began our research.

We started by studying the astronomical features of the mounds, and soon recognized the need to record as many of the earlier accounts as we possibly could. This line of enquiry had been completely neglected hitherto. We were astounded by our immediate discoveries, but sometimes felt as if we were violating a kind of taboo by revealing things that were considered secret, hidden and forbidden. Indeed, the story of the light in megalithic mounds is one of the strangest in all the annals of archaeology.

This photograph was taken during the 1880s or 1890s and it is the earliest known photograph of Newgrange. The entrance to the passage is shown, with a measuring rod over the entrance stone.

As it first appears in print, the account of light at Newgrange takes on a weird and mysterious form, and comes to us in a dramatic treatment of legend entitled 'A Dream of Angus Oge', written by George Russell in 1897. The significant passage is, 'As he spoke, he paused before a great mound grown over with trees, and around it silver clear in the moonlight were immense stones piled, the remains of an original circle, and there was a dark low narrow entrance leading within – He took Con by the hand and in an instant they were standing in a lofty, cross shaped cave, built roughly of huge stones. "This was my palace. In days past many a one plucked here the purple flower of magic and the fruit of the tree of life . . ." And even as he spoke, a light began to glow and to pervade the cave, and to obliterate the stone walls and the antique hieroglyphics engraven thereon, and to melt the earthen floor into itself like a fiery sun suddenly uprisen within the world, and there was everywhere a wandering ecstasy of sound; light and sound were one; light had a voice . . . "I am Aengus, men call me Young. I am the sunlight in the heart, the moonlight in the mind; I am the light at the end of every dream . . . I will make you immortal; for my palace opens into the Gardens of the Sun".'

In this passage Russell is definitely referring to Newgrange. We know this because in his autobiography of a mystic, *The Candle of Vision* (1918), he records a similar experience: 'To one who lay on the mound which is called the Brú on the Boyne a form like that the bards speak of Angus appeared and it cried: "Can you not see me? Can you not hear me? I come from the land of Immortal Youth . . . Oh, see our sun is dawning for us, ever dawning, with ever youthful and triumphant voices. Your sun is but a smoky shadow: ours the ruddy and eternal glow . . . My birds from purple fiery plumage shed the light of lights".'

As imaginative and visionary as Russell's prose is, it is extremely unlikely that he would have conceived certain images – the light, the engravings, the glowing floor – without first-hand or second-hand experience of the actual entry of the sun into the chamber. It is known that during the 1890s Russell made frequent excursions from Dublin to the mound. We also know that after 1849 the entrance to Newgrange had been cleared sufficiently to allow light to enter the passage. In 1849, William Wilde wrote in his *The Beauties and Antiquities of the Boyne*: 'a few years ago a gentleman, then residing in the neighbourhood, cleared away stones and rubbish which obscured the mouth of the cave, and brought to light a very remarkably carved stone, which now slopes outwardly from the entrance.' Once the entrance was cleared, the light of the rising sun at winter solstice would have penetrated the passage as far back as stone L19, regardless of a certain amount of collapse closer to the opening. The sun's rays would have illuminated the triple spiral engraved on L19, later confused in folk tradition with the triple spiral in the chamber, which was in fact only illuminated again by the sun when the roof-box was opened early in the 1960s. As it is nearly 9 a.m. when rays of the rising sun penetrate the passage at winter solstice (as opposed to 5 a.m. for the summer solstice sunrise), someone, sometime after 1849 must have observed the phenomenon and perhaps realized it had some significance and meaning.

To Russell, who was primarily a poet and a painter, the light had mystical significance. Vallancey is frequently dismissed as having been of the astro-mystic school of megalithic research, but in reality he was not. It was Russell who founded that school. If only to help define what the truly mystical approach is and clarify terms, it is worth considering Russell's work.

In 'The Childhood of Apollo' he uses the imagery of *A Dream of Angus Oge* in a different context, substituting the cave of Diotima for Newgrange: '"Tell me have you ever seen a light from the sun falling on you in your slumber? No, but look now. Look upward." As she spoke the cavern with its dusky roof seemed to melt away, and beyond the heavens the heaven of heavens lay dark in pure tranquillity, in a quiet which was the very hush of being. In an instant it vanished, and over the zenith broke a wonderful light.

"See now," cried Diotima, "the Ancient Beauty".

'So from age to age the Eternal Beauty bows itself down amid sorrows, that the children of men may not forget it, and their anguish may be transformed, smitten through by its fire.'

Russell constantly uses the recurring words and images of light, dark, shadow, starry, shining and stone in his prose and poetry. 'A Vision of Beauty', 'Dawn Song', 'Immortality', 'The Memory of Earth', 'Morning', 'The Fountain of Shadowy Beauty', 'Winter', 'The Message of John' and 'Star Teachers' are some of the poems in a collection called *The Earth Breadth and Other Poems* (1897) that utilize these themes. 'The Cave of Lilith', 'The Story of a Star' and 'Voices of the Stones' are other works in which the shadow of Newgrange may be seen.

As a Celtic Revivalist, Russell was not so much concerned with the builders of Newgrange as with the ancient Irish vision of the mounds as inhabited by immortal gods of light. To him megalithic sites were 'cyclopean crypts and mounds once sanctified by Druid mysteries, and divine visitations and passings from the mortal to the immortal.' He dramatized the legends concerning Newgrange because he felt, 'perhaps, the time is not altogether wasted in considering legends like these, for they reveal, though but in phantasy and symbol, a greatness we are heirs to, a destiny which is ours though it be yet far away.'

Russell died on 17 July 1935, at the age of 68. He never explicitly stated anywhere how he came to learn of the light entering Newgrange. Although clues appear in his autobiography, perhaps one cannot expect detailed observations in what has been called 'one of the most important records of the mystic life ever written'. Interestingly enough, the friend who is with him at Newgrange in the autobiography could be W. B. Yeats.

Since his death, Russell's name has remained in comparative obscurity. But Russell himself felt that one day his work would be fully appreciated. Today it is clear that he was the first writer to recognize and respond to the meaning of the light entering Newgrange.

The light at Newgrange was not the only one to be ignored. In a more scientific work, *The Book of Sundials*, published in 1872, Mrs Alfred Gatty pointed out similarities between ancient sundials and the Neolithic rock engravings at Loughcrew and Dowth. She observed that a stone on Patrickstown Hill, Loughcrew, shows a rayed circle with a central hole 'very much like some of those sundials we still find on churches'. The book comments on the radial designs at Dowth, 'some of the early dials or circles may have been used as horizontal dials for finding the north only, by means of morning and afternoon observations of the shadow of a vertical gnomon'. In 1980, Jack Roberts and I were able to discern actual fully-worked-out diurnal sundials at Knowth.

By the end of the nineteenth century an architect, George Wilkinson, had already begun to challenge the colonization theory, claiming that the mounds could 'not be works of temporary invaders or intruders'; and the astronomer, Sir Norman Lockyer, pointed out that 'neither Newgrange and Dowth on the Boyne, nor Gavrinis in Brittany bear any internal proof of being specially prepared as tombs'. Certainly the isolated views of architects, astronomers, mystics and sundiallers were not going to make the model of prehistory advanced by archaeologists crumble, but already the cracks were beginning to show.

To catch a sunbeam

Neolithic astronomy and twentieth-century archaeology

At the turn of the century Newgrange was rapidly beginning to regain some of its former prestige. Not only was its appearance gradually improving, but soon the passage had a gate and a caretaker and the beam of light entering the mound was becoming part of local folklore and tradition. The caretaker, Mr Robert Hickey, and his wife were apparently partly responsible for establishing the oral tradition. It must be emphasized that although numerous testimonies confirm that the oral tradition existed, there is nothing to indicate that it had its origins in an ancient tradition, and its source appears simply to have been observation of the event by local people. The sun's entry must have become increasingly noticeable and dramatic as debris was cleared away from in and around the passage. The Hickeys are known to have attributed great significance to the beam of light and, over the years, by informing visitors and groups of school-children, the story evolved all the characteristics of a legend.

By 1960 the 'legend' of the sun's rays entering the mound on a certain day of the year had appeared in print, accompanying a colour photograph of Newgrange on a local calendar. At that time the archaeologist Glyn Daniel was residing in the Conyngham Arms Hotel, where the calendar was – and still is – on display. He was working on a book, *Newgrange and the Bend of the Boyne* (co-written with Sean P. Ó Ríordáin and eventually published in 1964), and in it he recalls the calendar and makes the first written reference by an archaeologist to the legend of the light beam at Newgrange. It is a 'strange wild-cat account', Daniel says, which 'needs quoting almost *in toto* as an example of the jumble of nonsense and wishful thinking indulged in by those who prefer the pleasures of the irrational and the joys of unreason to the hard thinking that archaeology demands.'

Any discipline may have difficulty in accepting new ideas, especially if they are presented in the form of folk tradition or dramatized legend. However, as early as 1909, Sir Norman Lockyer, an astronomer and Director of the Solar Physics Observatory, had clearly stated that Newgrange is orientated to the winter solstice in his book, *Stonehenge and Other British Stone Monuments Astronomically Considered*. Lockyer is very rarely given credit for being the first to draw attention to this fact on a scientific level. At much the same time, as a result of completely independent research, an American anthropologist, W. Y. Evans-Wentz, arrived at very similar conclusions. In 1907 and 1908 Evans-Wentz did preparatory work under the direction of the Oxford Professor of Celtic and during 1909–10 made folklore expeditions into Brittany and Ireland. In a

This photograph was taken in 1908, when a gate was installed at the entrance of Newgrange. The woman on the right is believed to be Mrs Hickey, one of the first people known to have witnessed the beam of light entering the chamber. The dry stone walling to the immediate left of the young girl is part of the original structure, but has been removed in the modern reconstruction.

section of his book, *The Fairy-Faith in Celtic Countries*, entitled 'The Testimony of Archaeology', Evans-Wentz not only drew attention to the fact that Newgrange was astronomically orientated, but also pointed out that mounds in Brittany, such as Gavrinis, had the same solar orientation. Thus, in the early part of this century, both an astronomer and an anthropologist had recognized an extremely important feature of Newgrange, and yet archaeologists seem to have been totally unaware of it. As another investigator of megalithic monuments in the 1920s, Admiral Boyle-Somerville, said: 'It is senseless to condemn [Astronomical] Orientation as being figmentary, or non-existent, as many do, without taking the trouble to investigate the subject practically by direct observation in the field.'

Much of the confusion and mystery surrounding Newgrange at this time was due to the lack of adequate documentation of the solar event itself. None of the contemporary published accounts can have been based on actual observations by the writers. Neither the mystic Russell, the astronomer Lockyer nor the anthropologist Evans-Wentz recorded a direct empirical observation of the light itself. Lockyer and Evans-Wentz referred to astronomical alignments and orientations and only hinted at light beams, while the light that Russell saw was purely visionary. Apparently the only people to have made true observations at Newgrange were the caretakers and a few local residents, and none of them published what they witnessed.

It is still hard to understand how the truth continued to elude archaeologists. I had the honour of meeting Robert Hickey in 1970, and during the time I lived in the Boyne Valley I was able to interview many of his close friends. While it is clear that Hickey knew that the sun's rays entered the mound at winter solstice, it is not known how a group of amateur archaeologists, in 1935, could have confused this with the summer solstice and mounted an excursion to the mound at precisely the time of year when the sun's position at dawn is in fact furthest from the entrance to the passage. The search for the sunlight began to resemble the search for the Loch Ness monster. The ill-fated expedition, equipped with tents for a three-night vigil, was doubly unfortunate in not having a single clear morning in which to view the rising sun. As a result of this fiasco the legend continued to remain unconfirmed, while the embittered caretaker continued to entertain visitors with his tales about the sun and the mound.

Undoubtedly archaeological attitudes and preconceptions were partly to blame. R. A. S. Macalister, who excavated at Newgrange (1928) and Knowth (1940) and knew of Hickey's claims, remarked: 'I may as well say here quite plainly that I have no faith whatsoever in correlations between the orientation of Rude Stone Monuments of any kind and astronomical phenomena and in reductions drawn therefrom.' Even when it was finally confirmed that the sun's rays did actually enter the mound, acceptance of the fact was reluctant and its full significance ignored.

Reluctance to accept or even test astronomical interpretations of the mounds spilled over into a rejection of all interpretations of the rock engravings which would suggest any connection with astronomy. George Coffey had seen the stars in the stones just as Eugene Conwell before him had seen them in cupmarks at Loughcrew, groups of which he thought were representative of constellations. The sun is in a sense the nearest star and early investigators quickly recognized the obvious solar symbols. In his book on Newgrange, Coffey is direct: 'Evidence of the solar cult is abundant at Loughcrew; rayed suns and wheel-like figures are plentiful. There is no reason to doubt that the cross-in-circle is a sun-symbol, the equilateral cross denoting the main directions in which the sun shines, becoming the symbol of the luminary itself.' Elsewhere he writes. 'The rayed cup-and-circle as found at Loughcrew is, no doubt, a solar symbol. The solar disc with rays proceeding downwards is a well known Egyptian sign for solar energy.' Like other investigators, Coffey did not follow up these initial insights, and was perfectly satisfied that the mounds functioned solely as graves. He therefore failed to connect the symbols with astronomical events at the mounds. He concluded finally that the engravings were decorative.

The reason why megalithic art has remained enigmatic for so long is not due to early man's inability to communicate ideas or to misleading associations surrounding the forms used in that art. The failure to interpret the meaning of the art stems from the failure to recognize the basic elements of the visual vocabulary. The investigators of the last century were able to recognize solar imagery, but could take their initial

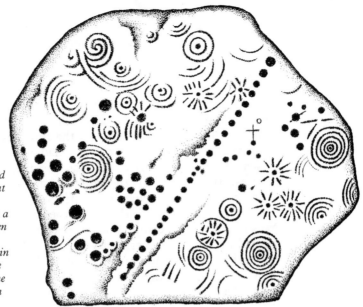

The stone roofing slab of a mound chamber, all that remains of what was once a complete structure. Today the slab stands upright in a field adjacent to the Sess Kilgreen mound in Co. Tyrone. When it was examined by George Coffey in 1899, he stated that it had 'some good stars with cup-centres. Some of the stars have lines going from them. . . .'

insights no further. In this century, solar imagery was almost completely ignored, because it could be too closely associated with astronomical alignments, which did not fit in with preconceived notions of prehistoric cultural development. The standard schemes of analysis of the symbols were originally worked out by Macalister (1921) and Breuil (1934), and these were elaborated or repeated by Piggott (1954), Ó Ríordáin and Daniel (1964), Lynch (1967) and Eogan (1968). In these schemes the engravings were initially reduced to being merely decorative or ornamental, and then later there was a futile attempt to derive human faces and figures from them. The solar emblems recognized by Conwell (1864) and Coffey (1892) became eyes of the 'mother goddess'. Flowers, axes, ships, male genital organs, feet, serpents and owls all appeared in these schemes, which seemed to include everything under the sun, yet managed to ignore the sun itself. It is unfortunate that the anthropomorphic interpretation gained such widespread acceptance, because there is not a single engraving which shows a convincing rendition of the human form. This misguided approach was first advanced by Abbé Breuil, who visited the mounds in the early 1930s. Breuil made inaccurate drawings, deliberately over-stressing the elements which he regarded as anthropomorphic.

Outside the field of archaeology other scholars in Ireland wisely maintained that many of the engravings were solar symbols. T. F. O'Rahilly, who was a Professor in the School of Celtic Studies during the 1940s, recognized a circle with rays leading out from the circumference as a *Roth Rámach* or a *Roth Fáil*, i.e. 'the wheel of light'. In 1957 the Spanish archaeologist, Albuquerque e Castro, argued that the juxtaposition of radial lines with a crescent found in an Iberian megalithic structure represented the sun and moon. These interpretations were not accepted as a convincing explanation. My own approach to the problem has been to establish a link between the light of the actual sun entering the mounds and its corresponding symbols.

During excavations carried out at Newgrange between 1962 and 1975, Michael J. O'Kelly discovered intact a curious structure over the entrance to the passage which he named the roof-box. The roof-box is a special aperture carefully constructed to admit light, not only down the passage, but into the very back recesses of the chamber. The top lintel, which was engraved with a rectilinear pattern, had become exposed as early as 1837. When the complete structure was unearthed it aroused a great deal of interest. It was seriously thought to be an offering cell for gifts to the dead or even a special entrance for spirits of the dead. All this of course was strictly in keeping with the tomb theory. O'Kelly thought that the real reason for the aperture could be connected with the local tradition regarding the sun's entry into the mound.

During the winter solstice of 1969 O'Kelly entered the chamber before sunrise to become the first archaeologist directly to observe the beam of light. He was familiar enough with the construction of the mound to realize that the straight line leading from the backstone to the centre of the roof-box aligns with the critical spot where the sun appears on the horizon. As a witness to the event itself he could only come to the conclusion that the seventeen-minute display of light he saw in the chamber was intentional and significant. He recorded his observations and presented the facts as best he could. The reaction was amazing: rather than face the implication of the new knowledge, a number of people at once raised objections, none of which would eventually be substantiated.

Based on flimsy and superficial data, some held that the probability of chance occurrence was one in ten or fifteen. This is a current fallacy, whose origins stem from a total unfamiliarity with sunbeam dialling and how it operates. Others held that the sun would not have entered the mound at the time of its construction. In fact, the event always has and always will occur, barring major catastrophe. In more desperate attempts to discredit the data, some went so far as to claim that O'Kelly reconstructed the roof-box himself in order to admit the light. This malicious rumour can easily be disproved by photographic evidence. To complicate matters further, although Jon Patrick had demonstrated in a survey that Newgrange provided by far the most convincing evidence for the astronomical orientation of some megalithic structures, no one, including O'Kelly, had recognized the degree of precision involved.

Amidst all the quibbling it was forgotten that a local tradition similar to the one surrounding Newgrange also existed in the Loughcrew Mountains, and that Newgrange itself was only part of a much larger system of solar constructs.

The shadow artists

Basic fundamentals of Neolithic sundialling

I arrived in Ireland in June 1970. My background is in art: I first studied it in New York City, where I was born, at the Pratt Institute, and later in Japan and Mexico, where I became interested in prehistoric rock engraving. My initial reaction to the ancient Irish art was one of awe and surprise at the exciting power and total abstraction of the elements. It is odd that this art, which represents the first major western European art tradition since the Ice Age, has managed to remain obscure and relatively unknown. Even histories dealing specifically with Irish art treat of it briefly and superficially. I think this is because of the profound enigma that has always surrounded it. The guide book available in the early 1970s stated that it would be futile for us *to attempt* to attach a specific meaning to the symbols. My training in art research did not allow me to accept this. The problem posed by highly abstract visual concepts is that, although narrow in intention, they are broad in extension, that is, they are capable of referring to many things. Only the context can reveal which meaning is intended. It is the context which decides whether a circle with extending radial lines refers to the sun, or whether no semantic function at all is intended, as in a wheel. A highly abstract design that bears little or no obvious resemblance to its referent must rely even more heavily on explanatory context to reveal its meaning.

I first began researching the art on a casual basis, but by 1976 I was involved in full-time documentation and analysis. I began with no preconceptions, but my regular visits to Newgrange at the winter solstice and other researches suggested to me by 1979 a possible explanation for both the rock engravings and the orientation of the mounds. My theory was not observer-imposed. The suggestion of solar and lunar images and the presence of actual sundials in the engravings, coupled with the spectre of the light entering Newgrange and the tremendous weight of tradition meant that all the needles were pointing in one direction. If the astronomical potential of the passage mounds in general was examined I was almost certain that it would demonstrate a close matching of the mounds to the movements of the sun and moon at this latitude. Just as the art displayed in a church could be expected to be religious, the art displayed in astronomical constructs could be expected to refer to the sun, the moon and the stars.

Another artist and amateur astronomer, Jack Roberts, was also concerned with the implications of Newgrange. We had met a few years earlier and he was aware of my work on the rock engravings. When he visited my studio one evening in February 1980 he was impressed by the small models I had constructed of Neolithic sundials. I explained that there are no textbooks on the very earliest forms of sundialling and that I had in effect to become a sundialler myself and learn through observing how the models operated. I also showed him how I was studying the interaction of the sun and earth and light and shadow by sunbeam dialling. I was investigating the behaviour of beams of light projected by the setting sun through the back windows of the studio at 10 ft, 23 ft and 27 ft. These distances are comparable to some of the smaller passages in the mounds and I was beginning to familiarize myself with techniques that were used very early in man's cultural development.

What excited Jack most was when I announced that I felt I was ready to start testing the theories in the field by direct empirical observation inside the mounds. Both the Boyne Valley and Loughcrew complexes are conveniently close to Dublin, and, as we have seen, these two groups of sites contain the bulk of megalithic art in Ireland. I thought these sites should be investigated first because, if the extant passage mounds could be demonstrated to be solar orientated, it would eliminate the possibility of chance occurrence and establish astronomical features as characteristic of the mounds. The research would be systematic, and would naturally extend to the few relatively isolated but similar mounds bearing the imprint of megalithic art. (This category does not include all the 150 passage mounds in Ireland, but enough to be a valid sample.)

Before telling the full story of our discoveries, some fundamentals of Neolithic sundialling need to be considered.

Figure 1 is a diagram of the sun's extreme positions as it rises on the horizon at various times during the year. Below this is a circle representing the year in time and how it is divided by these extreme positions. At summer solstice the sun is at its most northerly position on the horizon as it rises, and it assumes its highest position in the sky, 60° 18′ at noon. This day is called Midsummer's Day and is the longest one of the year. At winter solstice the sun is at its most southerly position on the horizon as it rises, and it assumes its lowest position in the sky, only 12° 18′, at noon. This day is called Midwinter's Day and is the shortest one of the year. These positions vary with latitude. Near the equator the solstice rising positions are much closer together. As one travels north or south these positions begin to widen. In the Boyne Valley at 53° 41′ north latitude the variation of these positions is large and to its early inhabitants this was probably one of the most striking variations in the natural world.

This annual solar movement along the horizon from one solstice to another and back again describes a year. It is an apparent movement that results from the earth's orientation in space and the motion of the earth in its orbit around the sun. The recognition of these movements along the horizon and the careful attention given to them by early man does not imply a recognition of the celestial mechanism which causes them. E. C. Krupp, who has done extensive research on prehistoric astronomies, has pointed out that astronomical events on the horizon are both indicators of

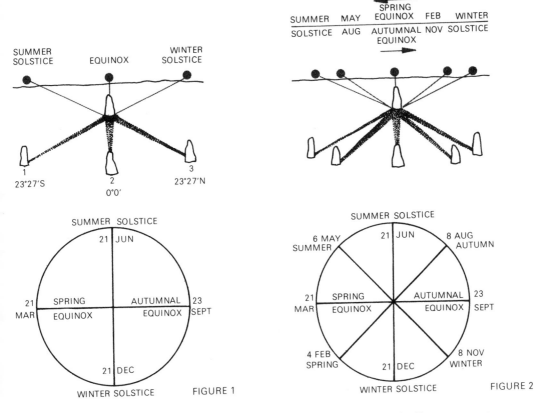

SUMMER
SOLSTICE   EQUINOX   WINTER
SOLSTICE

1
23°27'S   2   3
0°0'   23°27'N

SUMMER SOLSTICE

21 JUN

21   SPRING   AUTUMNAL   23
MAR   EQUINOX   EQUINOX   SEPT

21 DEC

WINTER SOLSTICE   FIGURE 1

SUMMER SOLSTICE

6 MAY   21 JUN   8 AUG
SUMMER   AUTUMN

21   SPRING   AUTUMNAL   23
MAR   EQUINOX   EQUINOX   SEPT

4 FEB   8 NOV
SPRING   21 DEC   WINTER

WINTER SOLSTICE   FIGURE 2

the orientation and motion of the earth in space and, in turn, the indicators of seasonal changes. To ancient peoples it might have seemed that the astronomical indicators were simultaneously the cause and symbol of the world's great forces. Our research in Ireland would tend to support this view. For our research it is therefore more pertinent to consider the apparent motions of the sun than the astronomical phenomena which cause the apparent motion.

As the sun moves from one solstice to another, its declination changes from 23° 27' south to 23° 27' north. This is the result of the angle of tilt of the earth's axis away from the celestial equator, which is 23° 27'. The celestial equator is the great circle in the sky which lies on a plane perpendicular to the earth's axis. The declination of the sun is its angular distance away from the celestial equator. Throughout the year the sun's apparent motion will be restricted to declinations lying between these two extremes. When the sun is above the celestial equator the days will be longer, and when it is below the celestial equator the days will shorten. When the sun is on the celestial equator its declination will be 0° 0' and day and night will be equal. This is called the equinox.

Besides defining the day and the year, the apparent movements of the sun also define the cardinal directions. At equinox, the sun will rise due east and set due west anywhere in the world. It will rise to its highest point in the sky at midday and define south. On any day of the year a line north and south will bisect the angle of its rising and setting positions.

It is the apparent geometric structuring of the heavens which gave rise to the geometric forms in megalithic architecture and art. The principal tool used for recognizing this structuring was undoubtedly the gnomon. In figure 1 I have positioned three stones which align to a central stone and the sun in a geometrical arrangement. The central stone is a gnomon, which literally means 'one who knows'. A gnomon is any vertical object that shows time by casting its shadow. It is an essential element in any sundial and may be used to show either the time of day or the time of year. Figure 1 indicates how it is used on the plane of the horizon as the position of the sun changes, so that the shadow strikes stones 1, 2 and 3 respectively at winter solstice, equinox and summer solstice. It has often been said that there is no human instrument more ancient or more interesting than the sundial; it is a visible map of time. The earliest must have been erected in the Old Stone Age tens of thousands of years ago; but among the oldest now known are those built in Ireland during the Neolithic period.

Besides the equinox and solstices there are two other positions of the sun on the horizon which were evidently important to Neolithic diallers. These positions are included in figure 2, and the circle below shows how the year is divided into eight parts when these positions are included. These new positions are called cross-quarter days, and they define half-time intervals between the solstices and the equinoxes. Notice that although they divide the year equally in time, their positions on the horizon are much nearer to the solstice positions. The reason for this is that the earth's orbit around the sun is not a circle but an ellipse. The effect is that the sun's rising position on the horizon changes rapidly as the year approaches equinox, and slows down nearly to a standstill as the year comes to the solstice. The term 'solstice' in fact means 'sun's standstill'. For a period of eleven days before and after the exact day of the solstice the sun's position on the horizon moves extremely slowly. By way of example, prior to the winter solstice in 1980 the declination of the sun changed from $22°\ 60'$ to $23°\ 26'$ during this period, whereas prior to equinox the sun's declination changed from $4°\ 8'$ to $0°\ 11'$ in the same period of eleven days. Thus it is much easier to determine the precise date of equinox than the precise date of winter solstice.

Cross-quarter days are extremely important because they express a rhythm which is linked to the seasonal cycle and which has an immediate application to the agricultural calendar. Solstices and equinoxes are primarily of astronomical interest only, whereas the cross-quarter days define spring, summer, autumn and winter and serve to announce times for planting and harvesting and moving domestic animals. This involves social organization and, as a rule, the more complex the social organization of a culture, the more complex the calendar will become. The Neolithic mounds are evidence in themselves that Neolithic people were not only farmers, but led a relatively complex way of life which included building permanent monuments. Farm surpluses allowed more time for the creation and exchange of goods and services, as well as for astronomical pursuits and probably ritual gatherings. Some of these activities may have

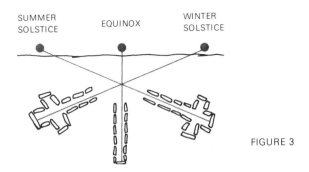

FIGURE 3

become the province of specialists, thus creating a division of labour and a central authority. The calendar was the device which regulated these activities through the year.

With the inclusion of the cross-quarter days in figure 2 the sundial calendar becomes far more useful and effective. Notice that the two cross-quarter-day stones operate twice a year, like the stone marking the equinox. Also notice that the dates given for the cross-quarter days are slightly different from the traditional ones. Modern festival days were adopted for convenience to the first day of the month, whereas in prehistoric times these dates could only have been determined by observing the sun and its shadow. Notice, too, that the dates given in the diagrams are the usual calendar dates of the events. In some years these may vary slightly either side of the usual dates.

In figure 3 I have substituted the ground plans of passages in megalithic mounds for the gnomons. The passage and chamber of a megalithic mound is a far more complex, precise and specialized instrument than a gnomon is. Instead of simply casting a shadow, the passage narrows a beam of light as it is projected into the chamber. The passage is aligned to particular points on or near the horizon. When the sun occupies these points at special times of year, light passes without interruption along the whole length of the passage to illuminate the backstone of the chamber. This type of sundialling is called sunbeam or light-beam dialling, and it represents a great technological improvement over shadow dialling with a gnomon. It does not require observation of the sun's shadow at the moment of sunrise, since it gives a clear definition of both the altitude and direction of the sun after the sun has risen. Not only is it more accurate, but it gives warnings of events and is a permanent construct that needs no re-aligning.

It is surprising that such Neolithic solar constructs have survived for so long, many of them intact and in working order. They are older than all the other known solar alignments of the Old and New Worlds. In Egypt Sir Norman Lockyer described how light-beam techniques were used at the Great Temple of Amun at Karnak for solstice observation, a description supported in more recent years by another astronomer, Gerald Hawkins. Lockyer pointed out that the technique was used in eastern observatories until the middle of the eighteenth century. Similar devices, less ancient than those of Europe and the Near East, have been demonstrated for the

New World too. In a book written in 1945, called *Mysteries of Ancient South America*, Harold T. Wilkins disclosed information about ancient American sites that was at the time considered fabulous and not taken very seriously. On page 172 he remarks: 'There are, it may be mentioned here, spots along the canyon of the Rio Colorado, where arrows cut deeply into the face of the sheer walls can be seen in certain lights and incidences of the solar rays.' Recently in Chaco Canyon, New Mexico, such a scheme was discovered: an arrangement of large stones was apparently positioned intentionally so that the rays of the sun would illuminate a set of spirals in ways suggesting special consideration for equinoxes and solstices.

On page 168 of his book Wilkins describes something even more interesting: 'When Cuzco was the capital of old Peru, it contained a Temple of the Sun, famed far and near for its magnificence. . . . In the west wall, the architects had contrived an aperture, in such a way that, when the sunbeams reached it, it caught and focused them inside the temple's nave and sanctuary. Stretching inside the temple, like a gold chain, from one sparkling point to another, the rays encircled the walls, illuminating the grim idols, and disclosing certain mystic signs, at other times invisible.' It transpires that remains in Peru do have alignments and the Inca did possess sundials. In substance it is likely that what Wilkins reports is true. Mayan temples have parallels to the basic strategies alleged to have been employed in Peru.

The problem that faced Jack and myself was that we were dealing with dialling methods about which we had no practical knowledge. We had to rely on direct observation in the field, supplemented by experiments with models in the studio. In the beginning our only actual experience was what we had seen at Newgrange. The only real description we had of the method was Lockyer's detailed discussion of the apertures and pylons of the Great Temple of Amun at Karnak. We were forced to start from the very beginning and explore the fundamentals until we ourselves became artists of light and shadow.

The wooden stakes depicted in figure 4 are aligned to define two dates. On day 1 a shadow is aligned with stakes 1A and 1B. On day 2 the shadow has moved to align with stakes 2A and 2B. Since the B stakes are placed twice as far away from the gnomon as the A stakes, they describe a difference in the angle of the shadow that is twice as great. The difference in the two days is doubly magnified and is made far more apparent by the B stakes.

The accuracy of any solar construct increases directly in proportion to its size. Let us suppose that two passages, one twice the size of the other,

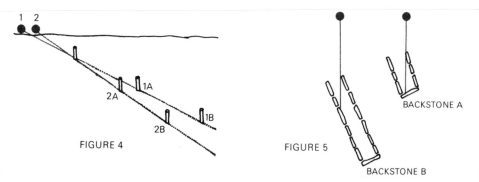

FIGURE 4

FIGURE 5

BACKSTONE A

BACKSTONE B

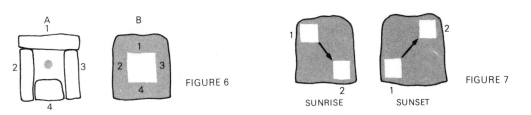

FIGURE 6

FIGURE 7

SUNRISE   SUNSET

are aligned to the same date (figure 5). The date is determined by the position of the light beam striking the backstone. The sun's rays are always parallel. On a particular day near the date of the alignment the light enters both mounds. An observer in the smaller passage must begin to consider the light as it strikes the backstone, whereas the observer in the larger passage knows immediately and at a glance that the intended date has not yet arrived.

Considered either architecturally or astronomically, no two mounds are the same, but they do exhibit similar characteristics, besides a preference for particular periods and events in the solar cycle. One of the chief aims of megalithic architecture is to reduce the light in the interior of the chamber. The darker the chamber, the more brilliant and magnificent the narrow shaft of light will appear to be. If the construct is intact, the beam of light will invariably be projected in the form of a rectangle, always aimed at the backstone with a few interesting exceptions. In figure 6, A represents a section of stones forming a typical passage and B is the backstone. The rectangle on the backstone is a beam of light projected by stones 1, 2, 3 and 4. Stone 1 is called a lintel or a roof-slab, 2 and 3 are passage stones or chamber stones, and stone 4 is called a sill. This basic construct is only a short step away from the concept of a roof-box, which is really a second aperture positioned above the roof-slab. If stones 1 and 4 are missing the orientation of the alignment can still be determined, but if stones 2 and 3 are missing, as a solar construct the mound is a ruin.

The daily movement of the beam of light traces the daily path of the sun, and will always move from left to right. Figure 7 depicts a backstone aligned to sunrise and a backstone aligned to sunset. As the sun rises the projected beam of light moves downwards, and as the sun sets the beam moves upwards. Each day the beam of light changes in exact accord with the daily change in the direction and altitude of the sun. The difference between one day and the next is amplified in proportion to the length of the construct. Besides this, the length of the construct increases the speed of movement of the light beam. If one of the stones in figure 7 is placed in a construct twice as long, the beam of light will take half as much time to go from position 1 to position 2. But in fact determining a specific date is not arrived at by timing the speed of the light beam, but by noting its varying position which is magnified by increasing the length of the construct.

It is unnecessary and impractical to design a solar construct so that the sun enters the chamber only on a single day. Not only would such a structure need to be hundreds of yards in length, but it would fail to give adequate warning of the approach of a specific date and would depend for its effectiveness on good weather conditions on that particular day. The

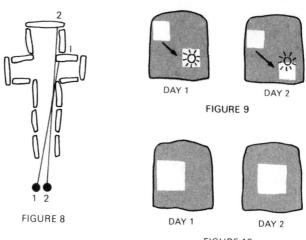

FIGURE 8

DAY 1   DAY 2

FIGURE 9

DAY 1   DAY 2

FIGURE 10

investment in extra time and labour would be immense, without any guarantee of success in solar observation. The typical megalithic solar construct is far more efficient, less delicate and equally accurate.

Figure 8 shows a beam of light entering a chamber on two successive days prior to the date of the primary alignment. On day 1, light is prevented from reaching the backstone. In a very small structure this may only be by a tenth of an inch, but the effect is the same – the two days are clearly visually differentiated to the observer. In all megalithic solar constructs the period during which the beam of light strikes the backstone is limited, and can be defined in terms of individual days. Let us say that this period is nine days and it is known to the observer from previous experience or marked on the stone itself. All the observer needs to do is count off the four days to the specific intended date of the alignment. Dependence on good weather conditions on that specific date is no longer required as the day has already been accurately determined in advance.

During the period in which the light beam strikes the backstone, individual days can be defined in terms of the varying positions of the patch of light. On day 1 in figure 9 the beam of light frames a rock engraving. On the subsequent day it is evident that the beam is no longer in direct alignment with the engraving.

Some backstones, however, have no engravings, and a specific day is determined solely on the basis of the position of the beam of light. In figure 10, on day 1 the beam of light is slightly off-centre, but on day 2 the beam is clearly in the central position.

There are special requirements for determining the exact date of a solstice. Unless the construct is of an extremely large size the varying positions of the light beam will be almost undetectable during the entire twenty-two day period of the solstice. Let us suppose that in figure 11 position 2 represents the sun on the exact day of winter solstice sunrise and position 1 represents a day prior to the commencement of the solstice. After reaching position 1 the sun will always move to its furthest rising position south on the day of winter solstice and return again to position

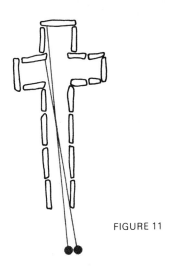

FIGURE 11

1 after the solstice. The exact date of winter solstice can always be determined by dividing the days the sun takes to return to position 1 by half. At Newgrange today the sun begins to enter the chamber on the eleventh day before the day of winter solstice. The construct actually gives a precise definition of the solstice period from which a specific date can easily be determined. Even if we assume that some of the stones in the passage have inclined inwards since the construction of the roof-box, the construct is capable of a high degree of precision.

A great deal is made by sceptics of the fact that the tilt in the earth's axis has changed slightly over the past 5,000 years, which would mean that the rising position of the sun is different from the ancient one. In reality this shift is only one half a degree to the north of the original position, and makes no significant difference to the accuracy of the alignment. At equinox the variation is so minimal that it need not be considered at all.

In order to test the theories in the field Jack and I decided in the spring of 1980 that the most promising monuments for research at that time of year were the two most prominent passage mounds in the Loughcrew complex, Cairns L and T. According to the ground plans we were using at the time both mounds seemed to be aligned slightly south of due east. If they were equinox indicators we assumed that they would be aligned due east. This caused endless speculation. The astronomical significance of the equinox is obvious, but we had no idea why prominent major mounds should indicate a date that would fall prior to the spring equinox and after the autumnal equinox. For all we knew, the mounds could be aligned to a particular rising of the full moon. We decided to start by checking all the possibilities. We would begin our vigil by observing the full moon on the evening of 1 March, and begin to observe sunrises from the following morning. Jack would record the events by photography and I would do the drawing, measuring and timing. We would concentrate on Cairn T first and investigate Cairn L when we had some idea of what Cairn T did. We decided to do Cairn T first partly because it featured an elaborately engraved backstone that had intrigued me for years.

Movements in the mountains

The first foray at Loughcrew

Located about 40 miles from the mouth of the Boyne, the Loughcrew mountains provide a commanding view virtually from coast to coast and into both northern and southern provinces of Ireland. On these heights, entire complexes of permanent public structures were erected, possibly sometime before the major mounds in the Boyne Valley were beginning to be built around 3700 BC. The Loughcrew sites have escaped the attention and well-documented archaeological investigation devoted to their Boyne Valley counterparts. Archaeologists have consistently maintained that they are later than the Boyne sites, even though there are no radiocarbon dates to support this view, and, as we noted earlier, rock-engraving techniques appear to be more primitive – and therefore older – at Loughcrew.

Within the Loughcrew complex, Cairn T, at over 900 ft, stands in the central position and takes the most prominent place on the highest summit of a megalithic area that may once have contained as many as fifty to a hundred mounds. The relative size and focal position of the mound indicates that, if it was a solar construct, the day that it defined must have had great significance for the builders. As Roberts and I began to realize this, we became more curious about the possible astronomical alignment. Unfortunately, adverse weather in the spring of 1980 prevented us from making a single observation of a sunrise. We stayed in the mountains the entire weekend of 1 March without getting a glimpse of the sun or moon. After returning to Dublin we tried changing our strategy. We took it in turns to study the weather conditions at 5 a.m. each morning, and, if the sky seemed clear, we would set off for Loughcrew at a moment's notice. The journey took about an hour and a half and we were usually positioned inside the chamber long before sunrise. On most occasions, however, clouds built up before dawn, thwarting our plans.

During the first part of the month Jack and I spent long hours in the dark recesses of the mound waiting for the light. The mountains were covered with snow and the prevailing winds from the east blew icy gusts down the passage of the mound. Meteorologists know that 5,000 years ago the climate was more favourable, being up to 2°C milder. Prevailing winds, however, remain relatively constant and one thing we learned quickly was that the passage was not orientated to avoid them. As the month wore on, the bad weather and the mystery of the mound became only more intense. The equinox would come on 20 March that year, and we were in danger of passing that date without having made a single observation.

On the morning of 17 March Jack telephoned with excellent reports of perfectly clear skies. He sounded excited and said that all the stars were out and he had been watching Mars in conjunction with Regulus in his telescope. We were assured of a brilliant sunrise and, although the regular car was not working, he was certain he could get the Land Rover on the road immediately. We left Dublin late, but for the first time in two weeks we were under a starry sky. By the time we passed Kells a faint glow of light preceding the break of dawn was already beginning to shine in the east, and from the elevated seats of the Land Rover we could peer over the hedges and pick out the ancient high places and monuments of Meath in the distance.

We were winding up the mountain road when the disc of the sun broke on the horizon. We felt as if we were ten minutes late for an appointment made over 5,000 years ago. From the top of the road there would be a climb on foot to the mound perched on the summit of the mountain. The lock on the modern door leading to the passage had frozen during the night, and as we struggled with it the rising sun was already above the horizon. When we drew back the door a narrow chink of light streamed down the passage and flashed into the end recess of the chamber.

On the upper left of the backstone a rectangular patch of light was rapidly beginning to take form (p. 94), brilliantly illuminating the entire chamber in a glowing splendour of shimmering golden orange light. It was dazzling, and when we entered the chamber we stood back and gazed in awe. Naturally, we had expected to see something similar to what we had seen at Newgrange. There, the low angle of the sun rising at winter solstice causes the beam of light to sweep across the chamber. Here, however, the light assumed a clearly defined geometric shape that was projected on to the upright backstone and moved diagonally across it, tracing the path of the sun against a mural of prehistoric art. What impressed us most was the careful and delicate modelling of the light beam by the huge stones forming the passage and chamber, and how the shape of the beam conformed to the patterns engraved on the stone. For the first time we were seeing the signs and symbols in the context in which the artist had meant them to be seen. Suddenly markings that had appeared to be random and haphazard became part of an intricately structured system that derived its meaning from the solar event we were witnessing.

Working with model sundials had provided invaluable experience which could be applied to dealing with real dials in the field. Further experience with real solar constructs would naturally develop our skill in predicting and estimating the behaviour of light in relation to daily changes in the sun's apparent position in the sky. What we had seen on 17 March indicated to us that the sun would not be striking the backstone for more than five or six days before and after the equinox, and on the day of the equinox, 20 March, the beam of light would sink lower on the stone and neatly frame a large engraved radial solar disc. In order to make an accurate determination of this we would need to make one other observation within the next few days.

It was clear to us that we were dealing with a solar construct capable of defining an individual day with far greater precision than Newgrange. The wider differences in the sun's apparent movement at equinox made it considerably easier to define the actual day of equinox at Cairn T than the day of winter solstice at Newgrange. Coupled with the help of the rock engravings, this created a remarkably precise astronomical instrument. What we had seen at Cairn T encouraged us to investigate Cairn L as well.

Cairn T is a major mound that dominates a group of smaller satellite mounds clustered around it on the summit of a mountain known as *Sliabh na Cailliagh*, the Mountain of the Sorceress, or otherwise Carnbane East (sometimes the entire range of mountains is referred to as *Sliabh na Caillaigh*). Cairn L is also a major mound, dominating a group of satellite mounds on Carnbane West. An unusual feature is a curious white standing stone positioned inside the chamber. We were now certain that this stone could be understood in terms of the behaviour of light inside the chamber. We agreed that Jack would lead a separate group to investigate Cairn L, and that I would form a group to continue monitoring Cairn T.

As the equinox approached, weather conditions deteriorated. When the day of equinox came and went without our having been able to make an observation, we grew anxious, knowing that the days during which sunlight would directly strike the backstone were rapidly diminishing. Both teams took up their positions every morning regardless of weather conditions, since even a brief break in the clouds could provide the information we required. On the third day after equinox the weather at last improved. Sunlight appeared along the passage of Cairn T, stopping temporarily at stone 3 before a beam of light dramatically flashed all the way to the backstone and the patch of illumination began to form. As expected, the beam of light was not framing the radial solar disc, but appeared low and off-centre in the same way that it was above and off-centre on 17 March. On 20 March, the day of equinox, the sun would definitely focus on what was apparently an image of itself on the backstone. We were simultaneously being initiated into the wonders of megalithic astronomy and megalithic art.

Suddenly Jack appeared at the passage entrance. He said that Cairn L was aligned to a position on the horizon that would not be occupied by the sun until much later in the year. These two major mounds – Cairns L and T – appeared to be orientated in the same direction according to archaeological surveys; however, in terms of real function, the equinox rising sun is focused on Cairn T, but does not approach anywhere near the passage of Cairn L. After that we never relied too much on surveys, and depended more on what we could see during the actual events. We again watched the dagger of sunlight move across the chamber floor at Cairn T. In two days time the light would no longer strike the backstone. Jack and I spent the Sunday afternoon (26 March) and evening in my studio going over the data from the two observations.

During these sessions we argue opposing views in order to arrive at agreed conclusions. We had no doubts that the alignment was pre-

TODAY'S WEATHER
Bright spells but showers of rain or hail. Rather mild.
(See Page 21)

Irish Independent

Vol. 89. No. 72 | TUESDAY, MARCH 25, 1980 | C | Price 14p | BIGGEST DAILY SALE IN IRELAND

Thatcher's no-nonsense timetable to end Northern impasse

GOLDEN SECRETS OF OUR HISTORY

The shape of the beam-sundial as it moved across the passage at Cairn T.

By GERARD O'REGAN

STARTLING new evidence, produced last night, shows that, 3,000 years before Christ, the Irish had a more advanced civilisation than has been previously thought.

And it may well be that in some areas we were even more advanced than the Egyptians and pre-dated the achievements of the Romans.

An American born expert on rock inscriptions last night suggested that the attached photograph shows that when it came to the "technology" then required for "astronomy and calender making" the Irish were in fact way ahead of their time.

"This is going to shatter a lot of the previously held beliefs about the state of Irish civilisation at that time," claimed Mr. Martin Brennan, who was born in New York of Irish parents but who has lived in this country for the past 10 years.

He has written a number of books on archaeology and related topics and his latest book, "The Boyne Valley Vision," which details the importance of the variety of ancient monuments in this area, is due to be published next month.

Mr. Brennan says that the inscription on the photograph was used by stone age Irishmen as part of a sophisticated process for denoting the passage of time and the different seasons of the year.

This inscription was photographed yesterday on the inside wall of the 5,000 year old structure in Co. Meath—and, as can be seen, the sunlight which filters through a space in the mound has gradually moved down through one of the circles which are believed to represent the sun.

Mr. Brennan said that in his opinion this mound and its complicated method of allowing sunlight to filter on to the wall inscriptions was part of a highly advanced method used by the Irish of the time to determine the date of the spring equinox—the date when day and night are of equal length.

"If that photograph had been taken on the 20th of this month the light would have focused completely on the top circle in the photograph," said Mr. Brennan.

"This latest discovery presents new and challenging evidence regarding the development of Stone Age technology and indeed questions the whole purpose of the mounds themselves.

"It is now evident that significant advances which were made in the fields of astronomy and calendar making in Ireland during that period have not been recognised," he said.

The mounds at the Loughcrew mountains are thought to be of the same period as the Boyne

Continued on Back Page.

Martin Brennan and Jack Roberts, who made the sundial discovery.

Bank rate to leap as Big Four seek 2½ pc

By COLM RAPPLE.
Our Business Editor

BANK interest rates are likely to take another jump within the next few weeks.

The Big Four associated banks have already held some discussions with the Central Bank and are believed to be seeking a massive 2½ to three per cent hike in rates above the current record levels.

It is doubtful, however, if the Central Bank would agree to such an imposition.

Some increase, however, is on the cards and the Building Societies have warned that any rise in bank interest rates would have to be followed by a rise in both their deposit and mortgage rates.

Loughlin Sweeney, Assistant General Manager of Allied Irish Banks, last night claimed that the Big Four banks could justify an increase of three per cent in their interest rates. But goodheartedly, he suggested that they might be content with 2½ per cent.

He pointed to the world-wide trend towards higher interest rates and to the fact that the anticipated drop in British rates now seemed unlikely.

The main worry of the Irish banks, however, is that their non-associated competitors — the merchant banks—have been increasing their rates in line with market trends.

It is this trend which has led to recent speculation that one of the Big Four banks might break ranks and push up rates on its own — breaking the cartel which has existed for decades.

Mr. Sweeney, however, ruled out such a development for the immediate future. Given the present tight credit position and the high level of interest rates, such a move would be to the detriment of the small man.

Last week the Banks Standing Committee raised the matter of interest rates with the Central Bank. Further discussions are scheduled. But it is unlikely that the Central Bank will

Continued on Back Page.

Mrs. Thatcher.

Take it or leave it Bill for the Commons

From JAMES KELLY,
Our Northern Political Editor

BRITAIN is to lay it on the line for the people of Northern Ireland with a "take it or leave it" Bill for the future Government of the area due for debate at Westminster in December or January next, followed quickly by a Northern Ireland General Election or Constitutional Referendum in February next.

I learned last night that this is the timetable which the Thatcher Government has laid down as the end result of hectic new negotiations on a British Cabinet White Paper to be submitted to a Stormont Conference, probably in July.

There will be provision also for wider consultations with Churches, trade unions and other interested parties, in addition to the political parties. After this process, the British Cabinet will produce the long-awaited legislation to end the North's Constitutional stalemate.

Last night Rev. Ian Paisley, the D.U.P. leader told newsmen at the end of the first phase of the Stormont conference that he believed, contrary to the expectations of the Official Unionists, that Mr. Thatcher was firmly determined to produce a

Continued on Back Page.

House law to be challenged in High Court

By JIM FARRELLY

CLEVER 1979 legislation to keep down the price of the 20,000 new private houses built annually in the State is to be challenged as unconstitutional in the High Court.

The challenge is by the powerful building industry which puts more than £500 million annually into private housing and papers have been served on the Government and the Attorney General.

The Construction Industry Federation, representing the builders, is seeking a declaration that the provision requiring that a certificate of reasonable value be furnished before mortgages for new houses be handed out is contrary to natural and constitutional justice.

The provision contained in the Housing (Miscellaneous Provisions Act 1979) was hailed last night, by Environment Minister, Mr. Sylvester Barrett, as "having the desired effect."

"I am encouraged by a decrease in the average gross price of new houses for which loans were approved by the four main lending agencies during the second half of 1979" he said at the opening of the First National Building Society Office in Gort, Co. Galway yesterday.

The main ground of appeal is that the Minister, Mr. Barret, has failed to make regulations providing a system of appeal to the Circuit Court for a builder aggrieved by a refusal to grant a Certificate of Reasonable Value.

Though there is provision for an appeal to the Circuit Court in the legislation the regulations necessary to bring the provision into effect have not been made.

Another grievance is that the builders are not being furnished with the reasons on which refusals are based.

Mr. Tom Reynolds, Director of the Construction Industry Federation, said last night that because of the legislation there had been a big drop in the number of private houses being built.

He claimed that the legislation was adding on greatly to builders' cocts.

The Act forbids lending institutions handing out a mortgage for a new house before the applicant for the loan produces a certificate of reasonable value issued by the Department of the Environment.

If the building society or the proposed house purchased contravenes the provision they will be guilty of an offence and liable to fines.

With the average cost of a new house standing at £28,000, Mr. Barrett claimed that the provision being challenged and other measures introduced by him last year were keeping down the average cost of new houses.

The other provisions are: Building societies must allocate 70 per cent of their available mortgage finance to house purchasers whose mortgage requirements are under £20,000.

They must allocate at least 40 per cent of their available mortgage finance for new homes.

The Minister said the building societies were fully cooperating with the government on all these measures.

Plan to solve traffic chaos

A free or reduced bus-fare week, coupled with the banning of private car parking in the city, should be introduced in the city and county area, members of Dublin County Council decided last night.

Some form of drastic action is urgently needed in a bid to ease the traffic situation, Mr. Frank Smyth said.

GAA protest at 'witch-hunt' by RTE's Frontline

G.A.A. chiefs are up in arms over an RTE "Frontline" programme tonight examining links between the G.A.A. and militant republicanism.

The three top men in the G.A.A., Mr. Pat McFlynn, president; Mr. Con Murphy, last year's president, and Mr. Liam Mulvihill, general secretary, have refused to go on the show.

G.A.A. sources last night described the show as a "witch hunt by RTE.

The three were invited on the show to discuss four "political motions" on the agenda for the G.A.A. annual conference this weekend in Newcastle, Co. Down.

The motions deal with the "occupation" of Crossmaglen G.A.A. club's football pitch by the British Army, support for the H-Block protest and the political affiliations of the G.A.A. as an organisation.

But it will also focus on recent paramilitary demonstrations which were linked with the G.A.A.

These include the Provo escort for the remains of John Joe Sheehy in Tralee, the Provo Protest in Casement park, and the support by the Tyrone G.A.A. for a "smash H-Block protest.

Last night Con Murphy explained why he did not go on the show which will go ahead without any of the G.A.A. hierarchy:

"Discusion and decision on these motions are the prerogative of the delegates and a public discussion on these issues by officials in advance would be improper", he said.

Frontline sources last night claimed that the "G.A.A. triumvirate are using Congress as an excuse not to go on the show", and that they had been offered "an easy ride" on the show.

Bullion hijack gang get record £4m.

A GANG posing as policemen hijacked an armoured bullion truck yesterday and escaped with gold and silver worth £4m., police in London reported. Police said it was even a bigger haul than the Great Train Robbery which netted £2½m.

A six-man gang, led by a man in a police uniform, waved the truck down as it was travelling on a main London road to the Docks. Thinking it was a traffic check, the truck halted.

The gang, armed with sawn-off shotguns overpowered the two guards and forced the driver to drive the truck to an underground garage where he was dumped out unhurt.

Police believed the gang transferred the loot to another vehicle somewhere and abandoned the truck. The gang escaped without a trace and there was no clues to its identity.

The truck belonged to a shipping company, Jeppessen Heaton Ltd.

Police said it took just one minute for the gang to halt the truck on Southend Road and take it over.

The guards told the police they had no suspicion anything was wrong until it was too late. They said they assumed it was one of the checks of vehicles carried out by police from time to time.

Most of the £4m. stolen yesterday was silver ingots, but some wsa gold.

The findings at Cairn T, Loughcrew, made a tremendous impact on the general public in Ireland. The 'Irish Independent' hailed the light-beam discovery as 'Golden secrets of our history' in front page headlines.

determined and intentional. Neither of us could be sure if the lower angle of the rising sun at the autumnal equinox would create a significantly different display of light, but defining the spring equinox alone represented a considerable achievement. We could not determine whether Cairn L indicated a particularly critical time in the solar cycle, but we were almost certain that Knowth, the largest mound in the Boyne Valley complex, was aligned like Cairn T to the equinox. Knowth was in the process of being excavated and so would be difficult to investigate, but what we had seen at Cairn T suggested that major mounds in both complexes showed that the equinox was regarded as a time of primary significance and importance to the megalith builders. We recognized that the equinox has universal significance and it therefore seemed logical for Cairn T to be in a focal position. The equinox alignments complimented the solstice alignment of Newgrange, and those who were prepared to dismiss Newgrange as either an accidental or vague ritualistic and prelogical orientation would now have to try to explain away the implications of a precise, accurate, equinoctial alignment still in excellent working order. We decided to bring our findings to the newspapers.

The reaction of newspaper editors on Monday morning was generally the same. They were all familiar with Newgrange and they immediately recognized the significance of what we had witnessed. In fact, what really perplexed them was how archaeologists had failed to make these discoveries themselves. We explained that archaeologists had dismissed the astronomical potential of megalithic mounds for generations, and it was unlikely that a change in attitude would come about overnight. We had no idea whether our story would be printed, so that when we woke up the next morning we were surprised to find that our discoveries had made headline news in the *Irish Independent*, and many other newspapers carried major articles. The story was also featured on radio and television news. Congratulations poured in all week; we had captured the imagination and support of not only the general public but also some professional astronomers and other specialists. Archaeologists closed ranks and publicly maintained a wall of silence. After our first venture into the field we were prepared to present our evidence, but no archaeologists approached us, not even privately. We did not know if they had valid criticisms to make or merely resented our intrusion into what they considered was their private domain. We wondered too if the full implications of our discoveries had been understood. Surely it was obvious that, if two of the major mounds investigated so far were solar constructs, others might be designed on similar principles?

Regardless of the lack of response from archaeologists, Jack and I had achieved a major victory in awakening public interest and awareness of our megalithic cultural heritage. Newly introduced methods of farming are rapidly destroying many smaller unprotected sites, and we are deeply concerned about the alarming increase in wanton destruction. By publicizing the cultural achievements of the past one is at least going part of the way to protecting the sites.

The second light

Lunar observations during the summer of 1980

One of the more positive results of the publicity was that it put us in touch with professional astronomers and specialists abroad. Several of them wrote to us during the course of the year. Receiving communications from professionals in no way implies that they immediately accepted any of our claims. We were artists who had entered the new and complex field of archaeoastronomy in the process of doing art research. But as artists we were very much encouraged by the fact that our work was taken seriously by scientists. The letters we received were neither for nor against our conclusions, but they were immensely helpful in that they showed us how much interest there was amongst modern astronomers in the astronomy of the Neolithic period. Derek McNally, Assistant Director at the University of London Observatory, wrote, 'My interest in positional astronomy is kept alive by its possible application in the field of archaeo-astronomy'.

One of the first specialists to contact us was Alexander Marshack of the Peabody Museum of Archaeology and Ethnology. Not all professional researchers, it seemed, were prepared to dismiss our finds without further enquiry. Professor P. Q. Wayman, of Dunsink Observatory outside Dublin, wrote to us regarding our method of direct observation: 'This approach has certain strengths and weaknesses. It is the strength of these observations that they carry conviction without the need either to make or to comprehend the detailed survey of the site or to establish the relatively abstract connection with the celestial sphere (which tends to be only properly understood by astronomers, surveyors and navigators, but which, in fact, is really quite straightforward). It is also the strength of this method that it presents a visualizable, impressive picture to a person witnessing it. This approach, however, has the disadvantage (a) that suitable weather conditions may not be adequately frequent; (b) that it is necessary to wait for the particular time of the year before progressing with the unravelling of the data.'

It was these disadvantages, particularly the need to wait for the right time of year, that caused us to refine our method by including lunar observations in our programme. We had considered them before, but had not realized their potential for indicating solar positions at various times of the year. Our main problem after the spring equinox observations at Cairn T was that two key major mounds, Cairn L and Dowth, were obviously aligned to the rising sun sometime in the winter months. A number of important smaller mounds were also obviously winter alignments. Our concern was primarily with the major mounds: we had already begun to suspect that they were aligned to indicate the most critical dates and that the smaller satellite mounds had supplementary functions. The two large complexes of the Boyne Valley and Loughcrew contained only five major mounds. The astronomical significance of two of them, Cairn T and Newgrange, was already known. Knowth was almost certainly aligned to the equinox. It was only Cairn L and Dowth that remained a mystery, and the only way they could be studied through observation during the summer months was by using the silvery light of the moon.

The first observations of the behaviour of moonlight inside the chamber of a passage mound were made on the night of 1 April, just ten days after our equinox findings. We were back at Cairn T waiting to observe the rising of the full moon, just as we had attempted on 1 March to see the sunrise, except that this time we had some idea of what to expect and the weather was now in our favour. In order to illuminate the chamber of a passage mound aligned on or near the horizon the full moon must rise after the sun sets. If the sun has not yet set the sky will still be very bright and the moonbeam will not project into the chamber. Usually it is on the night after the full moon that these conditions are fulfilled, and so it was on 1 April. On that night the declination of the moon was 2° 36′, which closely corresponded to the sun's declination (2° 33′) on 14 March. In other words we had an opportunity to get a good idea of what happened in the chamber six days before equinox, and this allowed us to check our estimates.

The first thing we noticed was that observing moonbeams is quite different from observing sunbeams. Before the sun rises the sky begins to brighten in the east and diffused light enters the chamber. On the night of 1 April we sat in total darkness. We were surprised by the sudden appearance of a mysterious thin shaft of silvery white light which penetrated the passage and created a glowing patch of brightness on one of the chamber stones. We watched in amazement as the size of the patch of light diminished rapidly until it disappeared before our eyes. It was like an apparition, and we were grateful that David O'Hehir was present to photograph it (p. 99), as it was singularly the strangest and yet most beautiful event we had witnessed inside a passage mound. After that I never doubted that, whatever the achievements of the megalith builders in the field of astronomy, the structures they built had a strong element of ritual observation in their function.

The entire event took less than twenty minutes, whereas the sunbeam had appeared in the chamber for over one hour. The position of the moon's beam on chamber stone 6, to the right of the backstone, clearly demonstrated that six days prior to the equinox the sun's beam would still be far away from the backstone, contradicting our original estimate that it would fall on the stone by that stage. Light would not start directly illuminating the backstone until about four days before the equinox, which implied that as a solar construct the mound was even more sensitive than we had thought.

Soon we were prepared to start using lunar observation as a means of estimating what we would expect to occur during the winter months, when most of the mounds go into operation. By this time we had reason to suspect that virtually all the mounds in the Boyne Valley and at Loughcrew were solar constructs. Around the time of summer solstice the full moon would rise approximately in the same position on the horizon as the sun at winter solstice. Thus it would be possible to determine if Cairn L could represent a solstitial alignment. In order to examine all the possible alignments we needed more recruits. We made plans to put four teams in the field. Jack and his group would be at Cairn L, Sheila Lindsay and her group would be at Tara. I would go to Newgrange with David O'Hehir and another group. Cairn U would be checked by a recent recruit from the United States, David Wollner, who had no previous knowledge of astronomy or archaeology but, like Jack, had tremendous determination and an inquisitive mind.

The night of 29 June was overcast except for a narrow area that stretched along the horizon. This break in the clouds directly above the horizon was essentially all that we required. The appearance of moonbeams on the backstone of a passage mound is the result of a complex lunar cycle known as the Saros Cycle. Whereas the sun repeats its cycle exactly every year, the moon's more erratic movements are duplicated in a period of 18.6 years. I knew that the moon's beams could not directly enter the chamber of Newgrange until June 1983, but I was still interested in seeing a partial entrance of moonlight into the passage and comparing this with data collected by the other teams. David O'Hehir photographed the rising moon as it was seen that night through the roof-box of Newgrange. At all the other sites the teams reported that the moonrise was far to the right of the intended alignment.

On the night of 28 July the same teams were used to monitor the same sites, except that I accompanied Jack to Cairn L. The moonrise on that night was closer, but still out of range of all the passages. It was not until the moon rose on the night of 26 August that moonlight streamed in, flooding the chambers of all three mounds (Cairns L and U and Tara). The position of the moonbeams indicated that the alignments were directed to the position of the rising sun on or near the cross-quarter day in November, and that consequently these structures defined the commencement of winter and were probably used again on the cross-quarter day in February to mark the beginning of spring.

The calendar in operation during the Neolithic period was basically the division of the year by solar observation into eight parts, determined by equinoxes, solstices and the cross-quarter days. Local tradition regarding the function of these mounds, as first reported by Vallancey and Beaufort, was essentially correct. Early in the twentieth century the astronomer, Sir Norman Lockyer, had explained the eight-part calendar fully and noted its use in megalithic orientations. He had also pointed out as far back as 1909 the alignment of Newgrange to the winter solstice. These mounds are not as mysterious as they seem.

A fourth passage, the largest of two at Dowth, might also have been on our list of cross-quarter day alignments (to the setting sun in November), had Lockyer been taken more seriously in his day. Instead, twentieth-century archaeological reconstruction has completely ignored any possible astronomical function, a modern artificial entrance has been built and the original entrance sealed like a tomb. A reconstruction that ignores the possible astronomical importance of a passage mound is no more nor less than an act of vandalism.

The series of lunar observations during the summer served a very useful purpose in giving us an insight into the totality of the Neolithic system of time reckoning without having to wait until we could make solar observations in the winter (although later we were able to make these winter observations). One of the things that fascinated us about 'these latest observations was the possible role of the megalithic mound in communicating calendrical information to the population. This idea was also derived from local tradition by Vallancey and Beaufort, and again it was advanced separately by Lockyer. Such a system may have been quite elaborate, and could explain the relationship of the mounds to each other and in relation to the landscape. A beacon lit from the top of Loughcrew could have been seen throughout much of the island. Many of the mounds are intervisible, and Tara is in a central position from which the Boyne Valley complex and the Loughcrew complex can both be viewed. In this context it is interesting that Tara was in fact the location of central rule and authority in Celtic Ireland. The lighting of fires at Tara is well documented in ancient Irish history and lore, as is its connection with the cross-quarter day in November.

Another interesting problem posed by our latest observations was determining whether or not the lunar orientations were deliberate in the way that the solar ones seemed to be. One primary reason for believing that they were was admittedly subjective. The sight of the moon's beams entering the chamber of a megalithic structure is even today a highly dramatic and impressive spectacle, and it seems difficult to imagine how the builders could have missed the phenomenon themselves. The present caretaker of Newgrange, Michael Smith, told me that for years he had recognized the possibility that moonlight might periodically enter the chamber without having any technical knowledge of astronomy. Provided that the moonbeams are observed over a long period of time, it is also hard not to notice the repetition of patterns over an 18.6-year period. Gavrinis, a passage mound in Brittany, appears to be aligned primarily to an extreme rising position of the moon, and its winter solstice solar alignment seems to be an important but secondary consideration. Perhaps the strongest evidence in support of the lunar as well as solar function comes from the rock engravings adorning the mounds. These display an intense concern with the moon and its phases (p. 135ff.). When one considers the size and number of astronomically orientated Neolithic mounds, together with the pronounced luni-solar character of many of the rock engravings, it seems to be flying in the face of the evidence to suppose that these early astronomers were not somehow involved in observing the intricate yet predictable movements of the moon.

The realms of light

Solar observations during the summer of 1980 and the autumnal equinox at Knowth

While we were making lunar observations at night we continued to make solar observations in ever increasing numbers during the day. Prior to summer solstice, Garreth Williams, who was a member of the team monitoring Tara, reported a possible solstitial alignment of mounds on Carnbane East, Loughcrew. This was a direct alignment of four mounds to summer solstice sunrise. Jack and I confirmed the alignment on the morning of 21 June, and then went over to the Boyne Valley to observe a similar alignment of three mounds that included Knowth and Newgrange and the summer solstice setting sun. Meanwhile, Toby Hall reported a summer solstice solar construct at Sess Kilgreen in Co. Tyrone.

After summer solstice Jack and I started making regular solar observations at Loughcrew. We waited for the sun to come within range of a series of satellite mounds that seemed to operate in a continuous sequential pattern. This was totally unexpected, as we had been thinking in simple terms of individual mounds indicating single special events. The concept of systematic continuous daily observation of the sun for an extended period of time by satellite mounds had not occurred to us. The fact is that from the cross-quarter day in August until the autumnal equinox, remaining mounds on Loughcrew chart the apparent movement of the sun on the horizon. The interesting point about this series of three satellite mounds and Cairn T is that the sequence follows the apparent movement of the sun in precise order, which indicates that the alignments must be intentional and pre-determined.

On the evening of 1 August the rays of the setting sun began to rest on the backstone of Cairn S, a satellite of Cairn T on Carnbane East. Further observations indicated that this Y-shaped construct was aligned to the setting sun on or very near the cross-quarter day on 8 August. In the mornings we were watching sunrises from Cairn F, a satellite of Cairn L on Carnbane West. When the sun was out of alignment with Cairn S in the evenings it came into alignment with Cairn F in the mornings. On the backstone of Cairn F a Neolithic artist had engraved a circle with extending radial lines and a series of crescents. These we now recognized as universal and ancient symbols of the sun and moon.

In August mists frequently form on the mountains and although this sometimes causes spectacular rainbows, it means one never quite knows when the skies will be clear. Our pre-dawn excursions were therefore frequent. When September came, the rays of the rising sun left Cairn F and began entering Cairn I, which is aligned to Cairn T on the horizon.

This warned of the approach of the autumnal equinox. By 18 September the rising sun's rays would shift from the backstone of Cairn I and begin to appear on the backstone of Cairn T four days prior to the equinox.

Jack went to West Cork early in September and arranged to be back in time for the autumnal equinox on 22 September. David Wollner had taken up temporary residence in the Boyne Valley, and together we continued the field research, which was now mainly monitoring Cairn I at sunrise and documenting the megalithic art of Loughcrew. David developed a deep interest in megalithic art from working at Loughcrew, and I showed him some of the documentation for the art of Knowth.

Compared with Loughcrew, the megalithic art of Knowth is monumental and spectacular. I explained that it first saw the light of day when Macalister began excavating the kerbstones around this gigantic mound in 1940. Macalister did rough but useful illustrations and then re-buried the stones. Now the stones are being re-excavated, but not fully uncovered. Knowth is strictly in the domain of archaeologists. It is completely sealed off from the enquiring eyes of independent researchers by a high fence topped with barbed wire. Inside, the mound is in the process of being cut apart like a layer cake, while its magnificent art treasures lie covered up under sheets of black plastic. Perhaps the comparative obscurity of megalithic art today is due to the fact that at Knowth some of its greatest examples remain quite literally cloaked in secrecy.

David was amazed that I had succeeded in documenting most of the art at Knowth in spite of the veil of secrecy. It had taken me about two years, and I had had to engage in painstaking archaeological espionage. Using Macalister's drawings, old photographs, aerial photographs and my own observations of the site at a distance with binoculars I had slowly pieced together the parts of the mosaic.

I had also become almost certain that the two passages at Knowth were aligned to both the sunrise and sunset at equinox. These passages are each about twice the size of the one at Newgrange, and would represent the largest and most impressive solar constructs known. As obvious and as blatant as these alignments seemed to be, it was unlikely that archaeologists would consider them anything other than tombs. In desperation I had telephoned an archaeologist requesting that the astronomical possibilities be investigated prior to reconstruction. I was informed that both passages were blocked up and that no observations would be possible. I naively accepted this explanation and, embarrassed by my apparent lack of information, apologized for enquiring.

Like most people, David had not been aware of the existence of Knowth and was curious about this unusual situation. He advised that I should keep to my own criteria for research, and at least attempt some preliminary observations this equinox. I explained that I had considered this myself, but felt the idea to be impractical. Even if the barbed wire fence were negotiated, once inside there would be nothing to see, because everything is sealed and meticulously covered over. In any case, the main purpose of our research was simply to determine the context of megalithic art so that we could understand it better. I argued, moreover, that on the evidence of Cairn T Knowth must be an even more advanced solar construct indicating the equinox, an assumption supported by the presence of accurate engraved sundials at the Boyne site, as well as art compositions that were clearly based on astronomical themes. While I agreed that the entrance of the sun's rays into such an enormous mound would be a spectacular event, I was already quite certain that it would happen.

Wollner was persistent and persuasive, however, and when we left our work at Loughcrew on Saturday 13 September, instead of going to the house we made a detour towards Knowth. We parked the car a good distance from the site and made our way silently through the fields until we reached a clump of woods north of the mound. From our vantage point we peered into the compound. As usual it looked like a top security prison. The majestic mound towered above its sixteen satellites, still retaining some of its Neolithic splendour. There was no one around and we were awed by the silence. Then I noticed something I had not seen in years. Much of the western side of the mound, including the entrance to the passage, was completely exposed. I could hardly believe what I was seeing through the binoculars. As the sun was setting a standing stone was beginning to cast its shadow on the entrance stone of the passage (p. 101).

We had no idea how archaeologists were going to reconstruct the entrances of the passages at Knowth, but for all we knew they could end up sealed like one of the passages at Dowth. Before us lay what might be our last chance to see the Knowth solar construct in operation. Jack and I had always felt that the responsibility for awakening an entirely new approach to Irish megalithic culture rested firmly on our shoulders. We welcomed archaeological criticism, but we regarded it as completely unfair to prohibit access to critical data while at the same time vehemently maintaining that our approach was 'speculative'. We were not vandals or treasure-seekers, we were serious researchers. If we were forced to gain information by scaling over barriers and obstacles placed in our path by archaeologists, we were bound to do so.

With these thoughts firmly planted in my mind, I indicated to David that we were ready to move in. We quickly and silently negotiated the fence and cautiously manoeuvred to the entrance of the passage, noting the position of the shadow on the entrance stone before crawling in. Inside, the narrow passage had partially collapsed, so that in some places the inclining stones left barely enough room for a thin person to squirm through, provided that arms and legs were fully extended and the person did not suffer from claustrophobia. I finally came to a section where there was enough room to look back. I was wondering how David was doing, when momentarily I was blinded by a brilliant flash of light. As I crawled further I noticed that, as long as David was not squeezing through a particularly narrow section of the passage, the light would come through. Deep back in the passage the beam was reduced to a narrow chink of light about 1 in. wide. It did not quite reach the stone basin at the elbow of the passage. The sun was beginning to set and we now had to move very quickly. I left David to monitor the light beam and myself went outside to see what the shadow was doing.

The entrance stone at Knowth has a vertical line engraved on it very similar to the one on the entrance stone at Newgrange. As the sun set the shadow of the standing stone inched away from the vertical line. The final shadow position on that day was to the right of the vertical line, but, as equinox approached (it was due in nine days time), the shadow position would gradually draw closer to the vertical line. I had suspected for some time that the standing stone outside the entrance of Newgrange projected a shadow on to the entrance stone at winter solstice and now I was convinced of it. Knowth, like Newgrange, was a complex solar construct that indicated time internally by means of a beam of light and externally by the clever use of shadow.

David crawled out of the mound and we looked at each other with the knowing feeling that we had just witnessed a remarkable event. We crouched down behind the entrance stone and waited in silence for the sky to darken. When night descended we crept out to the fields and back to the car. We telephoned Jack in West Cork and told him about what had happened. We also explained that at Loughcrew the beam of light from the rising sun was beginning to move off the backstone of Cairn I and would soon be illuminating the backstone of Cairn T. At the same time we would have to see what happened during the sunrise at Knowth. We thought that either the passages would be sealed on Monday or, if not, the archaeologists would have planned to observe the event themselves. We had no camera, we needed more observers and transportation, and the weather outlook was bad. Jack said that it would be difficult for him to come immediately, but he would try.

The next morning was Sunday and in the darkness before dawn we again slipped back into Knowth to observe the sunrise from the eastern passage, directly opposite the passage marking the sunset. The sky was cloudy, but in the early morning light it was clear that for the present the view of the horizon from the eastern passage was completely obscured by the current ground level, debris and clumps of trees. We spent the rest of the day at Loughcrew waiting for a break in the weather. Unlike the situation at Cairn T the previous spring, we now had enough experience in dialling to discern an equinoctial alignment on the basis of a single observation. It was still, however, eight days before autumnal equinox, and if possible we wanted to make an observation closer to equinox and photograph it.

The break in the weather came on Tuesday morning 16 September, six days before equinox. At Cairn I a narrow strip of the edge of the backstone, 6 in. wide, was illuminated by the sunrise. Wollner in Cairn T observed that the sunbeam was not yet striking the backstone. It was a glorious morning and our thoughts focused on Knowth and the sunset. We needed a photographer. In the afternoon we reviewed our situation over cups of coffee in the Conyngham Arms Hotel in Slane. Ironically, still hanging on the wall was the framed calendar depicting the entrance of Newgrange and under it the words that archaeologists had mocked so confidently fifteen years before, 'The rays of the rising sun at certain times of year penetrate the opening. . . .' Next to it were photographs of some rock engravings at Knowth. These were being studied carefully by a young woman with a camera.

Paula Miller was an American on holiday in Ireland. She was interested in megalithic art and fascinated by our project. It was now only six days to the autumnal equinox. The three of us waited until after six o'clock, when no one was likely to be around, before approaching Knowth. From the woods we watched closely and listened for a long time before venturing into the compound. The same silence permeated the site and we were surprised that the entrance remained open.

Paula was to photograph the beam of light in the passage while I monitored the shadows of the standing stone. David would communicate back and forth between us and maintain a look out for any sudden invasions of our privacy. We were nervous, but the work proceeded systematically and methodically. From 6.15 p.m. until the sunset at 7.30 p.m. we photographed, sketched and measured the lights and shadows. We then watched the shadow of night descend and, when the first glimmering stars appeared, we made our way across the fields. Behind us loomed the majestic mound.

Back at the house we compared the new data with data collected during our previous observation. As equinox approached the shadow moved closer to the vertical line and the beam of light penetrated the chamber. Knowth presents remarkably convincing evidence for a deliberate megalithic astronomical orientation. Furthermore, it represents the largest solar construct of its type in Europe, and there are no other passages even remotely approaching it in length. No one, not even a group of specialists, has the right to alter this mound in any way other than to restore it to its original form, and certainly no one is justified in hiding or darkening its light.

The triumph of the light

Solar observations during the winter of 1980

Jack finally arrived in Dublin on the evening of Saturday 20 September. That afternoon, John Michell, whose work on megalithic science and the origins and use of old stone monuments had deeply impressed Jack and me, had arrived from London. Although many professional researchers had expressed an interest in our project, Michell was the first actually to come and investigate the phenomena by first-hand observation at the sites. That evening an excited Wollner, who had remained in the Boyne Valley, came down to report that in the afternoon workers had sealed the passage at Knowth and covered the stones. It was now clear that the excavators either did not know about the light or, if they did, did not want it to be studied, by themselves or anyone else.

We discussed the implications of this new turn of events. After our well-publicized finds at Cairn T during the spring equinox, many archaeologists had tried to discredit our research. They insisted that the mounds were nothing more than mere tombs. However, the combined data from Newgrange, Cairn T and now Knowth clearly demonstrated, it seemed to us, that they were making an enormous assumption and that they were wrong. Traditionalists in Irish archaeology try to explain the passage-mound phenomenon as the result of cemetery-building invading colonists, who arrived from the continent and gradually spread to the west of Ireland after creating a giant necropolis in the Boyne Valley. As late as 1977 Herity and Eogan could state confidently in their book, *Ireland in Prehistory*, that 'About 2500 BC, the Passage Grave builders arrived in the Irish Sea from Brittany, and built their first tombs . . .' We seriously doubted both the tomb theory and the invasion theory, and new voices in Irish archaeology were tending to support us.

Presently, there is a revolution in Irish prehistory that has come about so suddenly that the implications of the new findings have yet to be assessed. Mesolithic hunters and gatherers, who represented Ireland's first settlers, were once thought to be nothing more than hungry strandloopers, unable to penetrate the island interior and able to do little more than scavenge a living along the shoreline about 6000 BC. Recent excavations carried out by Peter Woodman in the north and Michael Ryan in the very centre of the island, however, show that Mesolithic communities with substantial material equipment were flourishing in the interior by 7000 BC, or about 9,000 years ago. Göran Burenhult of Sweden uncovered an even earlier Mesolithic presence, dating back to 7500 BC, at Carrowmore in the far western extreme of the country. These are the earliest known habitation sites in Ireland, and they completely overturn the old notion that man first entered Ireland on the east coast after a short sea crossing from Britain.

Also overturned is the idea that the passage tombs originated in the east and spread westwards. The megalithic complex at Carrowmore excavated by the Swedes gave radiocarbon dates in the region of 4200 BC for the earliest structure, a thousand years before the construction of Newgrange. There were no burials at this level. All the evidence pointed towards an indigenous origin for megaliths, with an evolution from simple (Carrowmore) to complex (Boyne Valley). Moreover, the techniques of engraving at Loughcrew suggested to us that the mounds there came somewhere in the middle of this sequence.

Then, if the mounds were used primarily as tombs, where were the radiocarbon dates from human bones found in the mounds to prove it? No dates have been forthcoming so far. Some support for our attitude towards the monuments comes in a recent book by Elizabeth Shee-Twohig, *The Megalithic Art of Western Europe* (1981). 'Remarkably little study has been done on the burials from megalithic tombs', she writes. 'The size and sophistication of many of the monuments generally exceeded what would be required if they were built merely as burial places. It seems reasonable to conclude that they fulfilled some further role in society.' In

The illustration depicts in the foreground the remains of mound 7 at Carrowmore. On the horizon, 'Maeve's Cairn' and some satellites are seen on the top of the Knocknarea Mountain, which overlooks the Atlantic Ocean. The Carrowmore site included between 65 and 85 structures in the mid-nineteenth century. Originally it is thought to have contained twice that number. It remains one of the largest concentrations of megalithic sites in Europe, but now many structures are disappearing because of extensive quarrying in the area.

Until recently Carrowmore was considered a late site, representing the final phase of megalithic expansion to the west coast of Ireland. Completely overturning this model, Göran Burenhult has recently produced two well-related radiocarbon dates placing Carrowmore at the very beginnings of the Irish megalithic tradition, and establishing it as one of the earliest megalithic areas in Europe, antedated only by a few Breton dolmens.

Malta, she explains, 'excavation has shown that the megalithic temples of the third millennium were not used for burial but for some other purpose'. Moreover, 'at Dissignac, Loire-Atlantique, the eastern passage grave is orientated on sunrise at the winter solstice'. This is not the only description we have come across of an astronomical alignment in a continental passage mound. Even if radiocarbon-dated evidence of primary burials is eventually produced, the mounds cannot be simply regarded as tombs, and any burial function can easily be accommodated as part of a wider range of purposes and meanings.

Thwarted in our attempt to observe the autumnal equinox at Knowth, in the early hours of the morning of 22 September our research team (together with John Michell) set out to view it at Cairn T, Loughcrew. During the autumnal equinox the sun rises at a much lower angle than it does at the spring equinox, and as a result the patch of light in Cairn T is longer and thinner. But autumnal equinox is just as dramatic as spring, and the beam of light matches the rock engravings on the backstone equally well. We had in Cairn T without doubt recognized an accurate solar chronometer which measured both spring and autumnal equinoxes precisely and would continue to do so perpetually.

John Michell was deeply impressed. Much earlier he had written that 'Archaeology, which aspires to the status of a science in the modern, materialistic sense of the word, is ill equipped to investigate the stone instruments of the earlier, more comprehensive system, whose secrets cannot be excavated along with the bones and potsherds, but must be sought through the study of the megalithic science, the way which the arts of astronomy, architecture, numerology and every other branch of knowledge were united in one system to serve a common purpose.' Michell returned to London with additional material for one of his most critical books on archaeology, *Megalithomania* (1982). We were also saddened to say goodbye to David Wollner, who will be remembered for his exploits at Knowth.

During this period it seemed that every time we went into the field we came back with new and exciting findings. On 25 September Jack and I intended to make routine moonrise observations at Loughcrew. We spent the afternoon at the Ballinvally stone circle at the foot of the Loughcrew Mountains. In a heap of stones piled near the circle I noticed a beautifully engraved stone on top of the pile. Further examination revealed a holed standing stone in the same pile. It seemed extraordinary that these stones could have escaped the attention of generations of archaeologists. Later in the year, largely as the result of our discovery, the Ballinvally site was declared an official national monument, but our far more important finds were still being ignored.

Megalithic studies have been described as a war of ideas, but it is not understood that there are real casualties and many megalithic structures are being totally destroyed while researchers debate whether or not the light entering Newgrange is intentional and, if so, what effects minor changes in the obliquity of the ecliptic might have on the light beam.

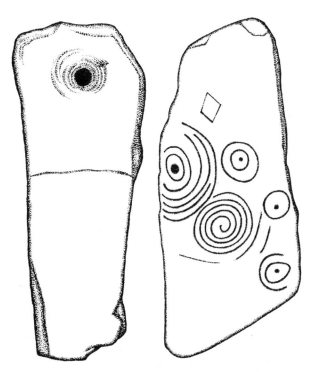

Ballinvally, loose stones, found in September 1981.

Archaeologists do not seem to be aware of the fact that at the beginning of this century, the only real protection the mounds had was the belief in the minds of ordinary people that vandalism would be swiftly revenged by spirits known as fairies. The disappearance of the fairies opened the way to large scale destruction. The results are disastrous. We have already destroyed an estimated 60 per cent of the archaeological monuments in Cork, 44 per cent in Kerry, 40 per cent in Antrim, 31 per cent in Tipperary and 29 per cent in Donegal. At this rate there will be very few possible astronomical alignments left to argue a war of ideas.

With the coming of the cross-quarter day at the beginning of November, the light of the rising sun began pouring in at Cairn L, Cairn U, and Tara. A satellite mound of Cairn L, designated Cairn H, provided a warning for this important date which marked the commencement of winter, very much in the same way that Cairn I was linked to Cairn T and warned of the approach of equinox. By far the most spectacular of these observations was the illumination of the white standing stone inside Cairn L, just as the disc of the rising sun appeared above Cairn M.

Now, all five major mounds in the two complexes had been shown to be astronomically orientated and only the second chamber at Dowth (Dowth 2) remained to be investigated. In addition, every satellite mound we had examined had without exception demonstrated a specific astronomical function. We had also identified a type of smaller supplementary satellite mound aligned due south, which marked the sun's passing of the meridian at midday. These are extremely obvious astronomical alignments, as is an alignment that is oriented due north, such as the construct at Baltinglass, Co. Wicklow. This type of construct demonstrates a concern with the stars, and was first noticed by Lockyer.

Had our findings come as a complete surprise to archaeologists there might have been some excuse for ignoring them, but Lockyer had in fact anticipated most of them and directly addressed archaeologists in his book, *Stonehenge and other British Stone Monuments Astronomically Considered* (2nd edition 1909), in which he called attention to the astronomical orientation of Newgrange. Referring to megalithic constructs he wrote: 'We made out that in the case of the temples devoted to sun-worship and to the determination of the length of the year, there was very good reason why all these attempts should be made to cut off the light, by diaphragms and stone ceilings, because, among other things one wanted to find the precise point occupied by the sunbeam in order to determine the exact day of the solstice.' Lockyer distinguished between star temples and sun temples, and said that these earliest astronomers 'used starlight at night for some of their observations, very much like they used sunlight during the day'. He concluded that 'The ancient priest need not have been a profound astronomer to build the monuments, which were simply calendars. I do not mean to say they were calendars and nothing more, but they were, from an astronomical point of view, simply calendars, enabling people to know and recognize from past experience the different parts of the year by the place of sunrise and sunset; and they were also night-dials, enabling them to differentiate between the early and the late hours of the night.'

Another intriguing and surprising find came towards the end of the year at Dowth. As winter solstice approached we gradually came to accept the possibility that Dowth 2 was aligned to the position of the setting sun at winter solstice. The realization came gradually because we found it difficult to believe that observers who had witnessed the rising sun's rays enter Newgrange could have failed to notice the rays of the setting sun entering Dowth on the same day. I had lived directly beside Dowth and cannot explain how I failed to recognize this. Perhaps it was because a hedge had blocked the view of both the horizon and Newgrange from inside the chamber. The hedge had been there for some 300 years, and after preliminary observations on 13 and 14 December we requested the Board of Works to remove it and let the light in. This they did. On 20 December, the evening before the winter solstice, we succeeded in taking photographs of the light streaming in at Dowth 2, half an hour before the sun sank below a bank of clouds. This event got widespread newspaper and radio coverage. It surprised archaeologists too, although they surprised us when Professor Herity called the findings 'of world-shattering significance, if true'. In fact, the strategy of synchronized alignments employed at Newgrange and Dowth replicates the similar strategy at Knowth, which we had not publicized. These sets of alignments together show that at particularly critical times of the year passages are orientated towards both the sunrise and sunset. One practical reason for this might be that, if weather conditions are unfavourable early in the day, there would still be an opportunity to make observations later on. In any event, the astronomy of Newgrange can no longer be discussed realistically without taking into account that it is part of an intricate system which includes Dowth and Knowth.

On the day of the winter solstice the rising sun's rays entered Newgrange, but cloudy weather in the afternoon prevented the setting sun from entering Dowth. In the morning out entire team was present at Newgrange for the grand celebration of light and measure which was to be our last observation of the year. An unusually large crowd of over 200 people came from all over the country to attend. Jack was inside photographing while I directed my attention to the shadow of the standing stone outside the entrance. An archaeologist had once confidently assured me that the shadow did not strike the entrance stone on winter solstice, but my drawings and elevations of the construct assured me that it did. The similar construct I had seen at Knowth meant to me that the scheme was pre-determined and intentional. The shadow clearly does strike the entrance stone (p. 101) and one should beware of hearsay, especially in matters concerning light and shadow.

After a full year of research in the field we had returned again to Newgrange on the shortest day of the year. We had completed a circuit that formed a gigantic calendar in stone. As artists we had explored a path that led us into many dark recesses of megalithic mounds. We found our way was always illuminated by the light of the sun, the moon and the stars. The mounds are not riddles or follies, they are a living testimony to the indomitable spirit of a Stone Age people, who built not only for themselves, but for future generations.

I am not ashamed to admit that our explorations were first inspired by intuitive feelings; our research did have a solid scientific basis, involving direct empirical observations, all of which are repeatable. An artist's mind and eye is trained to search for more than a superficial meaning in the works of other more ancient artists. We should recall that the world did not first hear of the light at Newgrange from an astronomer or an archaeologist, but from the artist and mystic poet, George Russell, who asked, 'What secret lies behind the lovely light?'

It was Russell's fellow poet and friend, James Stephens, who once wrote, 'The crown of life is not lodged in the sun. The wise gods buried it deeply where the thoughtful will not find it, nor the good. But the joyous ones, the adventurous ones, the careless plungers, they will bring it to the wise and astonish them. All things are seen in the light – how shall we value that which is easy to see?'

Part II

MEGALITHIC OBSERVATORIES

The Loughcrew complex

On the highest eminence of the Loughcrew Mountains in County Meath, commanding an extensive view of much of Ireland, a large complex of astronomically aligned megalithic mounds was constructed at a very early period, probably sometime in the fourth millennium BC. The Loughcrew Mountains are in fact a range of hills extending about two miles in an east-west direction and dotted with a carefully arranged system of mounds. As a laboratory for the study of megalithic science the region is unsurpassed. The hills and the immediately surrounding countryside offer what is probably the best-preserved example of a Neolithic landscape in the world. Originally there were fifty to a hundred mounds. Of those that remain, seven are still functioning, that is, sufficient stones remain in their original alignment for a beam of light to be projected into the chamber and against the backstone, presenting a clearly

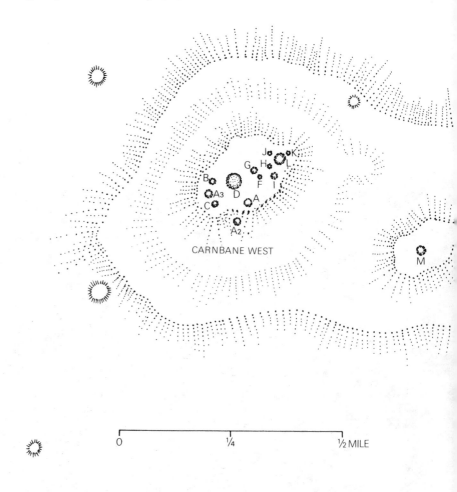

CARNBANE WEST

0   ¼   ½ MILE

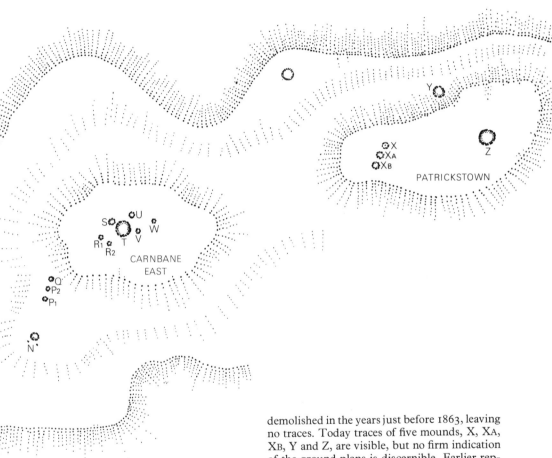

BALLINVALLY
STONE CIRCLE

Y

X
XA
XB

Z

PATRICKSTOWN

S U
T W
R1 V
R2

CARNBANE
EAST

Q
P2
P1

N

defined frame of light. The two most important mounds – Cairns T and L – are supplemented by smaller satellite mounds linked to their larger brethren by orientation and alignment. The number of mounds still functioning allows one to reconstruct the main elements in a planned astronomical and calendrical scheme.

The most severe destruction at Loughcrew has taken place on the eastern summit in the area called Patrickstown Hill. Immediately south of this hill twenty-one mounds were completely demolished in the years just before 1863, leaving no traces. Today traces of five mounds, X, XA, XB, Y and Z, are visible, but no firm indication of the ground plans is discernible. Earlier reports suggest that some of these five mounds were orientated towards the west. The unusual Y-shaped Cairn S is the only remaining mound that can be shown to be facing west today.

The view from Loughcrew is panoramic, from the mountains near Sligo in the far west to those above Carlingford on the east coast. Visible to the naked eye from this height are a number of important megalithic sites, including Fourknocks and Tara. In turn, Tara is visible from all three of the major mounds in the Boyne Valley – Knowth, Newgrange and Dowth.

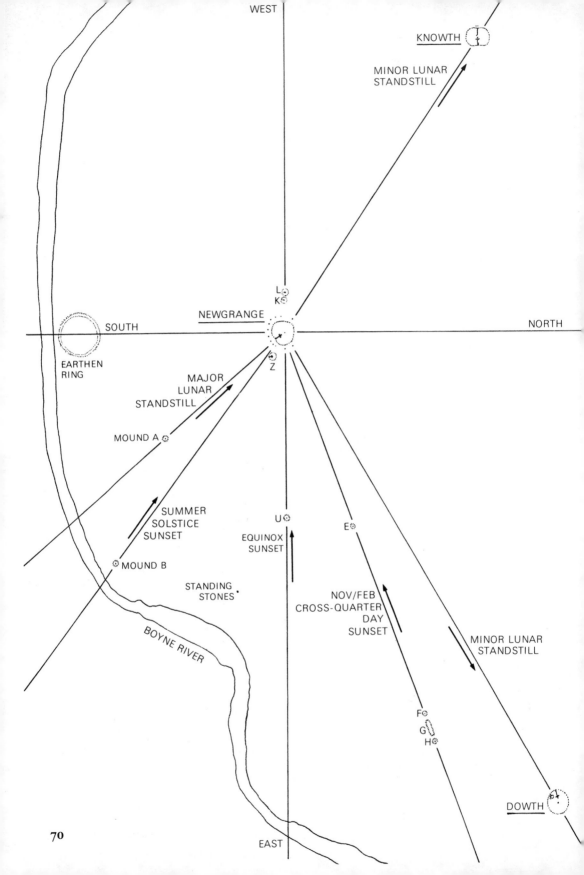

WEST

KNOWTH

MINOR LUNAR
STANDSTILL

L
K

NEWGRANGE   NORTH

SOUTH

EARTHEN
RING

Z

MAJOR
LUNAR
STANDSTILL

MOUND A

SUMMER
SOLSTICE
SUNSET

U   E

EQUINOX
SUNSET

MOUND B

STANDING
STONES

NOV/FEB
CROSS-QUARTER
DAY
SUNSET

MINOR LUNAR
STANDSTILL

BOYNE RIVER

F
G
H

DOWTH

70

EAST

Newgrange after reconstruction.

The Boyne Valley complex

'The mighty barrows by the banks of the Boyne' have for a long time been considered some of the most important prehistoric sites in the world. They represent the pinnacle of the Neolithic achievement and constitute one of the most impressive displays of Stone Age grandeur known. When all similar sites are compared one must conclude that it was in the Boyne Valley that Neolithic culture made its most ambitious and comprehensive statements in stone.

The map shows the area in the immediate vicinity of the three major mounds, Knowth, Dowth, and Newgrange. Not included are the satellite mounds of Knowth, which are currently being excavated. The map is based on a survey by Dr Jon Patrick, in which the mounds were co-ordinated by empirical photogrammetric procedures. From the data, Patrick concluded that 'there is evidence that some lines are deliberately orientated on solar phenomena', and he also pointed out lunar alignments. Independently, our own research team had recognized the solar lines by direct observation. We also noted that the alignment H, G, F, E and Newgrange is orientated towards sunset on the November and February cross-quarter days.

The cross-quarter day alignment is important because it corresponds to the solar light-beam alignment of the main passage at Dowth. Thus, side by side, there are two types of alignment indicating the same date: a solar construct within a mound, and an arrangement of solar-orientated mounds in the immediate vicinity. Patrick's bearings for the five aligned mounds are E–F 66°58′, E–H 67°17′, Newgrange–F 67°43′, Newgrange–H 67°50′, and Newgrange–E 68°27′. Patrick made a determination of the probability level at which parts of the proposed design plan could occur by chance and noted 'a rather large proportion of coincidences for a random distribution of points'. He concluded finally that 'It has been shown that the Boyne Valley monuments are probably laid out to a design plan.'

The map of the external design plan of the complex demonstrates a concern with solstices, equinoxes and cross-quarter days. Our own investigations took us into the interior of the mounds, where we found solar constructs with a similar concern but even more obviously intentional. I have divided our findings into groups which indicate these three fundamental divisions of the year. All the major mounds, and the vast majority of mounds in general, fall into these groups but I also include types of mounds that align south to the midday sun and north to the stars.

The solstice

Winter solstice at Newgrange

The illustration above shows the entrance stone, the entrance to the passage and, above the entrance, the roof-box. The roof-box is a special aperture which admits light from the rising sun at winter solstice. Note the positioning of the vertical line on the entrance stone and how it divides the spirals into left-handed ones on the left, and right-handed ones on the right. Megal-

ithic art will be discussed in detail in Part III. Here we should merely note the close relationship between art and astronomical orientation.

Below is the ground plan of Newgrange. The brown line indicates the bearing of the rising sun. Note that the astronomical alignment is the central consideration, and that it involves standing stone 1 and kerbstone 52 as well as the passage and chamber of the mound. The ground plan and the entrance suggest a symmetry derived from the inherent symmetry of the solar cycle.

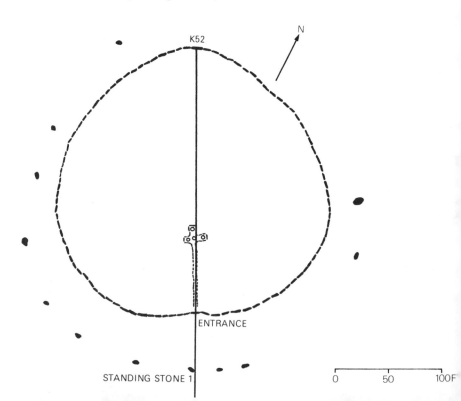

K52

N

ENTRANCE

STANDING STONE 1

0   50   100F

(Above) The sun's rays enter the chamber at Newgrange when the full disc of the sun appears above the horizon at 8.58 a.m. This photograph was taken on 21 December at 8.56 a.m., just moments before the light beam entered the mound. The sun will rise at an angle towards the right which places it in alignment with Newgrange. The line of the horizon is formed by a hill known as the Redmountain. (Below) Kerbstone 52 echoes patterns on the entrance stone and has an even more pronounced vertical line. Of ninety-seven kerbstones only three are fully engraved, and their astronomical positioning is highly significant. It is difficult to imagine how an astronomical alignment could be more explicitly expressed.

(Above) From inside the passage at Newgrange the rising sun shines through the roof-box. Outside the entrance, standing stone 1 aligns along its left edge with the vertical line on the entrance stone and the shadow of the winter solstice sun.

(Below) An early photograph of the roof-box. The lintel stone first began to be noticed in the last century. Excavators at that time tried and failed to remove it with crowbars, in order to find out what it was.

A cut-away illustration shows the solar construct at Newgrange as revealed by modern excavation. The structure is designed to house a narrow aperture 40 in. wide by 9 in. high. The light beam enters a narrow slit between roof-slabs 1 and 2. The lintel and corbel protect the diaphragm and keep it dry. Some of the stones are grooved to drain off water. Engravings on the lintel and the back of the corbel actually appear in the context of a solar construct.

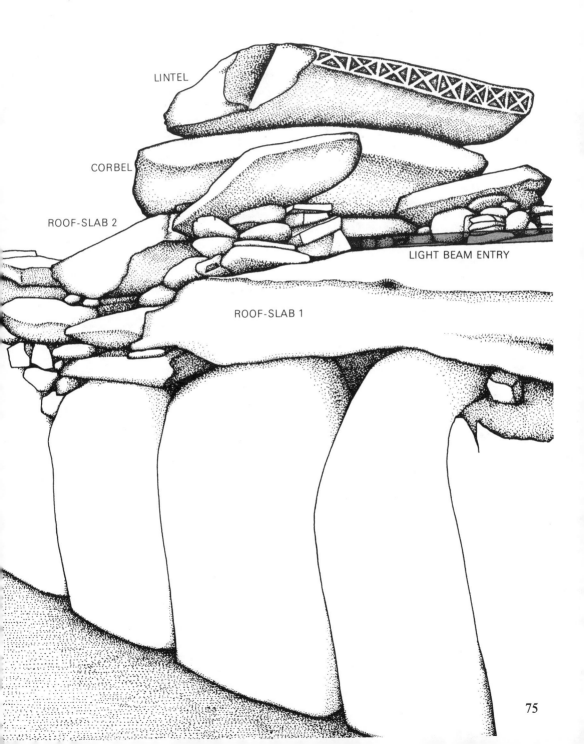

LINTEL

CORBEL

ROOF-SLAB 2

LIGHT BEAM ENTRY

ROOF-SLAB 1

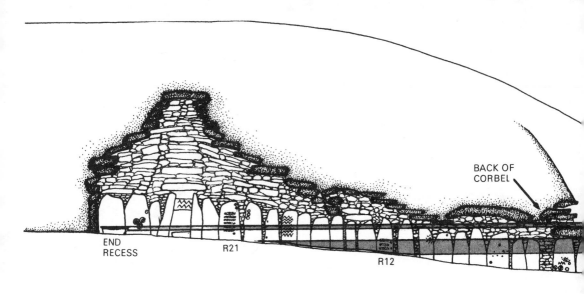

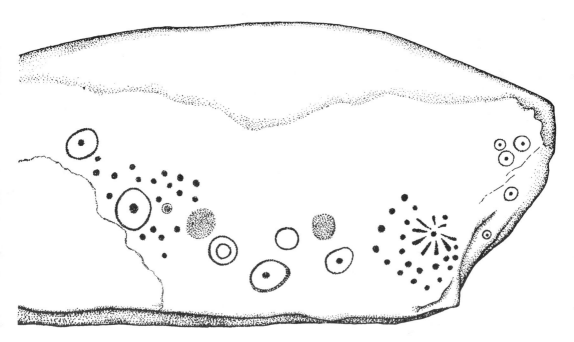

The Newgrange elevation shows the right side of the passage and chamber. A stream of light comes directly through the entrance and extends far back into the passage. The purpose of the roof-box is to allow a narrow beam of light to project into the end recess. After reaching the end recess, R21 narrows the beam of light until it is cut off from the chamber at 9.15 a.m.

The back of the corbel supporting the roof-box lintel is engraved with art that could not have been seen once the mound was completed. This 'hidden' art contrasts with the 'display' form exemplified on the entrance stone. Nevertheless, 'hidden' art at Newgrange is invariably positioned with reference to astronomical considerations.

An engraving on the right of the stone suggests the basic structuring of a sundial. Not a dial that was ever intended to function, but a dial as symbol of the sun. The image of the sundial is imprinted on a real practical dial – the megalithic structure itself. Time at Newgrange is both measured and symbolized.

LIGHT

SHADOW

RANCE
NE

STANDING STONE 1

The early photograph below shows, from right to left, standing stones 2, 1, 11 and 12. Stone 1 casts its long shadow on the entrance stone at winter solstice.

An early photograph of the Newgrange chamber and west recess shows a stone basin in the floor of the chamber where it was placed at the turn of the century. This was probably its original position. Now it lies in the east recess where it was found when the passage was excavated.

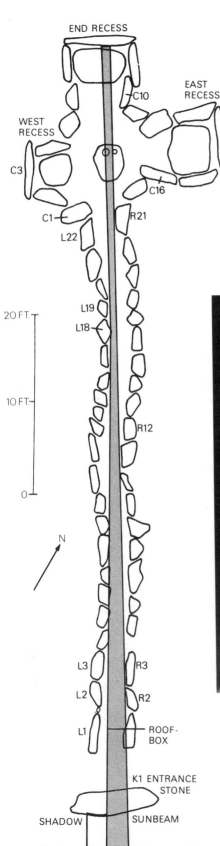

END RECESS

EAST
RECESS

WEST
RECESS

C10

C3

C16

C1

R21

L22

L19

20 FT

L18

10 FT

R12

0

N

L3

R3

L2

R2

L1

ROOF-
BOX

K1 ENTRANCE
STONE

SHADOW

SUNBEAM

The Newgrange ground plan shows the light beam striking the base of the backstone in the end recess. Jon Patrick's survey demonstrated that for this to happen the sun's declination must lie between 22° 58′ and 25° 53′, it must be in the azimuth range 133° 42′–138° 24′, and its elevation must lie between 0° 51′ and 1° 40′. The elevation of the horizon is 0° 51′, and a straight line from the back of the chamber to the centre of the roof-box aligns with the spot on the horizon where the sun rises at winter solstice.

The unambiguous definition of both the altitude and the direction of the sun means that the event would have taken place at the time of construction and will continue to occur regardless of slight changes in the tilt of the earth's axis. Patrick concluded that the alignment provided convincing evidence of deliberate orientation on astronomical phenomena.

The photograph shows the beam of light at the chamber entrance. After sweeping across the chamber floor for 6 minutes, the beam narrows again at 9.04 a.m., when it strikes the base of R21, on the right of the photograph. By 9.15 the beam is cut off from the chamber, and for the next hour it slowly moves down the right side of the passage.

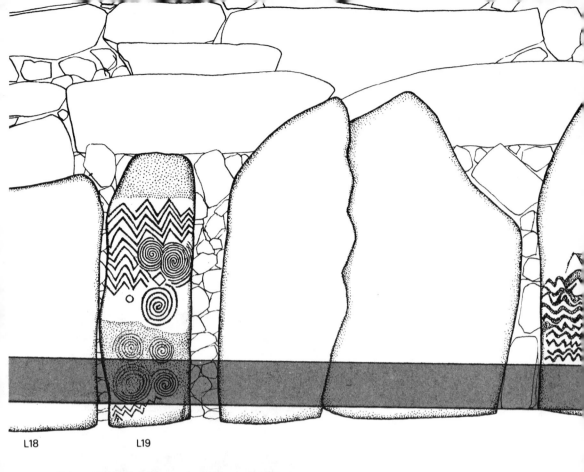

L18   L19

The diagram shows the beam of light entering the Newgrange chamber from the aperture in the roof-box. Light entering from the entrance of the passage extends as far back as stone L19 and illuminates the triple spiral on it. An early photograph (left) shows the engravings on L19. The photograph on the right shows light streaming down the passage from both entrance and roof-box aperture on the day of winter solstice.

Eleven days before the solstice a chink of light bypasses L18 and flashes into the chamber. After twenty-two days the light is again cut off by L18, which leans slightly forward. This could have occurred during the mound's construction, in which case the numbers eleven and twenty-two could have significance as day counts for determining the solstice. On L22 there are eleven rows or sets of markings. On L19 there are eleven rows of zigzags. Prominent engravings inside the chamber also indicate a count of twenty-two. Thus the engravings may have a numerical as well as symbolic significance related to the mound's function in the computation of time.

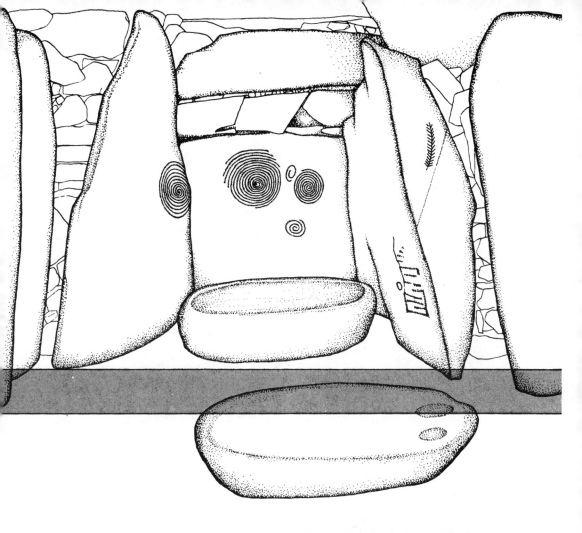

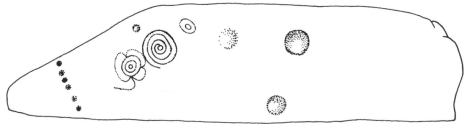

Winter solstice at Dowth

The entrance of Dowth faces out towards New-grange and the horizon beyond. Dowth acts as a synchronized counterpart of Newgrange. On the day of winter solstice the sun projects its rays into Newgrange at dawn and into Dowth at sunset. The passage and chamber at Dowth are about half the size of their Newgrange counter-parts, but the projected light beam is much larger, and it remains in the chamber for a longer period of time, creating an even more dramatic spectacle.

Parallels can be drawn between Dowth, and Loughcrew and Knowth, where passages are aligned to both the sunrise and sunset of a particular astronomical event. At Dowth a large circle hollowed into the entrance stone marks the position of the setting sun. The entrance stones at Dowth and Newgrange have similarities, but the Newgrange one is more formalized and clearly a later development in both technique and concept.

A second, larger passage at Dowth is also aligned to sunset. The original entrance to this passage was sealed during reconstruction. It seems to mark the cross-quarter days on 8 November and 4 February. The three gigantic mounds in the Boyne Valley, made up of hun-dreds of thousands of tons of material, in fact form a unified system that follows the circuit of the sun from the autumnal equinox to the spring equinox. It seems that after spring equinox interest shifts to lunar observation.

The photograph on the left was taken on 20 December 1980 as the sun's beam penetrates the chamber and moves towards the backstone. The photograph below shows the light beam about one hour before sunset as it touches the backstone (6). During the week preceding solstice the beam of light is projected against stone 5 at its entry. At solstice the range of the beam is narrowed to focus on stone 6. The beam of light moves gradually to stone 7 as the sun begins to set. At solstice the intense light reflected from stone 6 brilliantly illuminates solar emblems engraved on stone 13 in the large side recess of the chamber. Stone 13 is apparently angled to achieve this effect. The circular solar emblems on this stone and the entrance stone are echoed on a larger scale in the circular arrangement of stones forming the chamber.

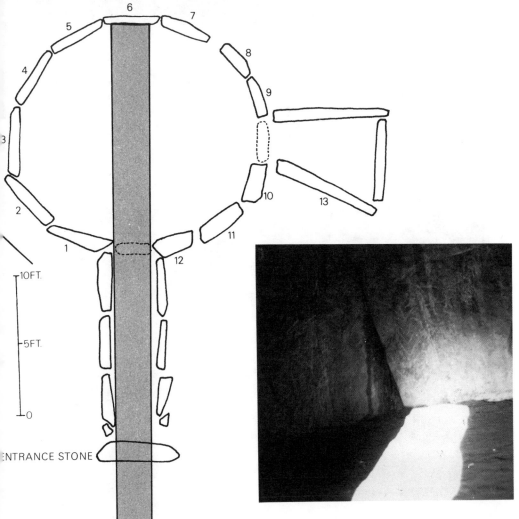

The photographs show two stages of the moving shaft of light as it appears one day before winter solstice in the Dowth chamber. In the photograph above, the clock indicates 3 p.m. as the light begins to ascend stone 6. A tape measure in the photograph records the fluctuating width of the moving beam of light. The photograph below was taken at 3.25 p.m. By this time the entire chamber and side recess is illuminated by reflected light from stone 6 and the effect is dramatic and awe-inspiring. At 3.30 p.m. the light beam begins to strike stone 7 and reflected light is cut off from the side recess. At 4.07 p.m. the sun has set.

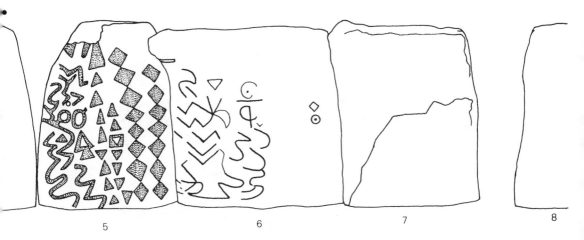

5

6

7

8

The engravings in the chamber at Dowth are for the most part confined to stones 5, 6 and 13. These are the chief stones that interact with the beam of light projected into the chamber. The symbolism and imagery of the engravings can therefore be said to relate directly to the event of the solstice itself. That this connection was deliberate on the part of the engravers is suggested by the juxtaposition in other megalithic mounds of similar incised symbols and astronomical phenomena.

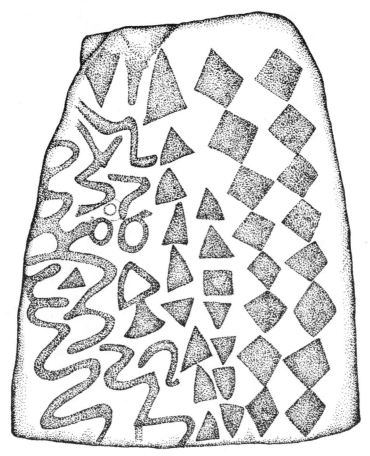

DOWTH
STONE 5

85

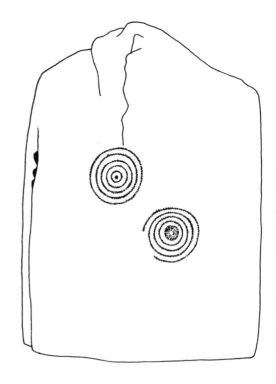

The photograph shows the remains of Cairn V in the foreground and Cairn T in the background. The drawing (right) illustrates the stone in the immediate foreground on the right in the photograph. To judge from the remains, it appears that Cairn V once marked the winter solstice sunrise.

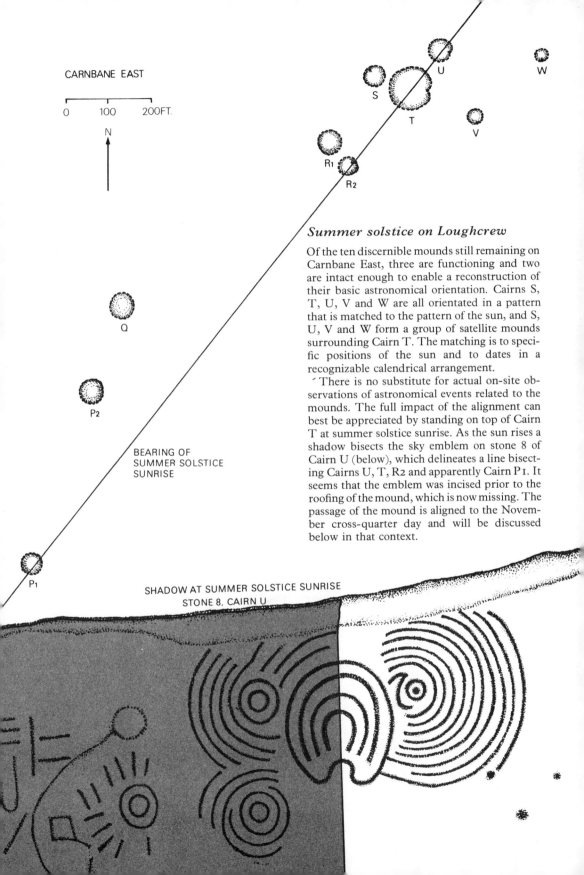

CARNBANE EAST

0   100   200FT.

N

Q

P₂

BEARING OF
SUMMER SOLSTICE
SUNRISE

P₁

S

U

T

W

V

R₁

R₂

Summer solstice on Loughcrew

Of the ten discernible mounds still remaining on
Carnbane East, three are functioning and two
are intact enough to enable a reconstruction of
their basic astronomical orientation. Cairns S,
T, U, V and W are all orientated in a pattern
that is matched to the pattern of the sun, and S,
U, V and W form a group of satellite mounds
surrounding Cairn T. The matching is to specific positions of the sun and to dates in a
recognizable calendrical arrangement.

There is no substitute for actual on-site observations of astronomical events related to the
mounds. The full impact of the alignment can
best be appreciated by standing on top of Cairn
T at summer solstice sunrise. As the sun rises a
shadow bisects the sky emblem on stone 8 of
Cairn U (below), which delineates a line bisect-
ing Cairns U, T, R₂ and apparently Cairn P₁. It
seems that the emblem was incised prior to the
roofing of the mound, which is now missing. The
passage of the mound is aligned to the November cross-quarter day and will be discussed
below in that context.

SHADOW AT SUMMER SOLSTICE SUNRISE
STONE 8, CAIRN U

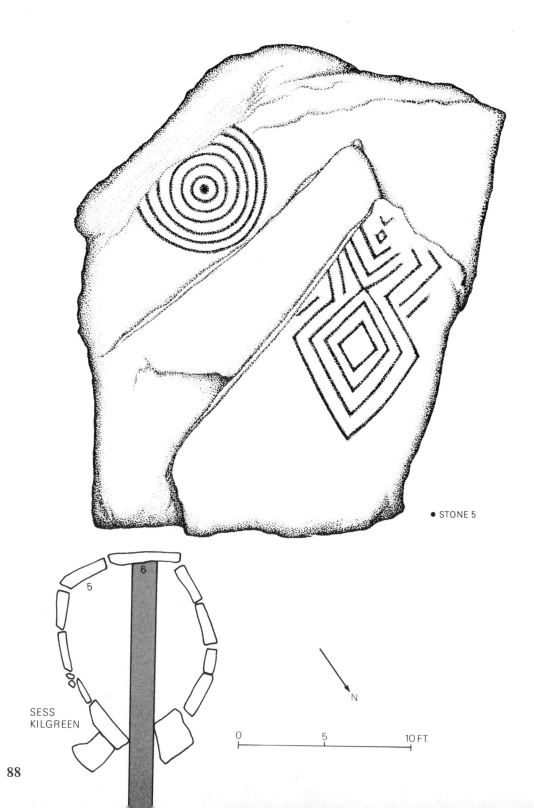

● STONE 5

SESS
KILGREEN

N

0   5   10 FT.

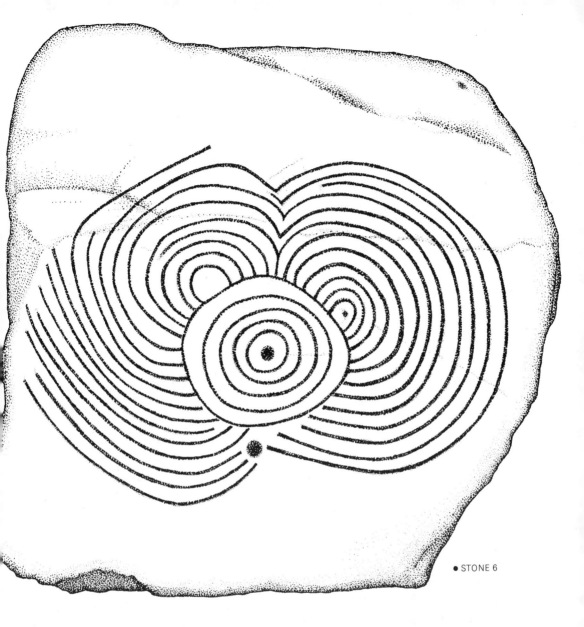

● STONE 6

Summer solstice, Sess Kilgreen, Co. Tyrone

As the sun illuminates the emblem at Cairn U, Loughcrew, a similar pattern is being illuminated 50 miles to the north at Sess Kilgreen in Co. Tyrone in a closely related scheme. The structure is 10 ft 10 in. long and 7 ft 5 in. wide. The accuracy and precision of these smaller mounds should not be underestimated. Before the large spectacular passage mounds were built, smaller mounds probably provided efficient and accurate sunbeam dialling for hundreds of years. It should be remembered that although these mounds are dwarfed by giants like Knowth and Newgrange, as sundialling instruments they are in fact constructed on a monumental scale.

The central engraved image at Sess Kilgreen is on stone 6. The correlation between this symbol and the emblem on stone 8 at Cairn U was noted by Michael Herity in his book, *Irish Passage Graves* (1974), where he states in connection with this, 'The work is so close in character to that of Loughcrew that master or pupil must have moved from there to Tyrone.' The master or pupil must also have seen the sun illuminate the emblem, and it was this image that was duplicated.

89

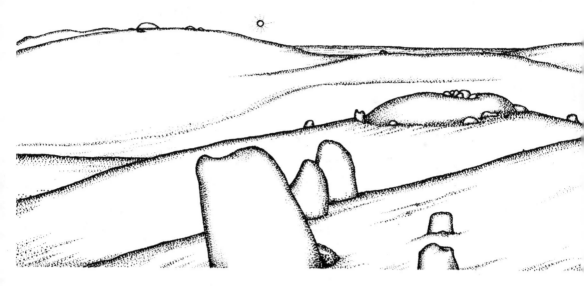

From Cairn F on Carnbane West, Cairn T is seen against the horizon as the dominant mound on Carnbane East. The drawing is based on a photograph taken on 23 March 1980 as the sun's rays entered the back recess of Cairn T.

The equinox

Equinox at Cairn T, Loughcrew

Equinox literally means 'equal night'. In terms of hours, equinox is the date when the hours of day and night are equal. The two extremes of this are winter solstice, when the night is longest, and summer solstice, when the night is shortest. In terms of the year, the equinox is midway between these points.

Astronomy has never been a simple science. Determining the exact day of the winter solstice requires careful measuring of the beam of light in the chamber as the sun changes position very slowly during the solstice. Near equinox the sun's position is changing rapidly, and sightlines need not be as narrow as solstitial sightlines. However, if the sightline is not focused on the horizon it must be orientated to measure the sun's beams at two different angles relative to the horizon. At equinox the sun is rising due east to the horizon. Cairn T is orientated about 9 degrees south of this and above the horizon, so that the beam does not enter the mound until the sun rises to the proper altitude. At the spring equinox the angle of the sun's path is very high in relation to the horizon, whereas at the autumnal equinox the angle of the ecliptic is lower. These factors directly affect the size of the sunbeam, and both of these angles must be considered in order to understand how the mound functions.

Damage done to the mound by partial reconstruction has fortunately had very little effect on the projected beam of light. The erection of a modern door at the entrance does affect the preliminary stages, but not the culmination. Changes that have taken place over thousands of years in the inclination of the earth's equator to the ecliptic plane of the earth's orbit are slight, and are negligible during the equinox. What we are witnessing at Cairn T essentially resembles the intended projection of light and its interaction with symbol.

Perhaps what is most impressive is the permanence of the structure. The stones upon which the shadows fall are fixed in position by closely packed small stones, and stand in silent testimony to the skills of their builders over 5,000 years ago.

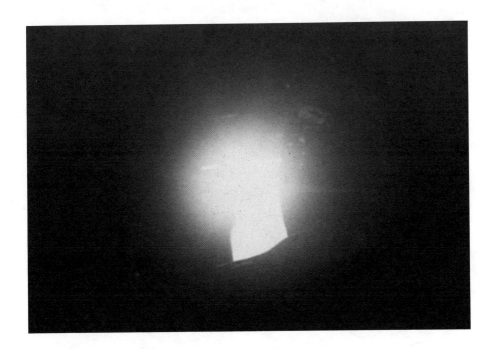

Above, the rising sun at equinox as it appears through the portals of Cairn T. Below, the ground plan of Cairn T takes the form of one of the most *ancient and universal sun symbols known, the 'equinoctial' or Greek Cross. The light beam at equinox is focused on stone 14.*

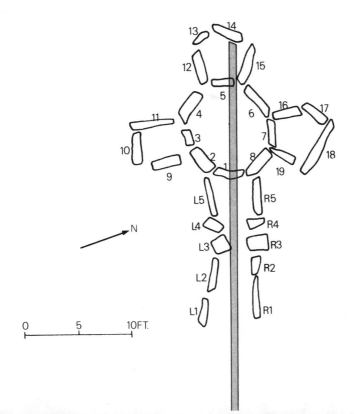

● CAIRN T,
STONE 14

The symbols on stone 14 in Cairn T may now be interpreted as the language of unknown archaic astronomers. The beam of light from the rising sun at equinox moves down the stone, illuminating key symbols as it progresses. The arrangement of the engravings in relation to the sunbeam reveals that there is quite precise time reckoning and careful determination of the equinoxes.

At spring equinox the patch of light is centred on the large circular radial sun sign on the right of stone 14. Above, three days after equinox the light beam is 6 in. below the equinox position.

Spring equinox, Cairn T

At dawn on the spring equinox the sun's rays begin grazing off the stones in Cairn T in a progression that culminates in the projection of a narrow shaft of light penetrating the length of the passage and focusing at the very end of the chamber. The interior is dramatically transformed as the beam of light moves slowly along the stones until it reaches stone L3. From stone L3 the light suddenly flashes on to stone 14, where it begins to widen and then descend. The engravings are an integral part of the interplay between light, stones and shadow. The stones become giant gnomons. The massive rocks are contrasted with the surprising delicacy of the narrowed shaft of light. The diagram illustrates various phases of the light beam in its journey through the recesses of the chamber. It progresses from left to right and gradually descends, reflecting the movement of the rising sun. It is the beam of light itself which finally and conclusively identifies the inscriptions as solar symbols. Moreover, the huge stones of the entrance and passage shape the light beam into a fairly regular geometric form. The rectangle of light disintegrates in the process of moving away from stone 14, on the left of the diagram. During this phase, reflected light illuminates the solar system on the lower left of stone 14. After disintegration, the rectangular shape reconstructs itself on stone 6 on the right of the diagram.

The entire sequence has as its focus the emblematic solar symbol reproduced on the opposite page.

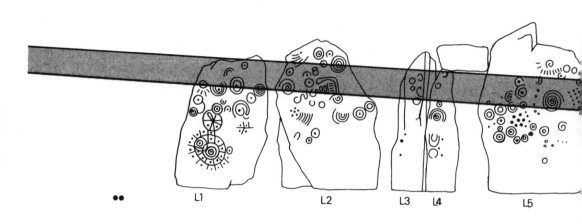

L1   L2   L3 L4   L5

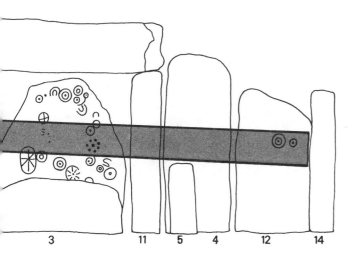

Spring equinox, Cairn T

The photograph shows the beam of light in the chamber as seen from the passage. A sillstone, stone 1 is in the foreground. The light is now being restricted by the lintel on top, L3 on the left, stone 8 on the right and stone 1 on the bottom. The diagram above shows the full extension of the light beam as it strikes stone 14 during the spring equinox. The drawing (right) shows stone 14 as seen from behind stone 1 in the passage.

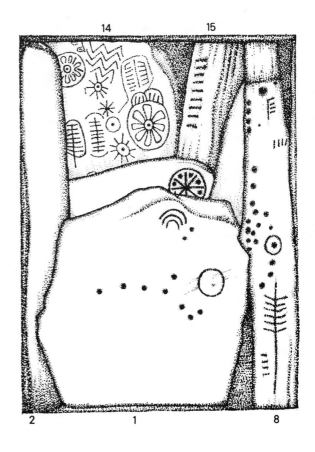

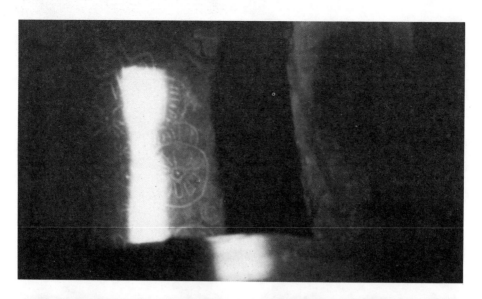

Autumnal equinox, Cairn T

This sequence of photographs was taken on the day of the autumnal equinox, 22 September 1980. It was observed that by 16 September the sun's rays were leaving Cairn I and beginning to enter Cairn T. On the equinox the sun rises at 7.11 a.m. Light immediately streams into the passage, but does not strike the backstone until 7.46 a.m. It takes 29 minutes for the patch of light to cross the backstone, moving at a rate of 1 minute 12 seconds per inch. It takes 1 hour 18 minutes from the moment the light strikes the backstone until it disappears on stone 6. The photographs show the culmination of light at

Cairn T as it crosses the sunwheel emblem. The beam of light clearly centres on the sun's disc, repeating the imagery of the spring equinox. The width of the beam is the same, but its length (c. $19\frac{1}{2}$ in.) is about double what it was in the spring. The focal image in both events remains the same, but the scheme is contrived so that different sets of engravings are utilized to measure the beam of light. In the first photograph the movement of the upper part of the beam is matched to a set of zigzags. In the second photograph it is matched to a set of segmented lines contained in an enclosure. A portion of the beam on the upper right is aligned to a series of horizontal lines on stone 15.

The first lunar observations in a passage mound were made on the night of 1 April 1980 at Cairn T. A narrow beam of light appeared for twenty minutes on stone 6 in the chamber. At that time the moon's declination was very close to the sun's declination six days before equinox, and the moon's beam would closely resemble the position of the sunbeam at that time. The photograph (right) shows the slender beam of light as it appeared in the chamber.

Spring equinox, Cairn T

The beam of sunlight (below) enters its final phase before leaving the chamber on 23 March. The long dagger of light on the left enters the chamber from an opening between stones 1 and 8. In the final phase, the rectangular form of the beam stops moving on stone 6 and begins to narrow from left to right until it disappears.

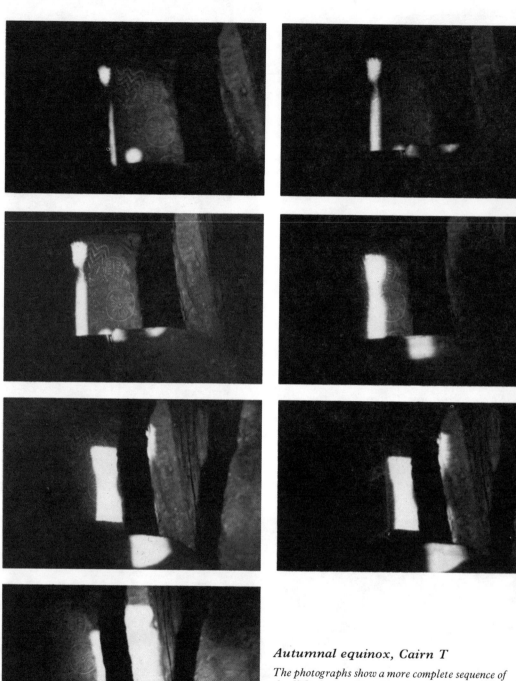

Autumnal equinox, Cairn T

The photographs show a more complete sequence of the light beam. Stages 5, 6 and 7 are critical, because this phase, which represents the culmination of the shaft of light, is unimpaired by the modern door at the entrance. The illumination of the sunwheel unambiguously links the art and the astronomy.

Equinox at Knowth

Knowth is the largest passage mound in Ireland. It is a massive structure covering an acre of land on a hilltop in the Boyne Valley. In architectural conception it represents the ideas and motivations of a society which we are only just beginning to understand. That society is very far removed from us, and indeed very far removed from even the most ancient civilizations that we do know something about.

In the illustration above, shadows from two standing stones are cast on to two kerbstones at Knowth at the equinox sunset. (Kerbstones are large stones surrounding the base of a passage mound.) The kerbstone on the left is the entrance stone of the western passage. This has a vertical line which replicates the vertical line on the entrance stone at Newgrange. The shadow of the standing stone seems clearly to have been intended to align with the vertical line on the kerbstone. Although the standing stone has been re-erected, it has been put back in its original socket, and observations made on 13 and 16 September 1980 seemed to indicate that the alignment was intentionally positioned to mark the equinox. This strategy has a clear parallel in the similar arrangement employed at Newgrange (below).

Solstice at Newgrange

During winter solstice sunrise at Newgrange shadows cast by standing stones 1 and 12 strike engraved kerbstones 1 and 93.

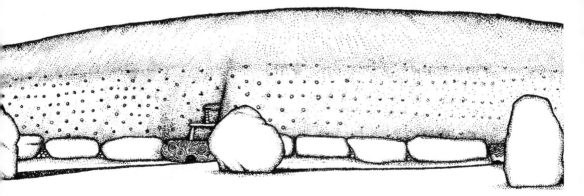

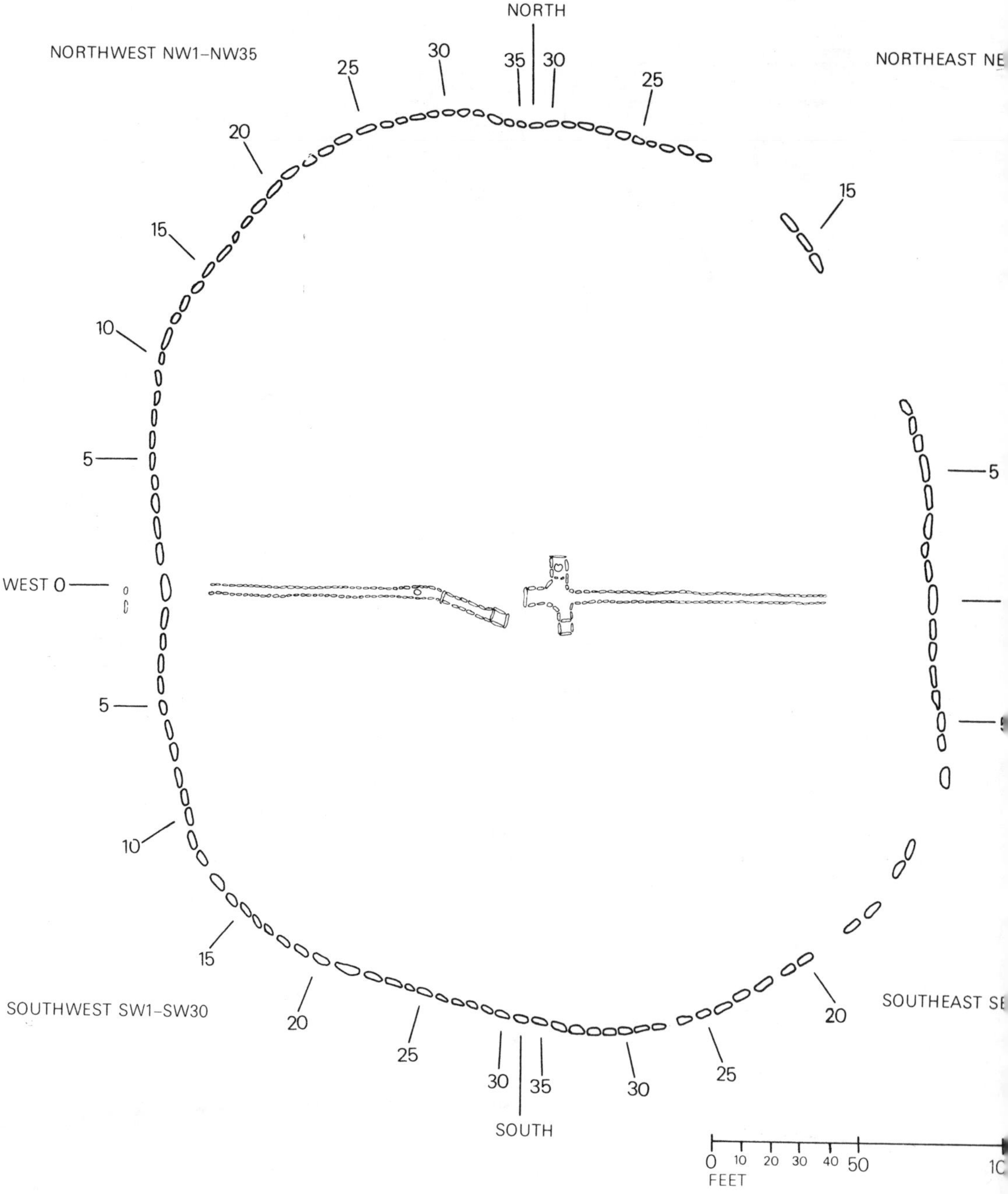

NORTH

NORTHWEST NW1–NW35

NORTHEAST NE

30

25

35 30

25

20

15

15

10

15

5

5

WEST 0

5

5

10

10

15

15

SOUTHWEST SW1–SW30

SOUTHEAST SE

20

20

25

25

30 35 30

SOUTH

0 10 20 30 40 50   10
FEET

Knowth

At Knowth a number of calendrical devices are synchronized in a single structure. The standing stones cast shadows, beams of light enter the passages (even though the entrances were damaged during the Iron Age) and smaller sundials are engraved on the kerbstones (numbered here according to the sequence given on the plan above). There are estimated to be 134 kerbstones, more than half engraved with major compositions and others with incidental markings. Many stones on the east side still remain buried, so that after number 8, the count is speculative. Heavily engraved stones are positioned in an area that extends clockwise from the northeast to the northwest, thus following a circuit that matches the movements of the sun and moon.

(Above) A section cut into the Knowth mound shows how layers of sods and brown clay are interspersed among layers of shale and pebbles. Layers alternate between organic and inorganic material. Current excavation is removing much of this material, and one wonders to what extent it will be replaced in the restoration.

(Below) Stones West O and East O are the entrance stones to the passages. The vertical lines indicate the positions of the rising and setting sun at equinox, and these are unambiguous astronomical alignments, closely resembling the alignment of the entrance stone and kerbstone 52 at Newgrange. A set of seven inverted arcs on NW1 duplicates the seven arcs engraved on SE1. The positioning of these markings demonstrates that their placement is intentional.

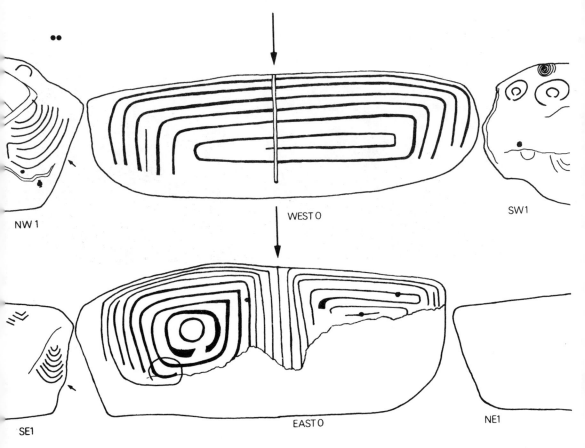

NW 1

WEST O

SW1

SE1

EAST O

NE1

The setting sun on 16 September 1980 approaches the standing stone outside the entrance of the western passage of Knowth. On the autumnal equinox, six days later, the sun would align with the standing stone as its beam penetrates deeply into the passage.

(Above) View of the western entrance facing north shows the standing stones and a peculiar arrangement of spheroid and ellipsoid stones whose purpose is unknown. To the north are two of Knowth's seventeen satellite mounds.

(Below) The standing stones contrast straight and narrow form with circular or ovular form. The straight standing stone is 7 ft 1 in. in height and its width varies between 15 and 18 in. It closely resembles in shape and measure the standing stone inside Cairn L, Loughcrew, which is also part of a solar construct. Its rectangular form is echoed in the engravings on the entrance stone and the vertical line. Behind the stones lies the entrance to the passage.

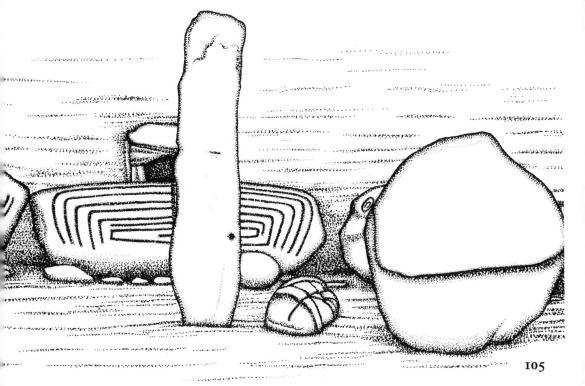

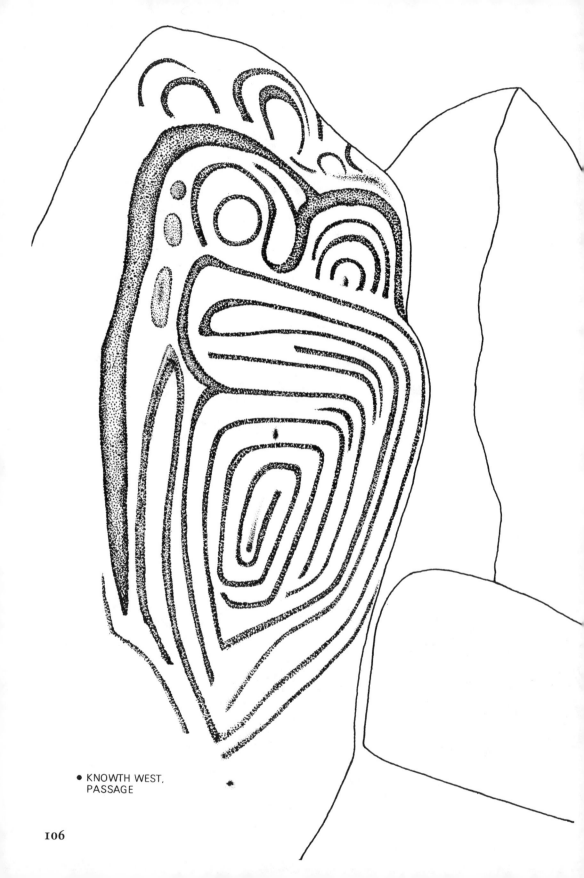

● KNOWTH WEST,
PASSAGE

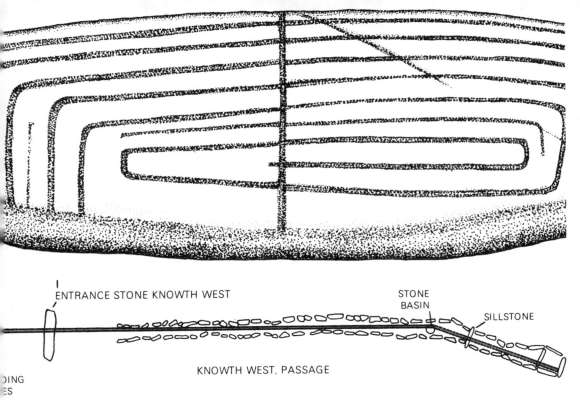

ENTRANCE STONE KNOWTH WEST

STONE
BASIN

SILLSTONE

KNOWTH WEST, PASSAGE

The beam of light entering the western passage at Knowth extends much further than the beam at Newgrange. According to radiocarbon dating Knowth was built about 500 years before Newgrange. The eastern passage, which cannot be observed because of obstructions, is about twice the size of the Newgrange passage. In the western passage the light beam extends nearly to the sillstone, beyond which the passage veers to the right. This sillstone is seen on the lower right of the illustration on the facing page. An engraved stone in the illustration combines elements from the western entrance stone (above) and the eastern entrance stone (below).

Because of their length and the time of year they indicate, the passages at Knowth are unsurpassed for their astronomical potential in accurately defining a particular day. The full extension of the light beam entering Knowth West can be observed from the back recess of the passage. From there the appearance of the light beam would indicate equinox. Some archaeologists believe that this area of the passage once formed part of an earlier and smaller mound, although at present there is little evidence to support the idea. In any case, as it stands today, as a solar construct, the passage represents one of the great wonders of the Neolithic world.

KNOWTH EAST,
ENTRANCE STONE

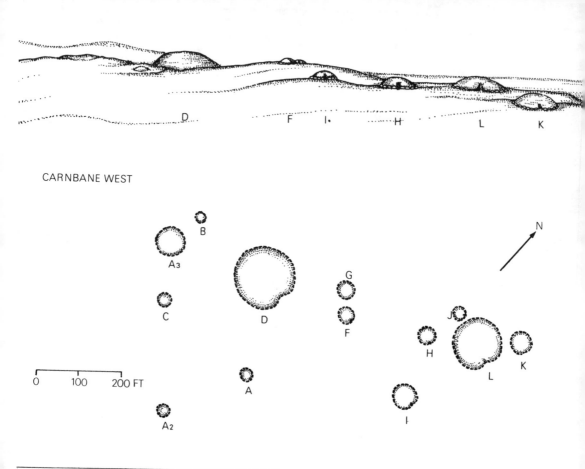

CARNBANE WEST

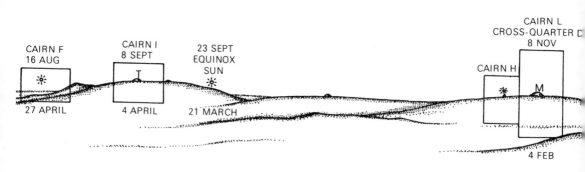

CARNBANE EAST

The illustration shows sunrise positions on the horizon as seen from Carnbane West. The rectangles represent approximate areas framed by remaining passages of mounds on Carnbane West. From August to November the sunrise positions move from left to right as light enters Carns F, I, T, H and L. In the spring, from February to April, the sun's position moves from right to left and light re-enters Cairn L on 4 February and then Cairn H. By spring equinox, 21 March, the sun's rays are again entering Cairn T on Carnbane East, followed on Carnbane West by Cairn I (4 April) and Cairn F (27 April). By 6 May, another cross-quarter day, rays of the setting sun are entering Cairn S on Carnbane East (not shown), to return again on 8 August, repeating the annual process.

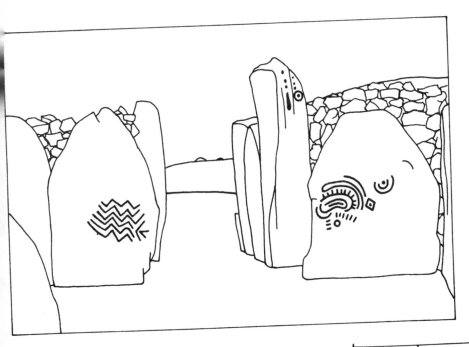

Between equinox and solstice

It is evident that the existing passages of mounds on Loughcrew are aligned to positions of the sun on or near the horizon, although on Carnbane West the passage of Cairn D has not yet been found and only Cairns F, H, I, and L are still functioning to any extent.

We have seen that equinoxes and solstices were the primary concerns of the mound builders. Next in importance were cross-quarter days, which fall exactly between the equinoxes and solstices, dividing the year into 8 parts. Some satellite mounds were apparently constructed to warn of the approach of an important date. Cairn I warns of the approaching autumnal equinox just as Cairn H warns of the coming of winter on the cross-quarter day in November. The view of Cairn T from Cairn I, illustrated above, is very frequently photographed. The two mounds are in fact closely related in a time sequence. At the beginning of September, the sun rises directly behind Cairn T and projects a beam of light directly on to the backstone of Cairn I (right). By 16 September the light beam is only 6 in. away from the right edge of the backstone, and simultaneously light begins to enter the chamber of Cairn T to mark the equinox. Cairn H duplicates this strategy as the sun's rays enter the chamber prior to the cross-quarter day in November when the sun comes into the range of Cairn L.

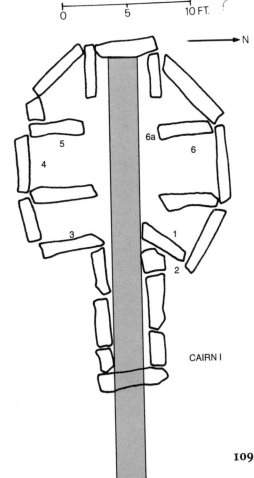

CAIRN I

109

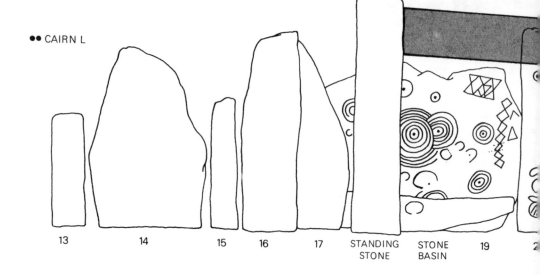

13   14   15   16   17   STANDING   STONE   19
                                     STONE   BASIN

Cairn L, Loughcrew

Cross-quarter Days, 8 November and 4 February

Some of the most unusual and dramatic sun-beam imagery in a mound occurs at Cairn L. Cairn L is unique among the Loughcrew cairns in having an asymmetrical chamber and a regularly shaped white standing stone positioned towards the right in the chamber. The stone is over 6 ft high and nearly 15 in. wide. It stands where it was found when the mound was first opened, isolated from the main structure of the chamber itself. Conceivably the mound could have been built as an elaborate housing for this special stone. Du Noyer records a single circle engraved on the bottom of the stone, but this is no longer recognizable and possibly never existed. The purpose of the stone has always been an enigma, but its function could be revealed in the light of the rising sun.

Teams were positioned inside Cairn U on Carnbane East and Cairn L on Carnbane West before dawn broke on the morning of 3 November 1980. Towards sunrise the stars began to fade, although the crescent of the waning moon remained a brilliant object in the sky. Near the moon, Venus and Saturn were almost in conjunction, and Jupiter could be seen in the east. The sun began to rise behind the knoll where the remains of Cairn M lay situated. As the sun rose, from Cairn L we could see the entire top of the knoll start to glow radiantly. The passage of Cairn M was probably aligned to this sunrise, and megalithic observers inside the mound may have viewed the sun's rays for about ten minutes before they appeared in Cairn L. As soon as the first limb of the sun appeared over Cairn M, a flash of light pierced the darkness of Cairn L and

STONE 20, DETAIL

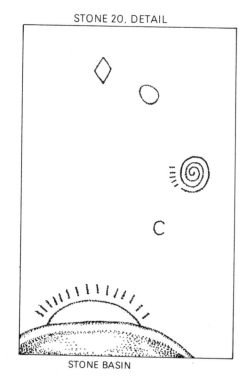

STONE BASIN

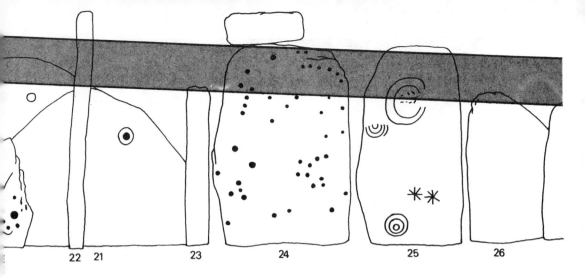

22 21   23   24   25   26

illuminated the top of the standing stone. Instead of the usual slow, progressive entry of the beam of light, it had penetrated the chamber instantaneously. The lower edge of the light beam was formed by the shadow of Cairn M, and stones inside Cairn L further modelled it, so that it illuminated only the standing stone and no other stones in the chamber.

On the morning of 3 November the beam of light was not in fact exactly centred on the standing stone, but directed a few inches to the left. This meant that an exact alignment would occur sometime on or very near 8 November. Unfortunately bad weather after 3 November prevented further observations until 12 November. But despite this, enough observations were made on 3 November to suggest that the cross-quarter day at Cairn L (and also Cairn U) was accurately designated.

The beam of light entered Cairn L at 7.40 a.m. on 3 November. In ten minutes it had moved down 7 in. from the top of the stone and was growing longer. By 7.56 a.m. the beam was over 30 in. in length and had shifted 9 in. from the top of the standing stone as it moved towards the right. Before leaving the chamber, the beam of light – by now rectangular – was projected on to stone 17 and brilliantly illuminated the entire recess. In the diagram above, the back of stone 17 is shown. The drawing shows a detail of the face of stone 20, which is opposite stone 17. The image of the rising sun is engraved at the edge of the stone basin. The engraved images are almost a pictorial representation of the astronomical event.

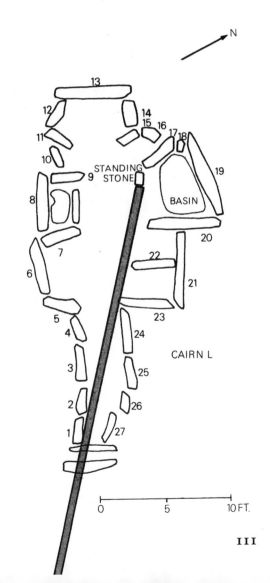

Moonrise, Cairn L

The photograph is of the full moon as seen from stone 13 at the very back of Cairn L on the night of 26 August 1980 at 10.15 p.m. At this time the moon's rays were simultaneously entering Cairn U on Carnbane East and the megalithic mound at Tara. This moon is known as the 'harvest moon', because it is low in the sky during August when the sun is very high, and during the harvesting of crops it provides a convenient light which allows work to continue into the night. When this photograph was taken a beam of moonlight was being projected on to the right side of stone 13, where it illuminated a hollowed circular depression in which was engraved a lunar crescent. From here the beam of moonlight moved downwards and to the right as it illuminated the lower portion of a standing stone, a stone basin and engravings on the lower edges of stones inside the chamber in a sequential pattern.

The photograph gives a good indication of the aperture as it exists today. Fortunately, when the mound was first opened over 100 years ago, Du Noyer was on hand and, from his drawing, it is clear that there has been no significant change in the entrance. The roofing of the chamber had collapsed, but the lintel forming the top of the aperture was still in place. It is possible that the portal as it exists today is, or closely approximates, the original scheme.

George Coffey referred directly to the symbols on stone 3 in his book New Grange (1912): they 'probably represent a symbol of the sinking or rising sun'. The twelve concentric circles could represent the year and there are two subsets of three arcs, likely to be an emblem of the rising sun and the year. Another luni-solar emblem appears on stone 4. In the photograph of the moon as seen from Cairn L, it is this stone which protrudes into the framing portal from the right. The left edge of this stone serves as a gnomon for the light beam.

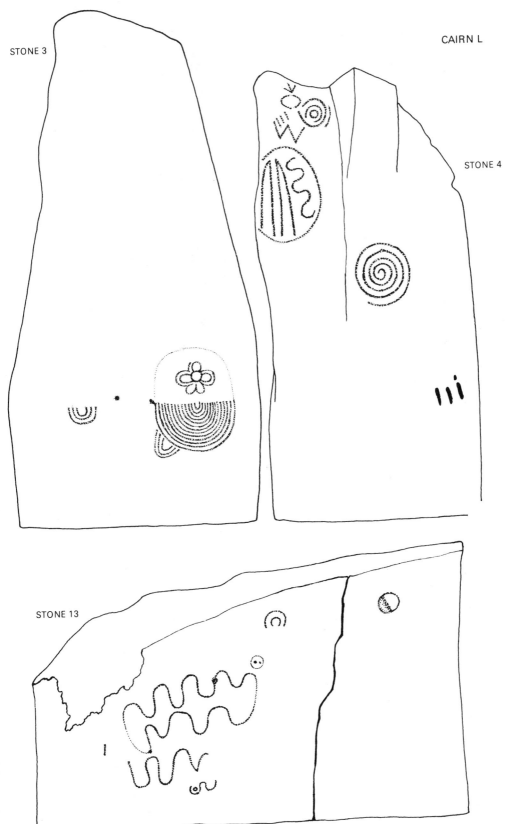

STONE 3

CAIRN L

STONE 4

STONE 13

Cairns H and F, Loughcrew

Just as Cairn H warns of November's cross-quarter day and the coming of winter, so Cairn F warns of May's cross-quarter day and the coming of summer. By mid-October the sun's rays enter Cairn H at sunrise and strike engravings on the edge of stone 4. As November approaches the rectangular light beam strikes the backstone. The sun then moves out of range of Cairn H and directly in line with Cairns L and M, which mark its position on the horizon on 8 November.

Similarly, the rays of the rising sun enter Cairn F late in April before marking the cross-quarter day on 6 May, when rays of the setting sun centre on Cairn S. The sun's rays return to Cairn S to mark the cross-quarter day on 8 August. By 16 August they again enter Cairn F, and continue to do so until the sun's rising position moves behind Cairn T and the light beam enters Cairn I, warning of autumnal equinox. Cairns I, T, F and S form the longest remaining sequential arrangement of alignments known.

One lintel only remains from the original roofing of both Cairns H and F, and at Cairn F the entrance is also partially blocked. Nevertheless, light is still projected on to the backstone. If it were cleared, light would not only touch the backstone (as at present) but also the sun-wheel on it.

Detail of stone 4, Cairn H

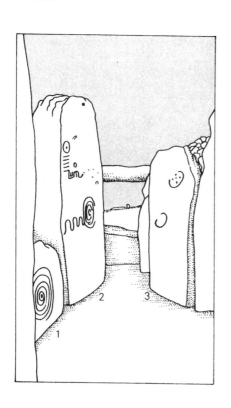

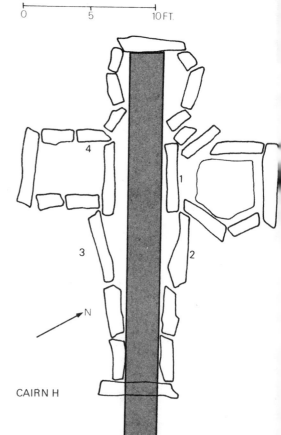

CAIRN H

The sun appearing at the portal of Cairn F, sunrise, 15 August 1980

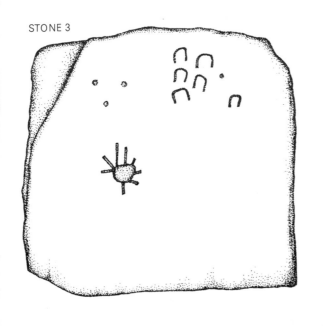

STONE 3

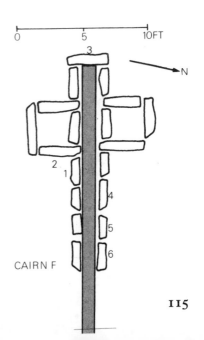

CAIRN F

Cairns S and U, Loughcrew

Cairns S and U are satellite mounds positioned in close proximity to Cairn T on Carnbane East. Cairn S indicates the cross-quarter day on 6 May and the cross-quarter day on 8 August, marking the beginning of summer and autumn. Cairn U is synchronized with Cairn L to indicate the cross-quarter days on 8 November and 4 February, marking the beginning of winter and spring. Thus, together the two satellite mounds of Cairn T serve to announce the four seasons of the year and in themselves form an agricultural and pastoral calendar.

Cairn S is abundantly adorned with engraved emblems of the sun. This is not at all unusual,

The photograph shows the setting sun as seen from the chamber of Cairn S early in August. Stone 2 may well be a pictogram of the event. As the sun sets, its image is beautifully reflected in Lough Sheelin, a lake near the horizon and visible from the chamber.

and in Part III solar imagery will be discussed as a general feature of megalithic mounds. The imagery on the backstone of Cairn U may represent the rising sun. On the cross-quarter days the set of elongated arcs is illuminated by rays of the sun.

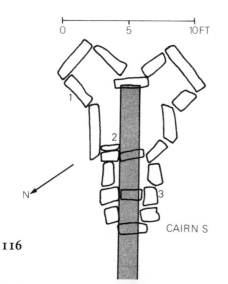

CAIRN S

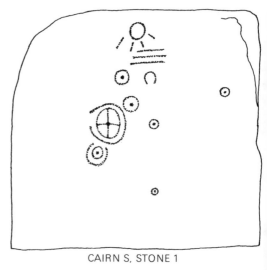

CAIRN S, STONE 1

MISSING FRAGMENT
OF STONE 2, CAIRN S

STONE 11

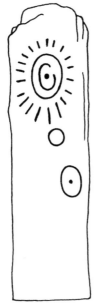

CAIRN S, STONE 2

Cairn S is the smallest passage and chamber encountered so far, but it is still a fairly accurate indicator of the cross-quarter days in May and August. After and before these dates the sun's rays enter the two side recesses. The right recess is now missing. Neither mound has any intact roofing, and collapsed cairn material partially blocks the entrance to Cairn S; yet both constructs are still capable of indicating the cross-quarter days by their orientation to the sun's position on the horizon.

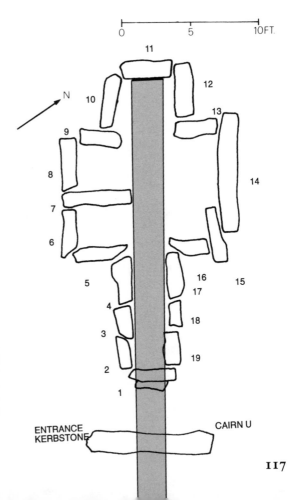

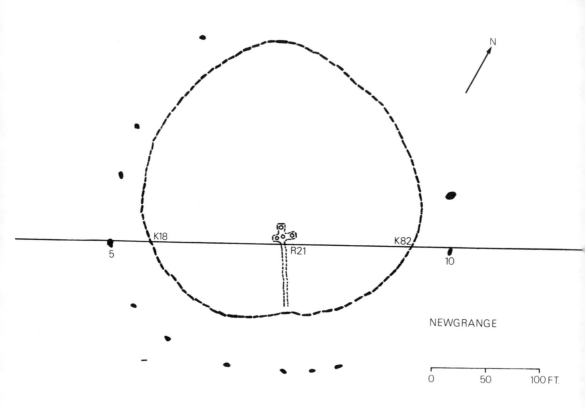

N

K18 R21 K82

5 10

NEWGRANGE

0 50 100 FT.

INNER SURFACE
KERBSTONE 18

Newgrange, cross-quarter days, 6 May and 8 August

Of the ninety-seven kerbstones at Newgrange, three are known to be fully engraved on their inner surfaces. All three are astronomically aligned, and in each case at least one standing stone marks the alignment. These are in addition to the back of the corbel stone of the roof-box, which is also engraved, aligned with a standing stone and to R21, a stone which directly affects the beam of light entering the chamber at winter solstice. The architecture of Newgrange embodies many astronomical alignments. Standing stones 5 and 10 are aligned to R21 and the rising sun as it appears on the horizon on 6 May and 8 August, the beginning of summer and autumn. On this alignment the builders have placed K18, with its engraved inner surface (now hidden by the mound) facing the rising sun. The stone was engraved before being positioned and before the mound was built, but probably after the standing stones were aligned.

The alignment of K18 with the other stones serves no practical or decorative purpose; one must assume it is ritual.

(Below) The shadow of standing stone 10 at the moment the sun's disc appears above the horizon. The position of the top of the shadow is marked by hollows engraved on kerbstone 82.

(Above) This early photograph of the interior of Newgrange shows stone R21 as viewed from the passage. A pattern of interlinking triangles is engraved on the upper part of the stone.

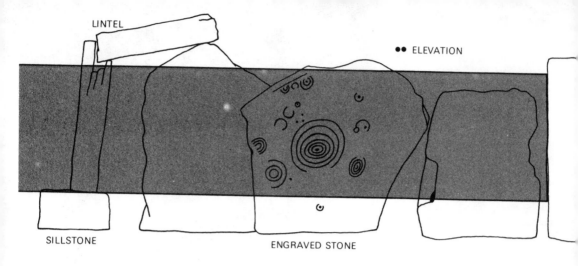

LINTEL

•• ELEVATION

SILLSTONE

ENGRAVED STONE

A view of the mound from the southwest.

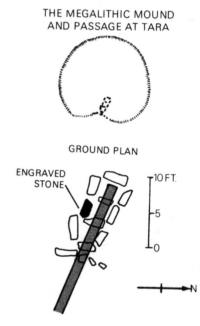

THE MEGALITHIC MOUND
AND PASSAGE AT TARA

GROUND PLAN

ENGRAVED
STONE

10 FT.

5

0

N

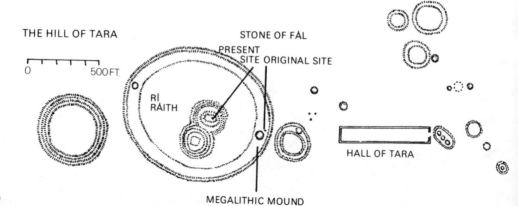

THE HILL OF TARA

0   500 FT.

STONE OF FÁL

PRESENT
SITE   ORIGINAL SITE

RÍ
RÁITH

HALL OF TARA

MEGALITHIC MOUND

Tara, cross-quarter days, 8 November and 4 February

An aerial view of the Hill of Tara. The megalithic mound is to the right of the circular earthworks.

Cairns L and U on Loughcrew, and, according to the ground plans, passage 1 at Dowth in the Boyne Valley, are all aligned to mark the cross-quarter days in November and February. Solar and lunar observations made at Tara during 1980 by our research group, and further observations made in February 1981 by local researchers Denis McCarthy and Patrick McNamee, confirmed that Tara is synchronized to Cairns L and U. This group of four mounds indicating the commencement of winter and spring shows that these points in time had major significance in the calendar of the mound builders. Cairn L and Dowth are both large focal mounds. Compared with this only one passage mound, the diminutive satellite, Cairn S, remains to indicate the cross-quarter days in May and August marking summer and autumn. It is the corresponding alignments of the four mounds in the November-February group that present the most convincing evidence for cross-quarter day observation.

The beam of light that enters the chamber of Tara is formed by a sillstone, a lintel and two uprights at the entrance. These form an aperture 24 in. wide, allowing a stream of light to strike the 48-in.-wide backstone. The sillstone is aligned to the horizon, so that the light beam strikes the backstone at the moment when the sun's disc appears above the horizon. The cross-quarter day is indicated when the patch of light is centred on the backstone. As a solar construct Tara could not be as accurate as Cairns L and U, where the passages are twice as long, or Dowth, which is at least three times as long. Yet, considered essentially as a sundial, Tara is still monumental in scale and daily changes in the position of a 13-ft-long sunbeam are more than adequate to determine specific dates.

Tara lies 10 miles southwest of Newgrange and, like Newgrange, it is steeped in ancient myth and tradition. It has always been associated with *Samhain*, the Celtic observance of the year's turning in November, and this event is well documented. Mythologically, the mound also has associations with the Tuatha Dé Danann, or the 'Lords of Light'. They arrive from the air and cast a darkness over the sun for three days. They bring four talismans, one of which is the Great Fál or the 'Stone of Knowledge'. According to the Dindshenchas, the ancient lore associated with features of the landscape, this stone was one of four stones positioned in the cardinal directions on Tara. It may be significant that the Hall of Tara, the political centre of ancient Ireland, is aligned north–south.

North and south alignments

The recognition of the cardinal directions, north and south, is the most fundamental observation in astronomy. Before the magnetic compass was invented these directions could be determined only by direct observation of the sun during the day or the stars at night. The astronomer, E. C. Krupp, remarks in his book, *In Search of Ancient Astronomies* (1977), 'True sun worship would amount to a sensible recognition of the sun's importance to cycles of life on earth and practical observation of the sun's behaviour, which reveals the pattern of its effects. The moon and the stars may well have been understood in similar terms.' Another astronomer, Lockyer, believed that the megalith builders incorporated alignments to stars in their architecture and 'used starlight at night in some of their observations, very much like they used sunlight during the day'.

Baltinglass, perched 1,288 ft up in the Wicklow Mountains, gives clear evidence of an alignment to the stars. Aligned due north, there is little doubt that it is focused towards our polestar today, and what was the polestar in the Neolithic period (see p. 186). The intention is accentuated by a vertical line engraved on the stone basin in the chamber. A vertical line marks

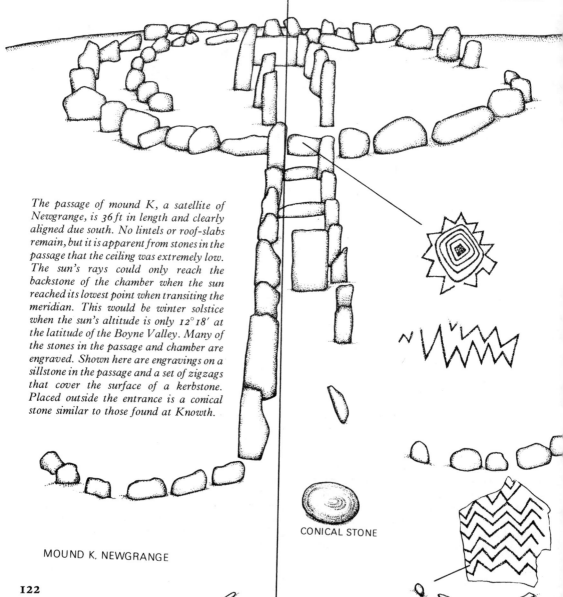

The passage of mound K, a satellite of Newgrange, is 36 ft in length and clearly aligned due south. No lintels or roof-slabs remain, but it is apparent from stones in the passage that the ceiling was extremely low. The sun's rays could only reach the backstone of the chamber when the sun reached its lowest point when transiting the meridian. This would be winter solstice when the sun's altitude is only 12° 18′ at the latitude of the Boyne Valley. Many of the stones in the passage and chamber are engraved. Shown here are engravings on a sillstone in the passage and a set of zigzags that cover the surface of a kerbstone. Placed outside the entrance is a conical stone similar to those found at Knowth.

CONICAL STONE

MOUND K. NEWGRANGE

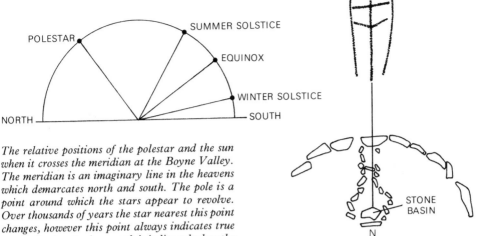

The relative positions of the polestar and the sun when it crosses the meridian at the Boyne Valley. The meridian is an imaginary line in the heavens which demarcates north and south. The pole is a point around which the stars appear to revolve. Over thousands of years the star nearest this point changes, however this point always indicates true north. During the day, south is indicated when the sun crosses the meridian at midday and reaches its highest point in the sky. The sun is highest at summer solstice ($60° 18'$) and lowest at winter solstice ($12° 18'$). In between these positions is the equinox ($36° 48'$).

Above, the megalithic construct at Baltinglass, Co. Wicklow, is aligned north and marked by an engraving on the stone basin. Below, Knockmany, Co. Tyrone, aligns due south.

many important astronomical alignments. The most obvious and explicit alignment due south occurs at mound K, a satellite in close proximity to Newgrange. Although this mound was re-buried after excavation, the intended alignment is clear from the dig records. A fascinating aspect of this solar construct is that the sun's rays would appear to strike the backstone during winter solstice at midday. The scenario in the Boyne Valley is far more complex than expected: it involves the sun's rays entering Newgrange at dawn (8.54 a.m.), mound Z at 10.15 and mound K at 11.20, remaining there until 12.26 Greenwich Mean Time (equivalent to noon local apparent time). Immediately afterwards the beam would enter mound L, remaining there until 1.09. Between 1.09 and 2.20, when a thin shaft of light appears in the chamber of Dowth 2, the sun's rays may have illuminated mound Z1, adjacent to Z. This mound has been completely destroyed, although there is some evidence of it in aerial photographs. By 2.53 the light beam has moved to the back of the Dowth chamber. Reflected light illuminates stone 13 in the side chamber from 3.04 until 3.30. Light is cut off from Dowth at 4.03, when the sun's disc begins to disappear below the horizon. The sun sets at 4.07. The intention seems to be continual observation of the sun throughout the shortest day of the year. Satellites aligned due south appear to be a feature of other major complexes. Cairn T on Loughcrew has one and Knowth also has at least one.

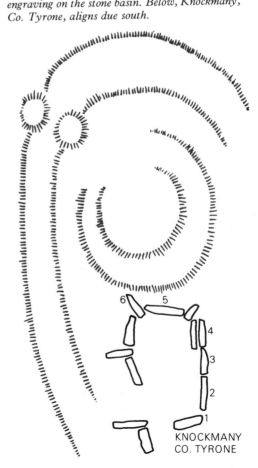

CAIRN W,
STONE 3

CAIRN W, STONE 1

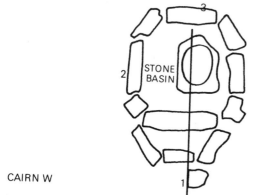

CAIRN W

```
0        5        10FT
```

SOUTH

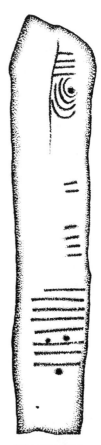

KNOCKMANY,
STONE 6

Cairn W and Knockmany

Cairn W was known as the 'Pot' Cairn, since unlike all other mounds on Loughcrew, the earth was dug away below the surface for its construction. This may have been to allow the sun's rays to penetrate the chamber when the sun is at its highest. Cairn W lies 128 yds east of Cairn T and is considerably removed from the main group of mounds on Carnbane East. Only fragments remain of a small passage mound that was once about 7 yds in diameter. Its stone basin, which was hollowed out to a depth of 3–4 in., is missing and engravings on stones 1 and 3, originally recorded by Du Noyer, have

now disappeared. It aligns due south, and markings on stone 3 probably indicated various positions of the sun at midday. Stone 6 at Knockmany probably had a similar function.

Knockmany is situated in Co. Tyrone, on a hill 779 ft above sea level, overlooking the plain of Clossach. It aligns to the sun at midday and is clearly not focused on or near the horizon. The diagram of the elevation shows the height of the sun at extreme positions as it transits the meridian. These are drawn from the most probable position of a lintel at the entrance. A 14-ft chamber of this type could have been used to determine dates and seasons by the height of the sun throughout the year. The entrance opens directly towards Loughcrew, 50 miles due south, an extraordinary distance if the alignment is intentional.

Above, an illustration of Knockmany based on early photographs. Below, an elevation of the stones on the right or east side of the chamber, and various positions of the sun at midday. Stone 2 has been re-erected and is here reconstructed according to Coffey.

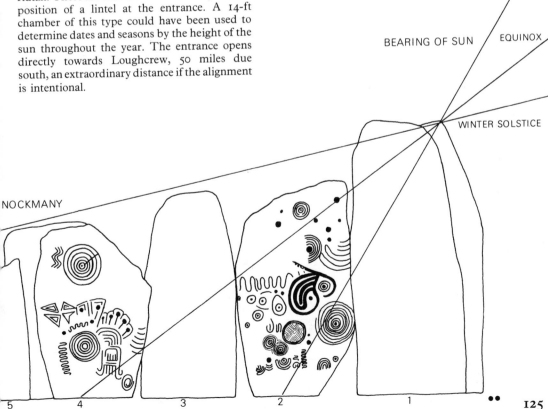

SUMMER SOLSTICE

BEARING OF SUN   EQUINOX

WINTER SOLSTICE

NOCKMANY

5   4   3   2   1

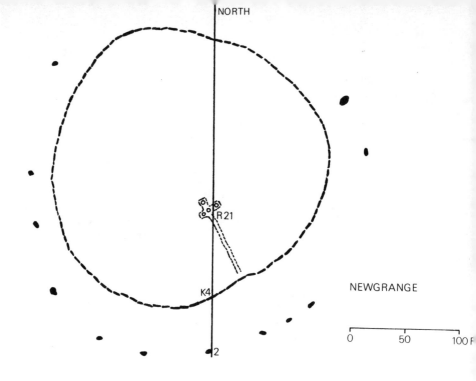

NORTH

R21

NEWGRANGE

K4

2

0   50   100 F

A north-south alignment is embodied in the architecture of Newgrange. The arrangement conforms
to a pattern of aligning a standing stone (in this
case, no. 2), a kerbstone (no. 4), which has been
engraved on its interior surface, and stone R21 at
the immediate entrance to the chamber. These
alignments strongly suggest that stone R21, the
standing stones surrounding the mound and certain
key kerbstones were erected first as baselines before
the mound was built. Thus, the structure of the
mound has its foundation in astronomical and
cosmological principles.

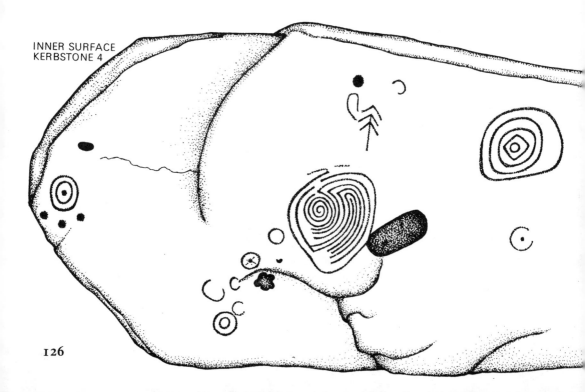

INNER SURFACE
KERBSTONE 4

126

Part III

MEGALITHIC ART

Megalithic art is not art in the ordinary sense of the word. It displays some of the improvisations of art, and at times acts as ornament or decoration, but it also exhibits the basic characteristics of a form of symbolic writing. Although each megalithic composition is unique there is a limited, identifiable and relatively consistent range of symbols which appear in widely different places.

The art as it exists in Western Europe can be succinctly defined as engraving or painting executed on megaliths. In Ireland, where the largest concentration is found, it is always engraved on a type of megalithic structure known as a passage mound. The art is harmoniously integrated into the architecture of the mound, and it is this relationship that identifies the art as monumental and links it directly with astronomical considerations.

Three main factors are generally recognized in the development of astronomy as a science. The first is observation of celestial bodies for the purpose of performing rites and rituals – this is detectable in Neolithic astronomy. The second is the correlation of celestial with terrestrial phenomena – the presence of this factor is a possibility, but there is no definite evidence for the development of a predictive 'science' of astrology. The third factor is calendrical: astronomy develops as a method to facilitate the measurement of time – this is the most readily

Rock engravings at Dowth 2 are clearly positioned with reference to the setting sun at winter solstice. Above, reflected light illuminates a spiral on stone 13. Gradually the entire stone glows in the darkness of the side chamber.

perceptible factor in Neolithic astronomy, although it exists among other considerations.

Although the beginnings of truly scientific astronomy can be recognized this does not imply that Neolithic astronomy was scientific in character. Ritual considerations seem to dominate in all the structures, and in general the art represents a semi-magical projection on astronomy. It is likely that among the population both the mounds and the symbols were regarded as sacred to the sun and moon. Images of both dominate megalithic art and this recognition alone, to a large extent, explains much of the art.

The gaps in our knowledge are still enormous, but the process of decoding and re-reading has begun. Apart from luni-solar symbolism, light itself seems to be the chief focal symbol. There is also a deep concern with time. Many symbols seem to indicate numbers and counting, although because of the simplicity of the numbers involved and the various ways of interpreting them, it is not always easy to determine precisely how they are used. But it is certain that counting ability and computation were directly connected with timekeeping.

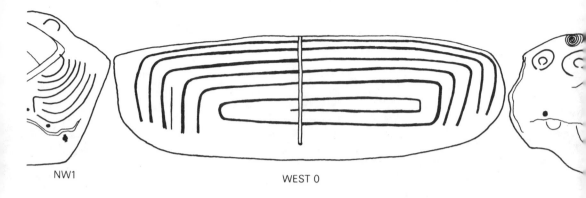

NW1   WEST 0

Rock engraving techniques

Megalithic art in Ireland exists solely in the medium of engraved stone. On the continent some stones are painted. Prior to engraving, the symbols were sometimes scratched on the surface of the stone with a pebble. A piece of flint or quartz was held in one hand and used as a chisel. The other hand held a stone hammer. Incisions were made along the scratched lines in a series of closely set pick marks, whose size was determined by the size of the chisel point and the pressure exerted. The point must have had to be constantly sharpened.

A more advanced technique, found in the Boyne Valley and on Loughcrew, was the use of various grades of point on the same stone. Later the picking technique was used in the Boyne Valley to create an outline and fill in the figure. Pick dressing also developed in the Boyne area. The thin outer layer of a stone was picked away to expose a new surface, removing superficial irregularities and improving the colour. The megalith builders carried the art further towards the three-dimensional, broadening the intaglio effect so that the image stood out in false-relief. They also developed the smoothing of pick marks by hammering. None of these innovations are evident at Loughcrew. The Boyne Valley engravings are also better preserved, because durable stones were used as opposed to the relatively soft local limestone at Loughcrew. The visual concepts and drawing skills are also far more advanced, indicating a development in both style and technique.

The enormous investment in time and energy suggests the engravings were too important to the community to have been mere artists' doodles.

Above, consecutive kerbstones at Knowth exhibit a wide variety of techniques. The standard technique of pickmarking is shown opposite, in the photograph of a detail of SW2. The form is an equable spiral which decreases in diameter by the same amount each revolution, and the tangents to the spiral make a constant angle to the radius. This was probably achieved by revolving a string around a fixed central post, making the distance between the lines equal to the circumference of the post.

Below, a stone from a Knowth satellite mound displays incised lines which outline the forms and subsequent pickmarking of twelve quadrangles and the beginnings of a thirteenth. The incised lines delineate the structure and form sub-sets of triangular patterns.

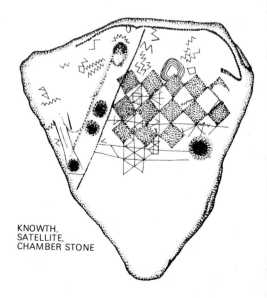

KNOWTH,
SATELLITE,
CHAMBER STONE

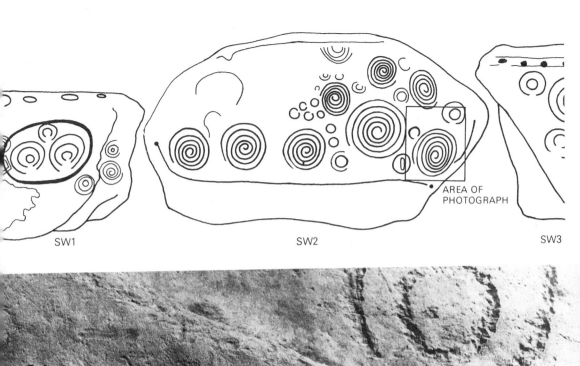

SW1   SW2   SW3

AREA OF
PHOTOGRAPH

The essential elements of megalithic art

Megalithic art is highly abstract and seems to be intentionally restricted to nine basic geometric forms, here called primaries because they combine to form all other marks and signs. The primaries are shown in the first row of the diagram opposite (*1* dot or cupmark, *2* line, *3* circle, *4* quadrangle, *5* arc or crescent, *6* zigzag, *7* wavy line, *8* spiral, and *9* oval or ellipse).

Primaries are clearly distinguishable from each other, they recur frequently and have a wide distribution. This classification eliminates elements which are clearly compounds of primary elements. It also includes ovals or ellipses, omitted from other classifications.

Row two shows the principal ways in which the primaries form sets. In row three, column four, two types of triangle are shown. They are not considered primaries, as it is the quadrangle, composed of opposed triangles, which generally

appears in the art. In column five, opposing variations are termed arcs (A), crescents (B), and elongated arcs (C). All three types can be shown to be clearly distinct in many instances. The C type is always distinct, but rarely forms compounds and is considered a variation of the arc rather than a primary. A and B types are indistinguishable in some instances and interchangeable in others. Note that the upright and inverted arcs of type A are one and the same symbol transformed by positioning. Likewise, the left and right crescents of type B represent different aspects of the same referent and one transforms into the other.

In row three, columns six and seven, the sets of zigzags and wavy lines are not in phase. These are variations of the more common form shown in row two. In column seven, A is termed a loop. It appears frequently and is related to the wavy line which in turn is related to the spiral. Spirals may be right-handed (A), left-handed (B) or retrograde (C), as shown in column eight. The ellipse shown in row one, column nine, is

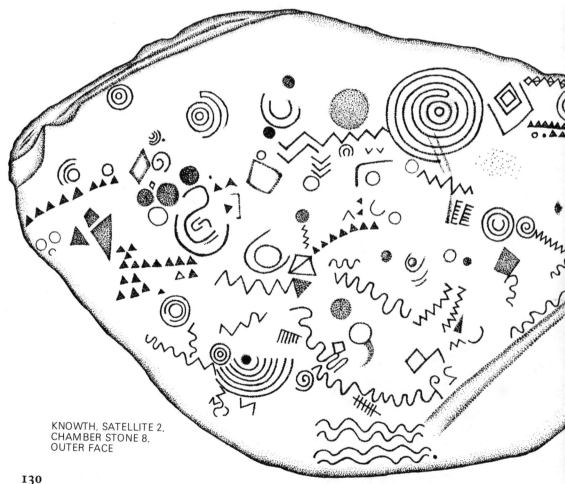

KNOWTH, SATELLITE 2,
CHAMBER STONE 8,
OUTER FACE

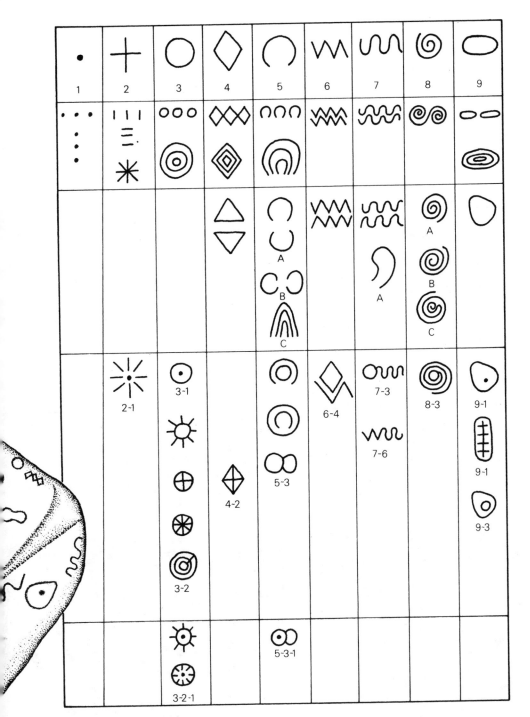

distinct from the oval in row three, column nine, but both are closely related and their numerous variants contain aspects of both so they are classified together.

Row four shows the most common simple compounds. These are emblematic forms or ligatures formed by two primaries. More complex compounds formed by three primaries are in row five. There are hundreds of compounds, many of which repeat, but these recur most frequently and are established standard symbols rather than innovations.

·	+	○	◇	◠	M	M	◎	○
1	2	3	4	5	6	7	8	9
20%	34%	53%	22%	39%	25%	28%	27%	17%

There are about 390 stones in Ireland known to be engraved with megalithic art. They are all found in passage mounds and, when these are accessible or intact, they have all been shown to be astronomically orientated, which reveals the context that the art appears in. The relationship between the art and astronomy is further re-inforced by the presence of engraved sundials, calendars and explicit solar-lunar imagery.

An analysis of the art shows that circles and arcs or crescents are the dominant forms. This results from the same pre-occupation with the sun and moon that is evident in the structure of the mounds. The chart above shows the primaries and the approximate percentage of stones on which they appear. Circles and arcs have the highest percentages. Of the 390 stones, 203 are illustrated in this book. These are selected to represent the entire corpus. They include all the major compositions, samples from each site and for the most part exclude only stones with minor isolated engravings. Of the 203 stones, at least half in some way express a relationship between the circle and the arc or crescent.

Stones on these pages are similar in that they are emblematic representations of the sun and moon and symbols of the year. The stone basin at Knowth is a ritual implement found in the context of an equinoctial solar construct. As ideally the equinoxes divide twelve months of the year into two equal parts, six radials are divided by a luni-solar emblem. The geometrical arrangement on the Bal-linvally stone is composed of twelve elements. Below, the number twelve is implied on stone SE28. The gapped arc could represent the thirteen possible full moons in a year. The crescent on the left is intentional and creates a polarity with the circle. This theme occurs regularly. Macalister recorded a left-handed spiral below the crescent.

KNOWTH, SE 28

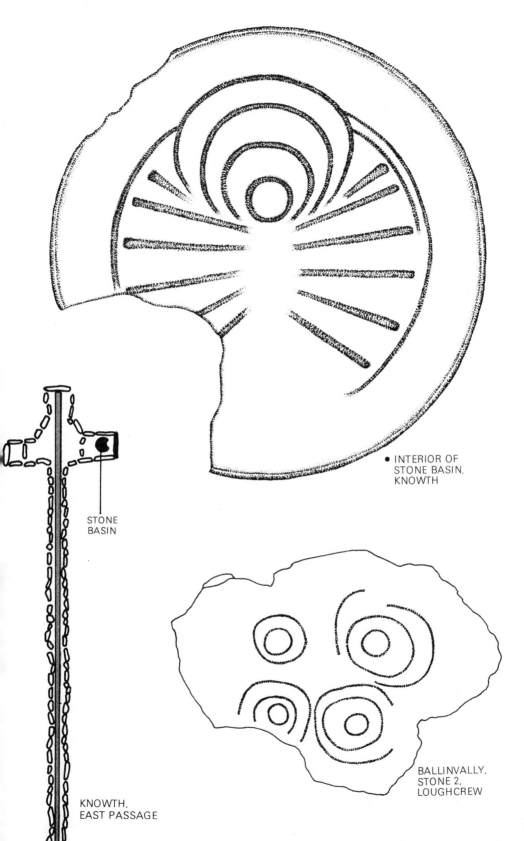

INTERIOR OF
STONE BASIN,
KNOWTH

STONE
BASIN

BALLINVALLY,
STONE 2,
LOUGHCREW

KNOWTH,
EAST PASSAGE

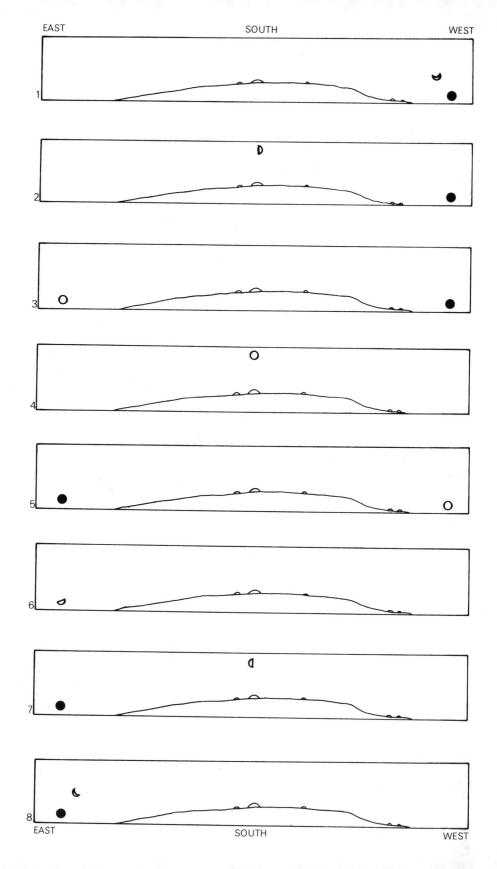

The moon in megalithic art

From earth the moon appears to be the largest celestial body in the sky; it attracts attention to itself constantly, changing its shape, size and brightness every day. These regular changes became the basis for the earliest calendar known – the megalithic lunar calendar. Lunar motion was undoubtedly seen to have an effect on the tides, and its phases were noticed to correlate with seasonal activities on earth, both agricultural and biological. Neolithic inscriptions are rich in lunar notation; it therefore seems likely that the moon's phases and positions in the sky were the subject of intense speculation. Thus to understand megalithic art one must first understand the moon. As a symbol, it has appeared in all human cultures. After forty years research into comparative religion, Mircea Eliade concludes that the cycles of the moon – its birth, growth, death and rebirth – reflect in a profound way the cycles of human existence.

The illuminated side of the moon always points towards the sun and shows the sun's position even when it has set. The lunar calendar requires observation of the first visibility of the new crescent on the western horizon. The diagrams on the opposite page illustrate approximately (and not to scale) various relationships between the sun and moon as seen from the north, looking at Cairn T in the Loughcrew Mountains. In diagram 1 the sun sets and the crescent moon makes its first appearance. The sun must be sufficiently below the horizon for the moon to be visible briefly before it sets. On the evening before, the moon was still too close to the sun to be seen. The moon is 'lost' in the sun for one, two and sometimes three days in each month. It is only when the sun and moon draw sufficiently apart that the first crescent will be seen briefly on the western horizon. This crescent will always face to the right and appear in the west. It is the simplest and most directly observable definition of the beginning of the month. The new crescent will appear not more than thirty days or less than twenty-nine days after the appearance of the last new crescent.

After the appearance of the first crescent, the moon seems to draw continually further away from the sun, appearing for a longer time in the sky and with an ever-enlarging crescent which still faces right. After seven days the crescent enlarges to the shape of a half moon. This is called the first quarter, and the moon appears at its highest point in the sky (or south) as the sun is setting (diagram 2). After this there are five nights of the so-called gibbous phase, when the moon is almost a complete disc, visible for much longer periods during the night. During all these stages the moon is said to be waxing, and its illuminated side is always on the right until the full moon. The moon can be considered 'full' for three successive nights, and at this stage it is always rising as the sun sets (diagram 3), reaching its highest point (or south) at midnight (diagram 4), and setting when the sun rises (diagram 5).

On the seventeenth night the moon noticeably begins to decrease in size and its waning period begins. It resumes its gibbous shape, but now the illuminated side is on the left. It rises later each night and its brightness declines. When it becomes a half moon again it is rising at midnight (diagram 6) and reaching its highest point at sunrise (diagram 7). This is called the third or last quarter, a mirror image of the first quarter. After this the moon rises very late at night and starts approaching the sun's rising position. The last old crescent moon finally rises at dawn just before the sun, and the last glimpse of the waning moon is seen on the eastern horizon. The next phase will be its period of invisibility when it is again 'lost' in the sun, before re-emerging in the west.

The cycles of the sun and moon provided not only an imagery that was easily transformed into meaningful symbol, but also the basis for a rough calendar, time-reckoning and direction-finding at night. The relationships diagrammed here are all amenable to visual observation without instruments. Serious astronomy can only begin when irregularities in the lunar month are recognized and measured. The basic tools required are fixed and permanent observation points, notation and counting ability, a system of measure and a mastery of dialling. All these ingredients were present during the Neolithic period.

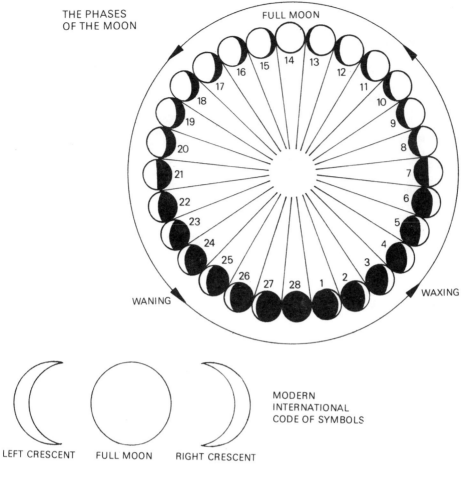

THE PHASES
OF THE MOON

FULL MOON

16 15 14 13 12
17   11
18   10
19   9
20   8
21   7
22   6
23   5
24   4
25   3
26 27 28 1 2

WANING   WAXING

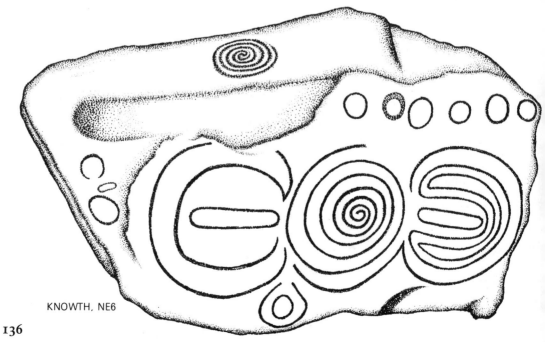

LEFT CRESCENT   FULL MOON   RIGHT CRESCENT

MODERN
INTERNATIONAL
CODE OF SYMBOLS

KNOWTH, NE6

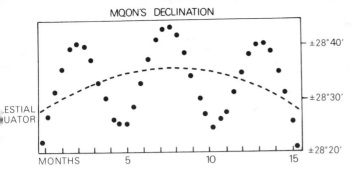

MOON'S DECLINATION

±28°40'

±28°30'

ESTIAL
QUATOR

±28°20'

MONTHS   5   10   15

The diagram shows consecutive monthly maximum north and south declinations of the moon during a year. The moon's path carries it in an ascending and descending motion, winding above and below the celestial equator through the year, besides meandering above and below the ecliptic every month.

The crescent and wavy line

The crescent and wavy line both represent the moon. In many cultures the moon is symbolized by a snake or dragon because of its motion in the sky, weaving above and below the ecliptic (the sun's path) each month. During the year the moon meanders in a wavy line above and below the celestial equator. The crescent is a pictorial symbol of the moon, and is included in the modern international code of symbols, a visual language recognizable worldwide.

The diagram opposite shows how the lunar cycle divides into recognizable segments. The waxing and waning phases divide the cycle symmetrically in half and there is a further division into quarters by the half moons. During the lunar month of 29 or 30 days there are 27 visible phases of the moon.

Stones NE6 and SW17 at Knowth show ways in which crescents and wavy lines measure time.

A set of 6 circles (6 months of the year?) extend across the right half of NE6 from above the centre of a spiral with 6 turnings. The circle and crescent (far left) also suggest the moon.

Wavy lines seem to be the primary counting units in megalithic art, and appear at most sites. They can enumerate days, months and possibly years, but which is not usually specified. Each turn of the line represents a unit. On SW17, a right crescent (confirming the moon reference) begins the count and transforms into a wavy line. Starting here the set describes a month of 29 days divided apparently with reference to the full moon. Below the main set, near the fourteenth turning there is a sub-set indicating 7. This could represent a division similar to our week. On other stones it seems that the megalithic artists divided the 27 visible phases into 3 periods of 9 days, a method later used by the Celts.

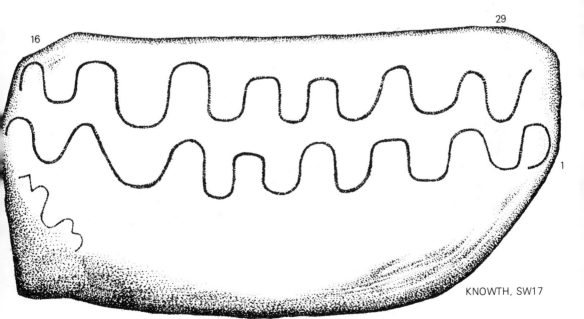

KNOWTH, SW17

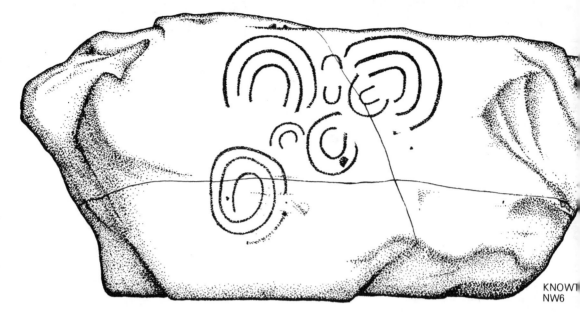

Stones NW6 and NE6 both feature a right-handed spiral and crescents, and are positioned opposite each other on the east and west sides of Knowth. The nucleus of NW6 are the 2 arcs juxtaposed in the centre of a series of 12 crescents. In ancient and modern astronomy these signs are used to indicate the point where the moon crosses the ecliptic or the ascending node, ☊, and the descending node, ☋. Note the way that the spiral ascends and descends across the horizontal line.

Stone SW9 is a variation of the same theme. There are six circles engraved on the upper surface

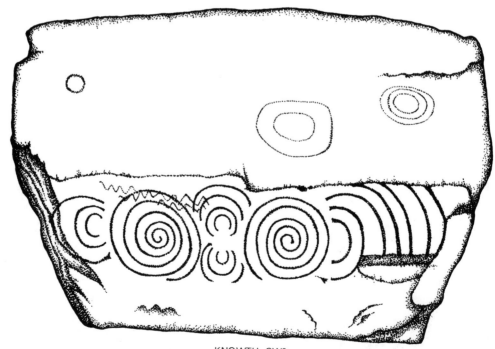

KNOWTH, SW9

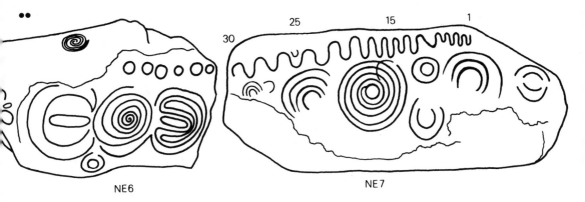

NE6   NE7

and a right-handed and left-handed spiral are juxtaposed. The same elements are on NE6 in a different arrangement. The wavy line indicating 30 on NE7 reinforces the lunar symbolism on NE6. Spirals on these stones are opposite and contrast each other. On NE7 a left crescent seems to emerge from the circle at the centre of the spiral. This may be a reference to the left crescent of the moon that begins to show after the full moon which occurs directly above in the wavy-line development. On NE6 the right crescent seems to merge into the right-handed spiral.

The symmetrical division of the year into two halves of six months is also the theme of SE29. The main element is a luni-solar emblem composed of a circle and 6 crescents. On the right, crescents are transformed into a set of wavy lines forming two counts of 6. Below that there are two rows of 6 chevrons which transform into a set of zigzags which merge and form a total count of 12. This partly encloses a quadrangle which thus becomes charged with meaning and symbolism as the division of the year into light and dark halves and four quarters.

KNOWTH SE29

MOUND G, BOYNE VALLEY

LOUGHCREW, CAIRN U, FRAGMENT

CARNANMORE, CO. ANTRIM

The stone found near mound G in the Boyne Valley is now re-erected upright near Newgrange. A crescent seems to emerge from the spiral. There are 6 crescents and a wavy line indicating 6. On a corbel stone in the chamber of Carnanmore there is a wavy line of 9 and 3 arcs. The same breakdown of the number 12 occurs on NW8 at Knowth. The central line indicates 12 and a small crescent refers the count to the moon. A line of 9 is below this and above, 3 turnings enclose a spiral. The entire set totals 24 and probably represents 24 months or 2 years. The damaged part of the stone does not seem to interfere with the engravings. There are other possible interpretations which imply the recognition of a complex lunar cycle of 9.3 years. We know there is a concern with number and numerical relationships, but although the references are here taken to be the moon, we cannot be sure.

The wavy-line development indicating 12 is common, particularly on the continent. Examples are shown here from the Boyne Valley and Iberia. The Iberian stone has 6 arcs and one pair frames crescents. Engravings on two stones at Kiltierney, Co. Fermanagh, echo patterns on the stone from Anglesey, and these suggest a concern with 6 and 12 and the division of the year. This similarity between Britain and Ireland is not surprising when one considers the close proximity of Ireland to Anglesey.

KNOWTH, NW8

MOUND K
BOYNE VALLEY

DOWTH 1

KILTIERNEY, CO. FERMANAGH

BARCLODIAD Y GAWRES,
ANGLESEY BRITAIN

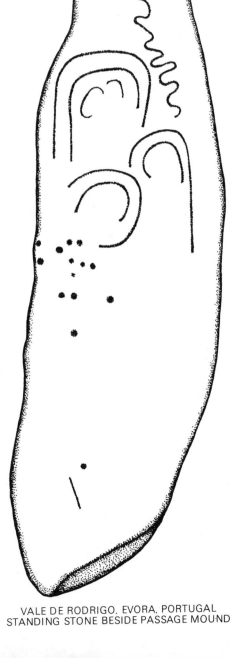

VALE DE RODRIGO, EVORA, PORTUGAL
STANDING STONE BESIDE PASSAGE MOUND

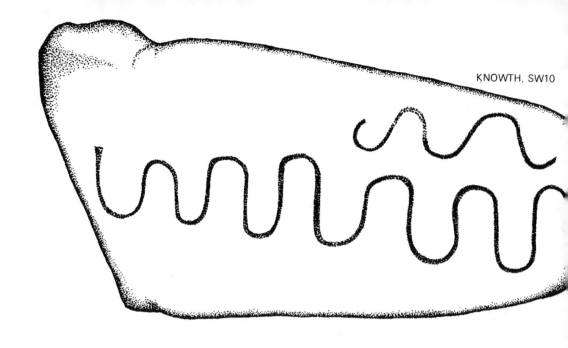

(Above) SW10 has a main line indicating 12. The top line of 5 begins from the seventh turning and appears to be intentionally out of phase. On the other hand it may be a continuation of the count to 17. Of the 12 stones of this distinct type at Knowth, 8 have wavy lines indicating 17. (Below) SE34 has a luni-solar emblem on the upper left. There is clearly a preference in these types of emblematic devices for positioning the sun on the right and the moon on the left. The main imagery is the 4 arcs above the wavy line of 8, which establishes a theme based on the division of the number 12. There are subsets of 6 arcs, a pair of 12 zigzags and 4 arcs which continue the count of the wavy line to 12.

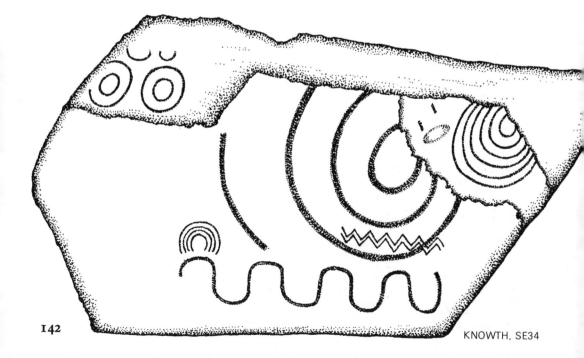

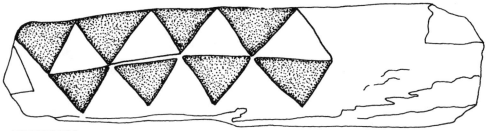

● NEWGRANGE
CORBEL IN CHAMBER

DOWTH 1, PASSAGE STONE

A set of 12 triangles at Newgrange also explores relationships between 4, 8 and the number 12 which are directly applicable to divisions of the year. We have seen in Part II how the orientation of the passage mounds divides the year into 8 parts. This is a natural division based on the sun. The division of the year into 12 parts is based on the moon. Symbols strive to combine the diverse elements of nature into unified forms. Approached this way, even a simple set of 6 arcs, like those on NW23, have purpose and meaning. The recognition of a basic symbolic use of simple numbers leads to the recognition that more complex numbers are likely to be used to deal with more complex lunar cycles. On the stone at Dowth a group of arcs and circles form sets of 6 and 12. To the right of this, 19 marks are framed in a cartouche. Significantly in the Metonic cycle – the basis for the Greek calendar – the phases of the moon recur on the same days of the same months after a lapse of 19 years.

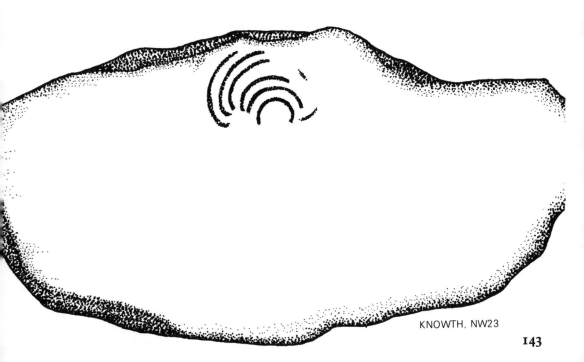

KNOWTH, NW23

143

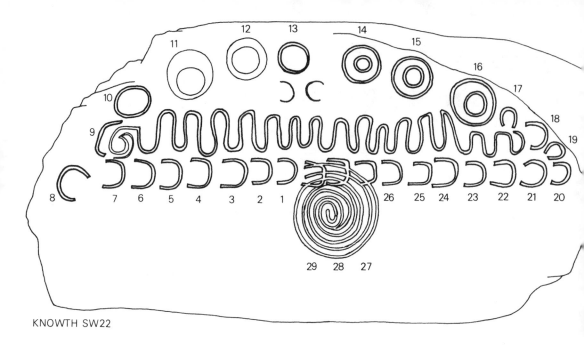

KNOWTH SW22

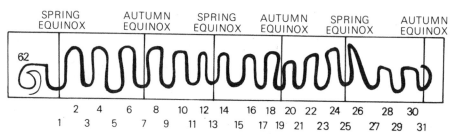

Calendrical engravings

Any genuine system of time reckoning must admit of numerical treatment, and it must consist of divisions and subdivisions of approximately equal length. Compositions such as SW22 draw on the simplest laws of written numerals, ordering and grouping.

The age-old problem of calendar making is in harmonizing the solar and lunar cycles. The basic formula for a solar-lunar calendar is 12 lunar months = 1 solar year. In practice, 12 lunar months are 355 days, falling short of a solar year of 365 days by about 10 days. After $2\frac{1}{2}$ years this amounts to nearly a full month. In other words, after 30 months, a month must be added to bring the lunar and solar cycles into harmony. In order to harmonize this with the seasons, two 31-month cycles or 5 solar years of 62 months need to be used. If the year is divided into two parts, let us say a light half and a dark half determined by the equinoxes, each 31-month period will consist of 5 seasons, and the 5-year period will contain 10 seasons which will begin and end at

the same equinox from which they start. This essentially was the basis of the ancient Celtic calendar, and a similar system is outlined above in a chart of the wavy line on SW22. Each turn of the wavy line represents one month, or a complete circuit of the distinct but related pattern of crescent and circle repeat units which are closely matched to the phases of the moon. The count moves to 31 and reverses back to 62, keeping in pace with the equinoxes. Crescents transform into circles as they approach the full moon when they become double circles. The eighth phase or quarter moon is represented differently, as is the seventeenth phase. The twenty-seventh or last visible phase begins to disappear into the spiral, which obscures the invisible phases. The same imagery is echoed on SW23, where crescents appear to emerge from a spiral, and wavy lines total 12. A similar device on the lower right-hand corner of SW22 is ambiguous and could have many applications. The Portuguese stone has 30 grouped crescents and a single thirty-first crescent which is related to a wavy line development of 12 turnings or months.

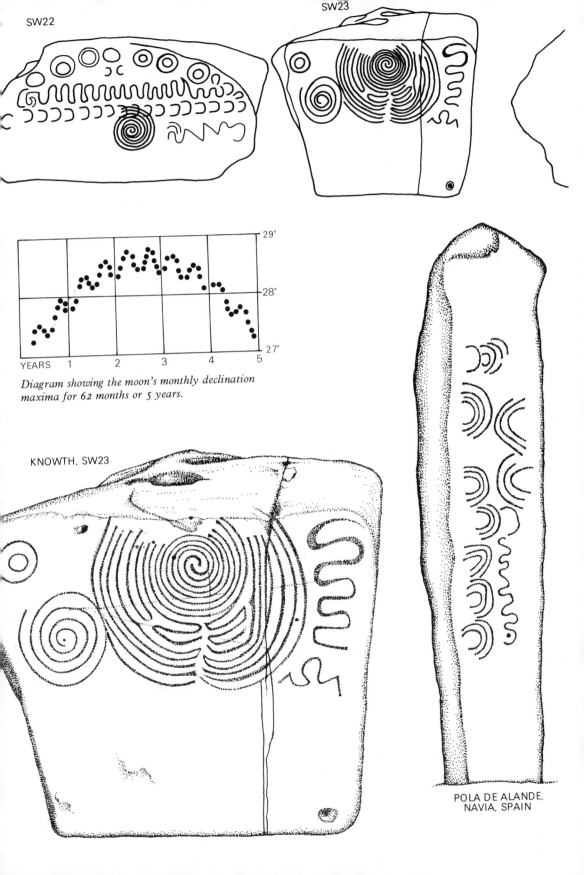

SW22

SW23

Diagram showing the moon's monthly declination maxima for 62 months or 5 years.

29°

28°

27°

YEARS   1   2   3   4   5

KNOWTH, SW23

POLA DE ALANDE,
NAVIA, SPAIN

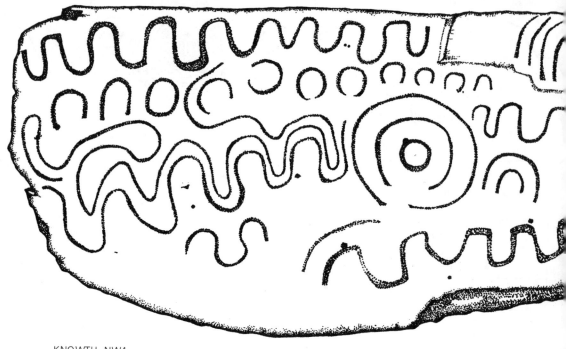

KNOWTH, NW4

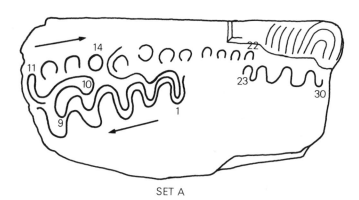

SET A

NW4 is a diagrammatic representation of the moon through the use of bijections or one-to-one correspondences with the phases of the moon. A ribbon-like development of the wavy line extends from the central image. This closely parallels the arrangement of SW22. The line follows a sequence shaped to fit the lunar month. The wavy line is transformed into crescents and then a full circle or full moon on the fourteenth count. A line divides the rest of the month, towards the end of which the crescents revert to the wavy line at the last quarter, defining a month of 30 days. This is the main set (A).

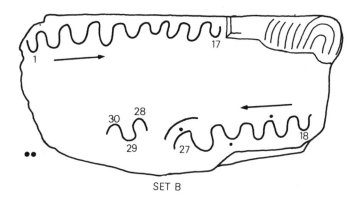

SET B

Set B is another way of ordering the month. The top line counts from the first phase to the seventeenth phase when the moon begins to wane. The continuity is then picked up below, where the sequence continues the count to the last visible phase indicated by a left crescent determinative. Following this, the final three invisible phases are represented.

146

KNOWTH, NW3

Lunar crescents supply the main imagery on NW3 and loops parallel those on NW4. These can be seen on SE31. The illustration is based on Macalister's record of the stone. Zigzags emanating from the spiral develop 12 turnings. Below this a wavy line, which is apparently damaged, seems to have in- dicated 17 and continues in a sequence of 14 to total 31. There sometimes appears to be a relationship between numbers expressed on a stone and that stone's numerical position in the mound, but this is in no way consistent.

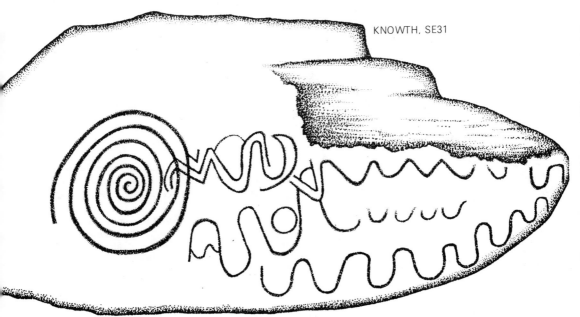

KNOWTH, SE31

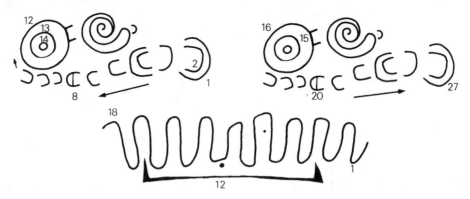

In the diagram of elements from NW19, the lunar phases are first counted from right to left, beginning with a right crescent. At the eighth phase or first quarter, a half moon is indicated. Circles match phases of the full moon. When the count is reversed the twentieth phase represents the half moon, making the last quarter. The engraved spiral and its adjacent small right crescent seem to indicate the way in which the sequence is arranged. The arrangement parallels the use of the spiral on SW22, where crescents emerge from and disappear into a spiral to represent the unfolding cycle of the month. The bar below the wavy line marks off 12 of the 18 turnings, perhaps indicating a year.

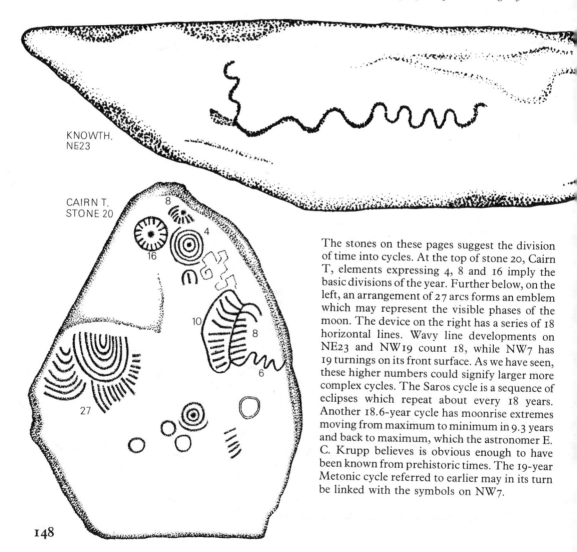

KNOWTH, NE23

CAIRN T, STONE 20

The stones on these pages suggest the division of time into cycles. At the top of stone 20, Cairn T, elements expressing 4, 8 and 16 imply the basic divisions of the year. Further below, on the left, an arrangement of 27 arcs forms an emblem which may represent the visible phases of the moon. The device on the right has a series of 18 horizontal lines. Wavy line developments on NE23 and NW19 count 18, while NW7 has 19 turnings on its front surface. As we have seen, these higher numbers could signify larger more complex cycles. The Saros cycle is a sequence of eclipses which repeat about every 18 years. Another 18.6-year cycle has moonrise extremes moving from maximum to minimum in 9.3 years and back to maximum, which the astronomer E. C. Krupp believes is obvious enough to have been known from prehistoric times. The 19-year Metonic cycle referred to earlier may in its turn be linked with the symbols on NW7.

KNOWTH, NW19

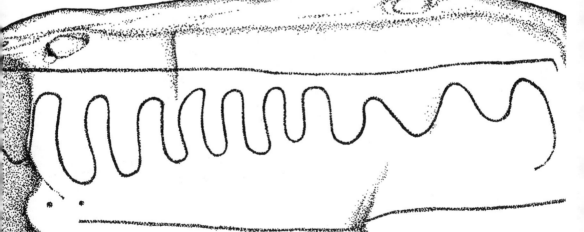

KNOWTH,
NW7

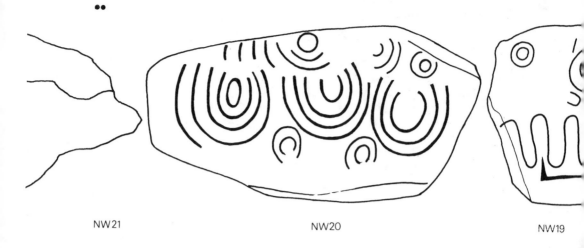

NW21   NW20   NW19

KNOWTH, NW20

*Three large groups of arcs and an oval form a large
set of 12 on NW20. This is surmounted by arcs and
circles to a count of 12. The total count on the entire
composition is 28. The composition is related to the
moon in both form and number, and these associations are reinforced by its positioning in relation to
other stones with explicit lunar imagery.*

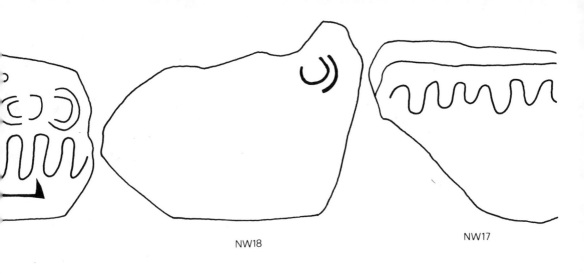

NW18

NW17

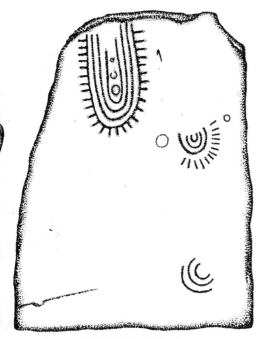

CAIRN T, STONE 15

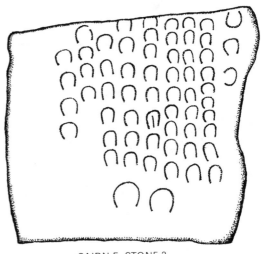

CAIRN F, STONE 2

The Loughcrew stones are important because many of the symbols and arrangements used in Boyne Valley art were anticipated at Loughcrew, and the Loughcrew complex may have provided the model for the astronomical orientation of the Boyne Valley mounds. On stone 15 at Cairn T a concern with lunar images and number is detectable, even though there are discrepancies on the actual counts involved in drawings of this stone.

Stone 2 at Cairn F clearly exhibits ordering and grouping of crescents, a method of calendrical computation that was fully developed at Knowth. The crescents total 62, and correspond to the basic calendrical fitting of 62 lunar months into 5 solar years. In size, form and technique these crescents are duplicated by those on the backstone of Cairn F (p. 115), which appear with a solar radial that is periodically illuminated by the sun and the moon.

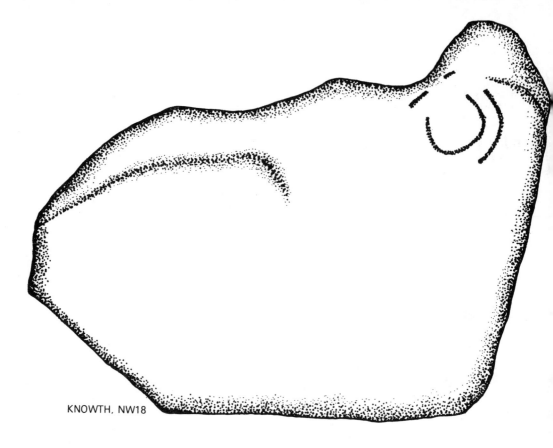

KNOWTH, NW18

● TAL QADI, MALTA

The number 17 is frequently given special significance in connection with the moon. It may have had significance in a calendar of ritual. Usually it is the seventeenth phase of the moon which appears on the horizon and projects a beam of light into the mounds. In other early cultures the seventeenth of the month had a symbolic significance. According to Plutarch, the Egyptians had a legend that Osiris's life came to an end on the seventeenth, 'on which day it is quite evident to the eye that the period of the full moon is over'. NW17 is one of the recurring wavy lines indicating 17. The relationship between the crescent and the wavy line is echoed on NW9, on which natural holes and cupmarks seem to provide a starry background to the lunar imagery. The stone from a megalithic site on Malta is about a foot wide and displays a lunar crescent among more explicit groupings of stars.

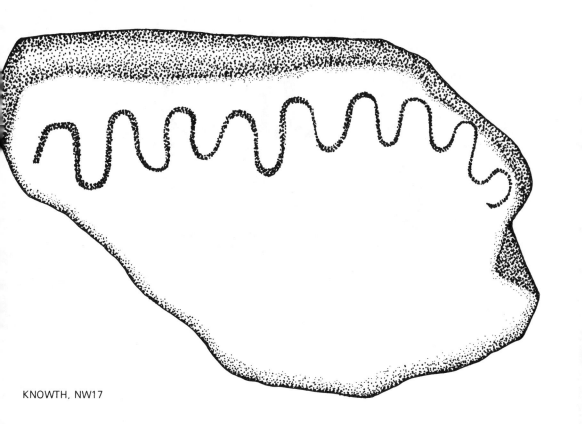

KNOWTH, NW17

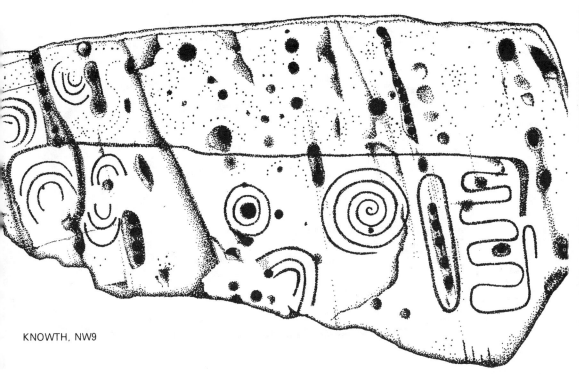

KNOWTH, NW9

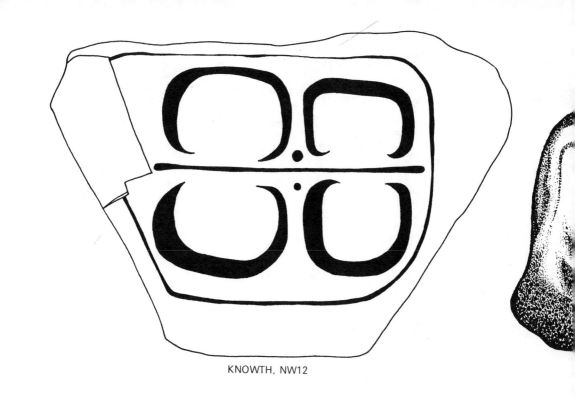

KNOWTH, NW12

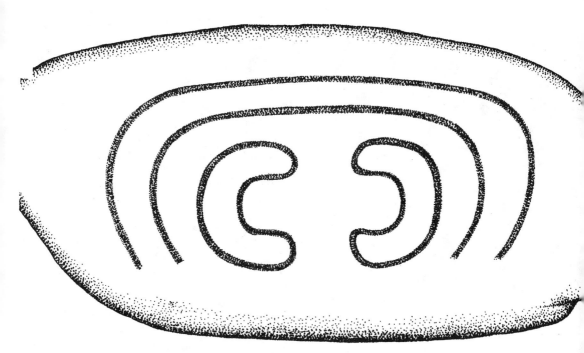

KNOWTH, SOUTH 0

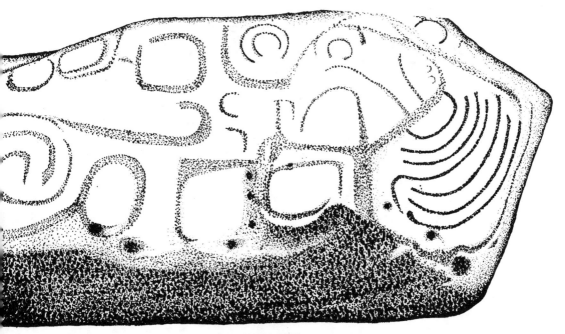

KNOWTH, NW1

NW1 is positioned immediately to the left of the entrance stone of the western passage at Knowth which is aligned to the equinox sunset. Lunar imagery predominates, and right crescents on the right seem to be transformed into left crescents on the left. The design is closely related to the entrance stone of the eastern entrance, and similarly suggests compartments or 'houses' of the sun or moon reflecting the concept of the mound itself.

The symmetrical compositions on NW12 and South O imply a recognition of the inherent symmetry manifested by the moon and the heavens. This also is reflected in the structure of the mound. Arcs enclosing the crescents on South O may

represent the dome of the heavens, and this element seems to serve as a generic sky symbol applicable to the sun, the moon and the stars. In 1885, Thomas Wise M. D. called it the 'horseshoe' and described it as 'the figure of the firmament, or Providence hovering over the world; this giving rise to its influence against evil spirits'. The horseshoe is still used as a talismanic charm today and its origins lie in the perennial human desire to connect the stars with fate. Its use in megalithic art implies a semi-magical projection on astronomy, and the abundant solar-lunar devices resemble emblematic charms rather than purely naturalistic representations.

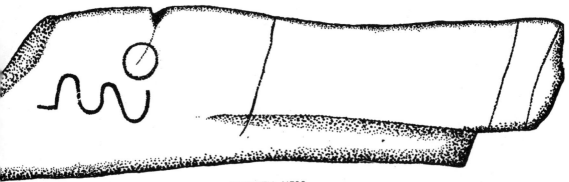

KNOWTH, NE28

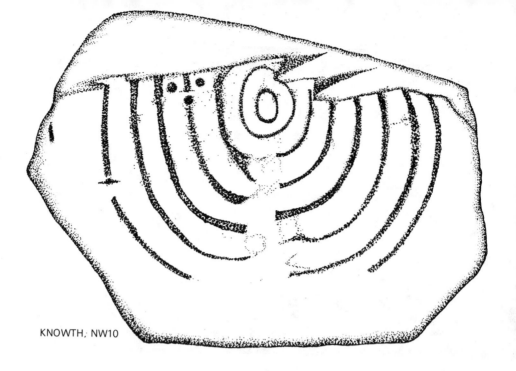

KNOWTH, NW10

The moon must have been immensely important in the daily life of societies without mechanical clocks and few distractions to divert attention from events in the sky. At Loughcrew crescents and arcs dominate the imagery, and at Knowth similar forms and numbers generated by the moon are pervasive. It is this profusion of lunar imagery in the art that supports the conclusion that the mounds were used for both lunar and solar observation.

The numerical and geometrical relationships expressed on SW3 are simple but extremely interesting. The main image is a concentric development of 9 elements including an ellipse and the beginnings of a spiral. Beside this there are 9 circles and arcs, 3 pairs of which are positioned in a triangular arrangement surrounding the main set of 3. NW15 has 30 circles and crescents that appear to revolve around two circles. This seems to be highly abstracted lunar imagery in which there is no apparent sequence in the transformations, yet the number and forms reflect patterns of the moon. It is essential to realize that in megalithic art the elements in a composition are frequently different aspects of one thing in a process of change.

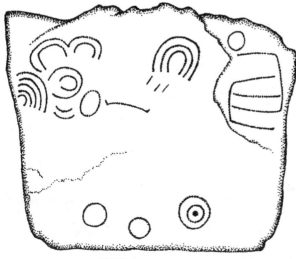

CAIRN L, STONE 8

CAIRN S, STONE 3

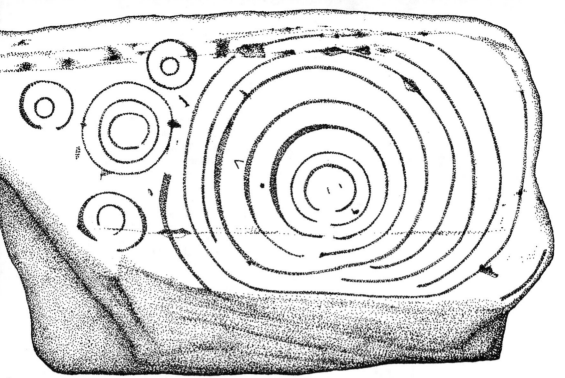

KNOWTH, SW3

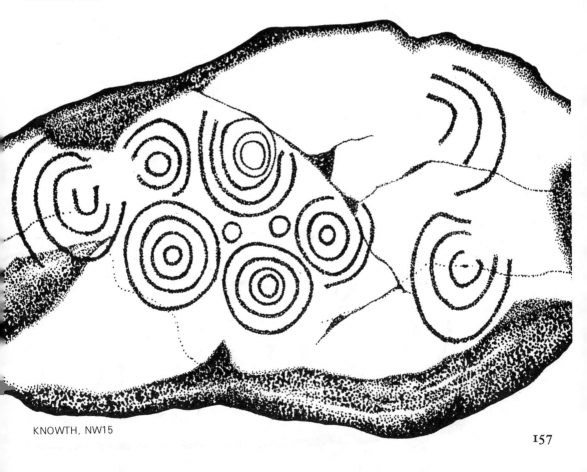

KNOWTH, NW15

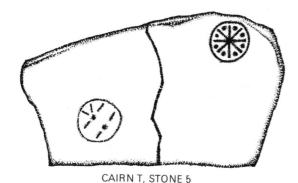

CAIRN T, STONE 5

The sun in megalithic art

Images and symbols of the sun are essential characteristics of megalithic art. Perhaps the most critical evidence in support of this is supplied by the sundial on the flat top of NE4 (in scale left, with position arrowed on NE4 below, and enlarged opposite), which directly leads to the recognition that radials, as exemplified by the engraving on stone 5 at Cairn T, are representative of the sun. The fact that this radial is illuminated by a contrived beam of light at equinox substantiates such a conclusion. Radials are the most important compounds in the art and appear on about 10 per cent of engraved stones in Ireland and Western Europe. The image of the cross in the circle is fundamentally the concept governing the basic structure or ground plan of the megalithic mound.

On the sundial at equinox, the sun rising in the east casts its shadow west, at midday it casts its shadow north and, as it sets, it casts its shadow east, completing a cross in its circle and defining time and space simultaneously. This forms the basis of one of the earliest geometrical expressions and has been regarded as the first and greatest of all talismans.

The dial measures what are known as the unequal or 'planetary' hours, which are shorter in winter and longer in summer. At the equinoxes it divides the day into 8 equal parts, which are further subdivided into 16 parts. This corresponds to the solar division of the year into 8 parts. The importance of the NE4 dial is immense as it is the earliest sundial known, preceding other known diurnal sundials by thousands of years.

Sundialling and sun symbols are inextricably connected in megalithic solar constructs. On NE4 emblematic images of the sun and moon appear directly below the dial. The dial of the

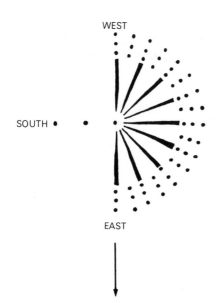

WEST

SOUTH

EAST

KNOWTH
NE4

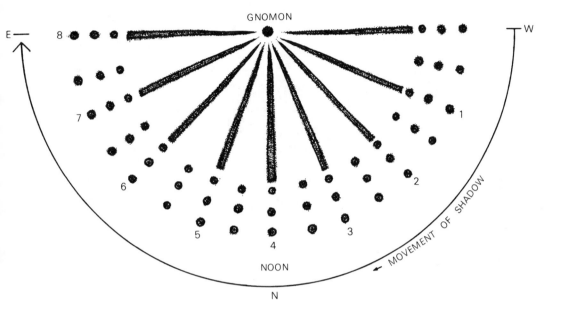

S

GNOMON

E — 8 ● ● ● ●

W

7

6

5   4   3

NOON

N

1

2

MOVEMENT OF SHADOW

day complements the mound, which is a dial of the year. At Newgrange radial solar symbols are engraved in the chamber and on the roof-box. There are other, more complicated, functional dials at Knowth, and there may be another dial lightly engraved on the remarkably smooth flat top of NE4. The NE4 dial has been shown to a number of professional astronomers who confirm that it is a dial with real and intentional fiducial markings. The dial is precisely orientated. In style and technique it is megalithic, as is supported by the fact that the engravings are weathered to the same colour as the surface of the stone.

CORBEL IN
CHAMBER

BACK CORBEL OF ROOF-BOX

● NEWGRANGE

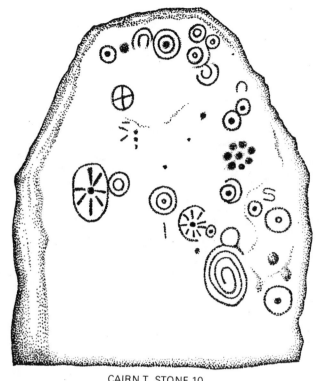

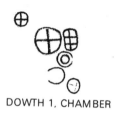

● DOWTH 1, CHAMBER

CAIRN T, STONE 10

DOWTH 1, CHAMBER

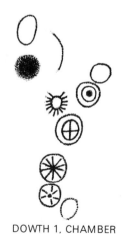

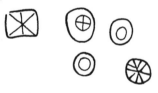

DOWTH 1, CHAMBER

● DOWTH 2, STONE 13

DOWTH 1, CHAMBER

CAIRN U

● DOWTH 2, STONE 13

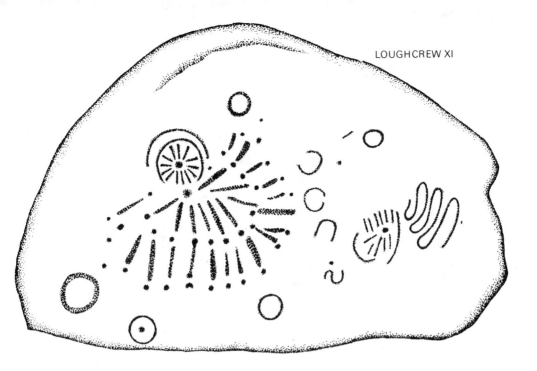

XI was probably the backstone of the chamber in Cairn XI at Loughcrew. At present it stands alone in a circle of kerbstones and faces towards the northwest. In this context it would have been illuminated by a beam of light. Like the backstone of Cairn T radials are the central images. On XI explicit sundial imagery is used as an analogue symbolizing the sun. It is not meant to be a practical sundial, but it contains all the elements of a functional sundial using the same system employed on NE4 at Knowth. The 9 large radials of the inner set form 8 segments and the outer set of lines form 16 segments. Although there is no attempt at precision in the geometrical arrangement, the symbol contains the same idea. The two smaller radial patterns are related to each other.

The opposite page shows various radials from Loughcrew and Dowth. The ones from Dowth 2 are incisions on stone 13 in the recess. This stone is positioned so that it is brilliantly illuminated by reflected light at the winter solstice. The designs show how the radial easily develops into triangles and forms the quadrangle, a relationship implying that they represent different aspects of one and the same thing. In fact they do not often appear together, and on sites where radials predominate, such as Cairn T, quadrangles are virtually absent.

Viewed from the centre of the stone circle at Athgreany, Co. Wicklow, the stone below is due south and is engraved with what seems to be a dialling device. It is situated in a field called Achadh Gréine, 'sun-field'.

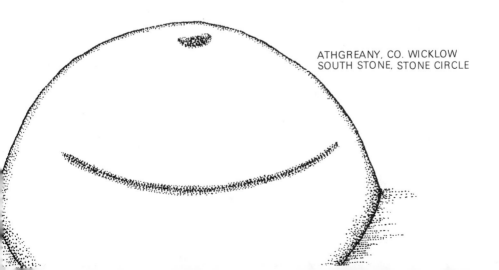

ATHGREANY, CO. WICKLOW
SOUTH STONE, STONE CIRCLE

• CAIRN T, STONE 1 DETAIL

The human mind, unless biased by preconceptions or in other ways pre-conditioned, will have a natural tendency to perceive forms such as those on the Portuguese stone (opposite) as representations of the sun. The association seems to be confirmed by the fact that the stone forms the entrance to a probable equinoctial solar construct.

The sun as a rayed circle appears as a day sign in the earliest writing systems. The counting of days in reference to the moon is a human tendency detectable in all cultures, because lunar cycles provide a convenient measure of solar cycles, being longer than days and shorter than years. One of the large sunwheels on the Iberian stone has 12 radials and the pair total 30. There is a large set of 12 lines, one of which transforms into a crescent. Evidently the artist is using abstract visual language to explore relationships between the sun and the moon.

The buried surface of stone 8 at Knowth (top) has a beautifully engraved radial on its pointed edge, and an array of symbols that include triangles and quadrangles.

Stone 1 at Cairn T displays a complex development of the basic radial form derived from the patterns and imagery of sundialling.

CARAPITO, BEIRA ALTA, PORTUGAL

JEREZ DE LOS CABALLEROS,
BADAJOZ, PORTUGAL

*These stones are from a probable equinoctial solar
construct in Portugal. They closely parallel stones
at Loughcrew, notably those in Cairn T.*

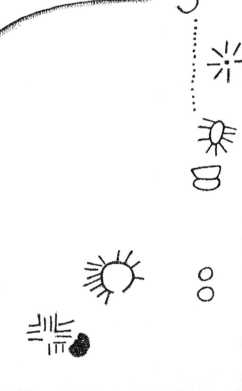

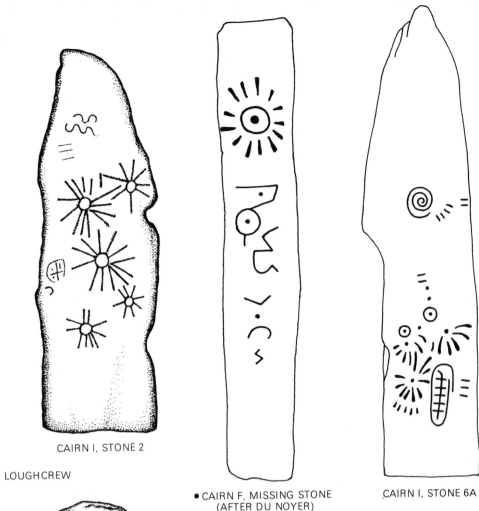

CAIRN I, STONE 2

LOUGHCREW

• CAIRN F, MISSING STONE
(AFTER DU NOYER)

CAIRN I, STONE 6A

CAIRN T, STONE 14

The main sunwheel on stone 14 at Cairn T is the focal point of the beam of light projected into the mound at equinox. This forms the basis for a division of the year into 8 parts according to the solar cycle of equinoxes and solstices which also divide the year into 6 months. These seem to be represented in the 6 radials of the sunwheel below and the 6 lines enclosed by attached crescents. The sunwheels belong to a set of 4 which contain a total of 31 radials in the form of elongated crescents, and together they make up the fundamental month count in the luni-solar calendar.

The segmented lines could be units of measurement calibrated to measure daily changes in the height of the beam of light. They correspond to a similar set at the bottom of stone 6A in Cairn I. A low narrow shaft of light strikes these marks on the days immediately preceding the autumnal equinox.

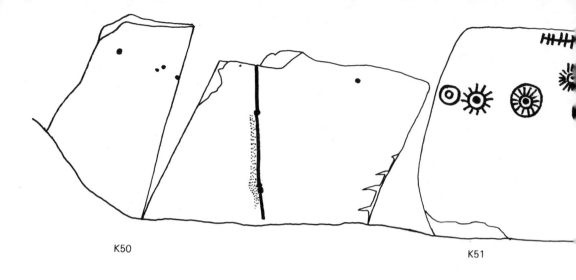

K50   K51

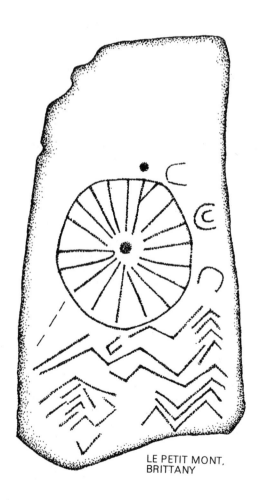

LE PETIT MONT,
BRITTANY

K51 and K52 are the only known major compositions on the kerbstones of Dowth. They face eastwards, approximately opposite the entrances of the passages on the western (far) side of the mound. The vertical line on K50 may have had a similar function to that on K52 at Newgrange. Sunwheels on K51 recall those at Cairn T and reveal a similar concern with calendrical fittings of luni-solar cycles. With 6 rayed circles there is also a rayed dot which appears to be a sunset. The luni-solar symbol on the left suggests that the stone represents a month count, because 12 radials extend from the circle. The next two discs with 14 and 17 radials give a total count of 31, reinforcing the idea of the month count. The count continues to 99 months, which brings the lunar cycle and the solar cycle into extremely close correlation in a calibration of 8 years (365 days × 8 = 2920 days, 99 months × 29.5 days = 2920.5 days). The 8-year cycle is a very important development in calendar making. Known as the 'Octaëteris', it was the earliest cycle developed by the Greeks. It neatly contains 5 Venus years (5 × 584 = 2920) and this gave the cycle symbolic as well as calendrical significance in many ancient astronomical systems.

The prominent displays of the number 8 may reflect the special significance given to it as representing divisions of the day and year and a cycle of 8 years into which 99 months and 5 complete revolutions of Venus neatly fit. On K52 the 8 circles and ovals very likely represent the 8 years which are reduced to terms of months on K51. Radials such as those on the stone at Le Petit Mont could represent luni-solar cycles of 18 or 19 years. In megalithic art significant numbers expressed in appropriate symbols seem to recur in prominent positions in astronomical settings, forming a system which is remarkably consistent and unlikely to occur by chance.

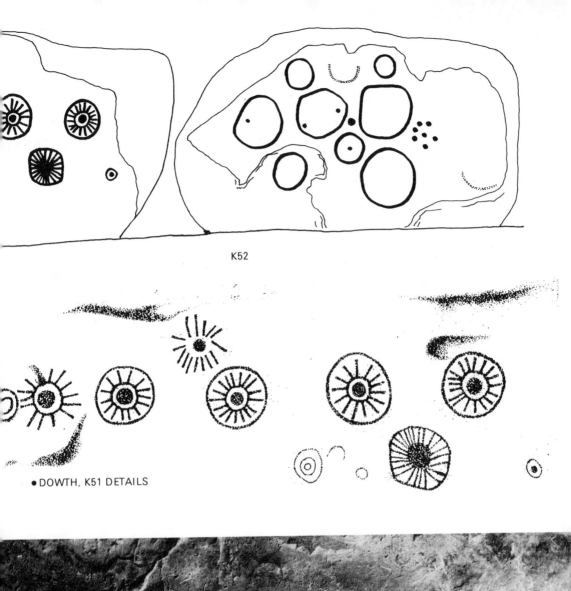

K52

● DOWTH, K51 DETAILS

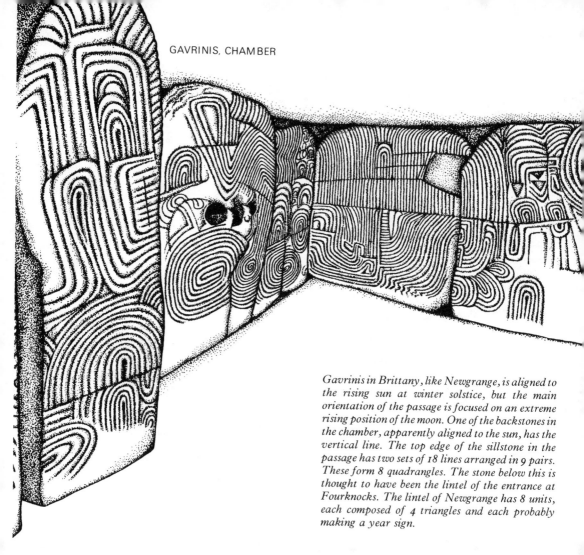

GAVRINIS, CHAMBER

Gavrinis in Brittany, like Newgrange, is aligned to the rising sun at winter solstice, but the main orientation of the passage is focused on an extreme rising position of the moon. One of the backstones in the chamber, apparently aligned to the sun, has the vertical line. The top edge of the sillstone in the passage has two sets of 18 lines arranged in 9 pairs. These form 8 quadrangles. The stone below this is thought to have been the lintel of the entrance at Fourknocks. The lintel of Newgrange has 8 units, each composed of 4 triangles and each probably making a year sign.

GAVRINIS, SILLSTONE, TOP EDGE

FOURKNOCKS, LINTEL

NEWGRANGE, ROOF-BOX LINTEL

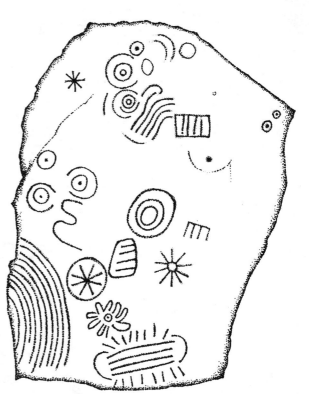

In the Irish passage mounds major compositions
have been found engraved on two roof-stones. In
both cases the stones have been engraved prior to
being positioned above the recesses. When the beam
of light strikes stone 14 at Cairn T, the roofstone is
brilliantly illuminated by reflected light. Sunwheels, notably those with 8 radials, echo the
pattern of sunwheels on stone 14. The Newgrange
artists may well have seen this stone because they
expanded brilliantly on the theme of the sun
manifested in its divisions and cycles of time. The
quadrangle is here directly linked to the sunwheel,
and there are two spirals of 8 turnings. The double
wheel suggests the sun and the moon and the
concentric development of 5 ovals possibly represents Venus.

CAIRN T,
CENTRE RECESS,
ROOFSTONE

NEWGRANGE,
EAST RECESS,
ROOFSTONE

169

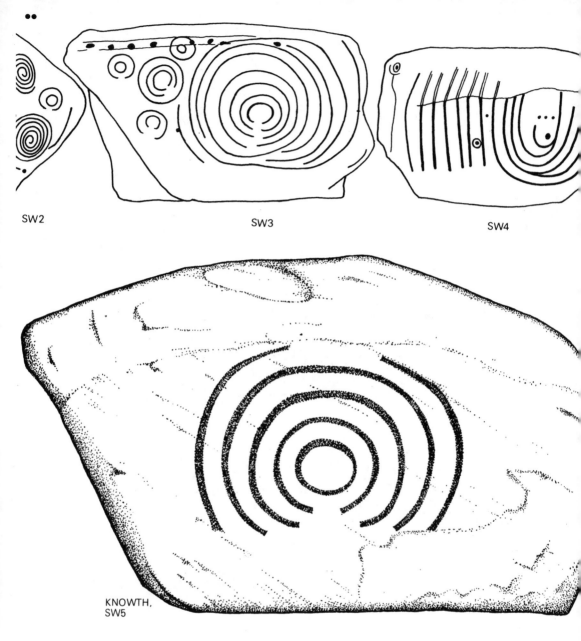

SW2

SW3

SW4

KNOWTH,
SW5

A luminous celestial object is the sole image on
SW5, representing either the sun, moon or Venus
looming above the horizon. These are the only three
celestial objects capable of projecting beams of light
and casting shadows. Because of its brilliance,
Venus frequently became an object of awe in early
astronomies. The 5 rings on SW5 could represent 5
cycles of Venus equated to the 8 solar cycles or years
implied on SW6. Venus only appears in the east
before dawn and in the west near sunset. Its path in
the sky bears a close resemblance to the elongated
arcs on a stone in satellite K.

NEWGRANGE, SATELLITE K

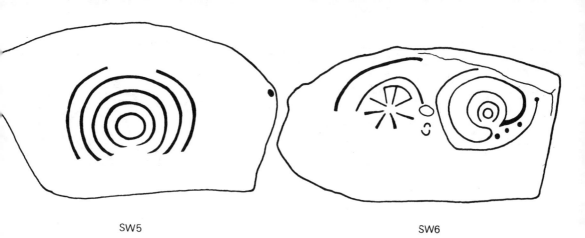

SW5   SW6

KNOWTH,
SW6

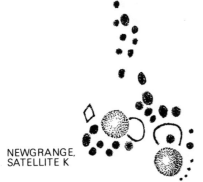

NEWGRANGE,
SATELLITE K

Compositions that place the sun on the right and the moon on the left are common to many cultures. It is the preferred arrangement in megalithic art. Notable exceptions seem to be confined to compositions on the southwest kerbstones of Knowth. On SW6 a sunwheel of 8 radials is balanced by lunar crescents forming a typical polarity. The circle, in the form of large hollows, is similarly balanced by crescents at satellite K. These circles, appearing amidst 30 cupmarks, may represent the full moon.

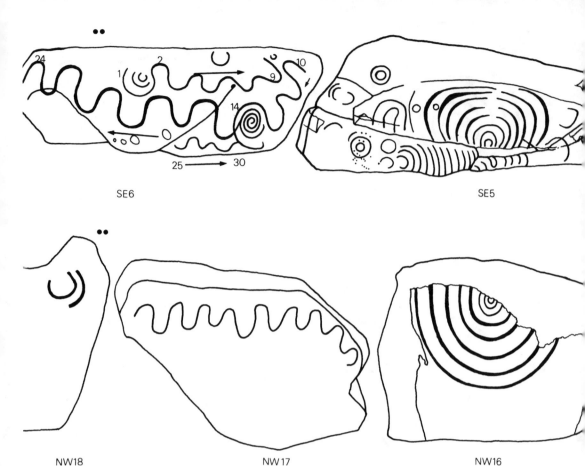

SE6   SE5

NW18   NW17   NW16

KNOWTH

EASTERN PASSAGE

Pairs of stones that juxtapose lunar and solar imagery appear frequently at Knowth, as shown by SE5 and 6, and NW17 and 16. Concern with the number 8 is evident as at Newgrange, and it is echoed in the kerbstones, for example SE5 and NW16. Note that SE6 has three wavy line developments of 9, 15 and 6 turnings totalling 30. Counting from left to right and then from right to left, the spiral is positioned at the fourteenth turning and begins the fifteenth turning, matching the full moon phase and echoing its usage on NE7.

Emblematic representations of the sun and moon are often enclosed in a cartouche, such as on NW5. The cartouche is a development of the oval. The Knowth artists developed powerful luni-solar imagery by synthesizing basic elements that had already emerged on the stones of Loughcrew.

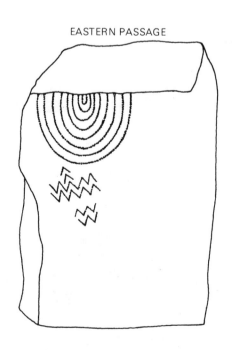

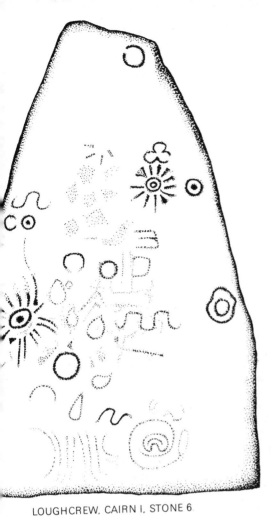

LOUGHCREW, CAIRN I, STONE 6

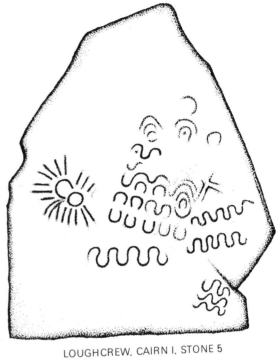

LOUGHCREW, CAIRN I, STONE 5

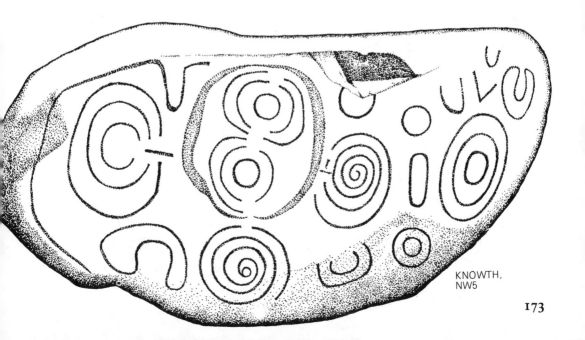

KNOWTH,
NW5

173

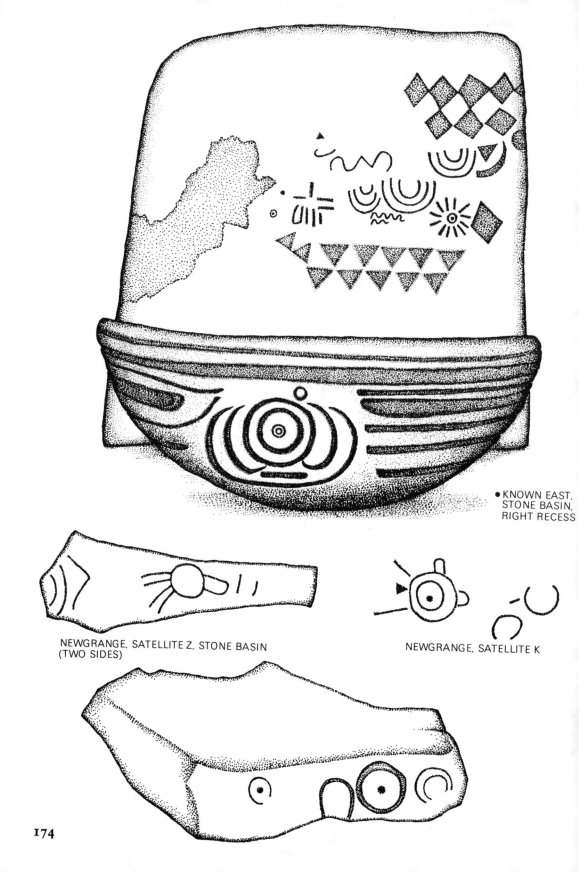

● KNOWN EAST,
STONE BASIN,
RIGHT RECESS

NEWGRANGE, SATELLITE Z, STONE BASIN
(TWO SIDES)

NEWGRANGE, SATELLITE K

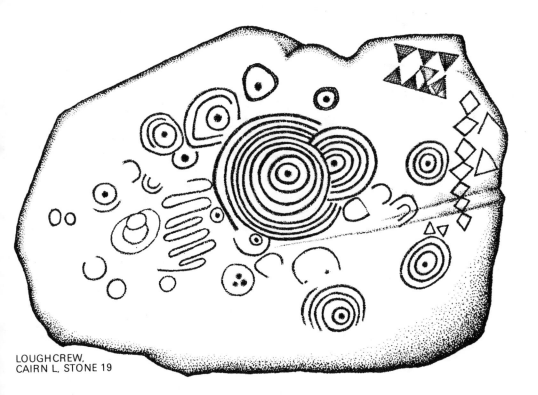

LOUGHCREW,
CAIRN L, STONE 19

Luni-solar images are frequently circles and crescents merged in a single emblem. The image makers usually, but not always, intended their creations to be seen illuminated by the light of the sun and/or moon. Stone 19 at Cairn L forms the backdrop for a stone basin, and is brilliantly illuminated by reflected light at sunrise on the November/February cross-quarter day. The recess at Knowth would also have been seen in the reflected light of the sun, and the imagery forms close parallels with Cairn L. Tara and Cairn L are orientated to the same sunrises and share similar luni-solar images.

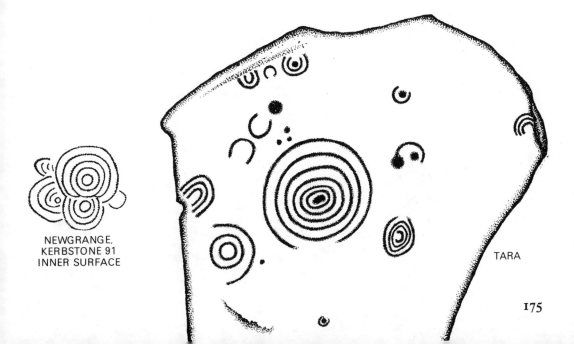

NEWGRANGE,
KERBSTONE 91
INNER SURFACE

TARA

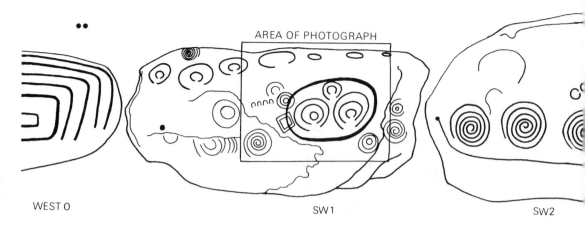

AREA OF PHOTOGRAPH

WEST 0   SW 1   SW 2

The triple form of the luni-solar emblem is a variant of the double image that includes another sky symbol to represent either Venus or the stars or both. Very early observers of the sky usually did not distinguish planets from stars, and Venus as the brightest star easily became representative of all stars. The sun, the moon and the stars form a trinity in the very early history of man's ritual observation of the sky. On Knowth SW1 a large emblem of the celestial triune is enclosed in a cartouche. Hovering above, on the top of the stone, are 8 luni-solar emblems.

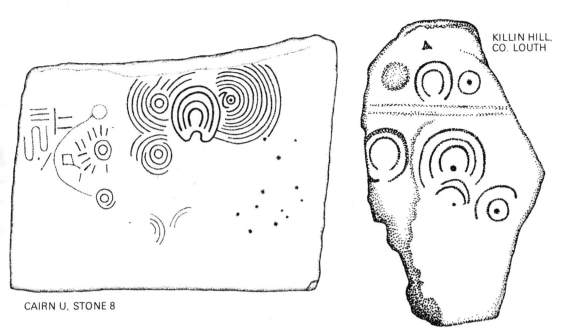

CAIRN U, STONE 8

The distribution of variations of the trinity emblem is widespread. At Killin Hill a triune seems to hover over a line representing a horizon. The moon is a hollowed circle, perhaps representing its receptive nature in reflecting the sun's light. The dot in the circle is used to represent the sun as at Cairn U, and this symbol of the sun persists in modern astronomy. The most comprehensive and developed imagery in megalithic art appears at Newgrange. The same concept is expanded to the power of 3 on kerbstone 52, and expressed geometrically in the form of triangles.

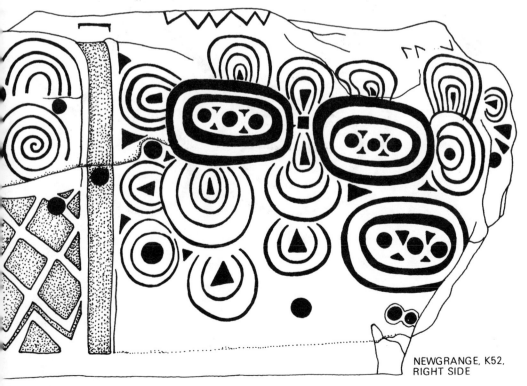

NEWGRANGE, K52,
RIGHT SIDE

NEWGRANGE, SATELLITE Z
(AT PRESENT IN THE NATIONAL MUSEUM, DUBLIN)

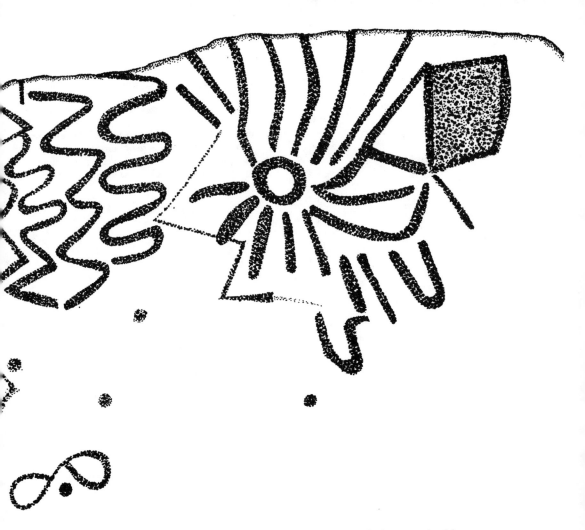

Megalithic art and cosmology

Megalithic monuments, whether viewed in the light of Newgrange at winter solstice sunrise, or Stonehenge at summer solstice sunrise, or through the theodolites of researchers such as Alexander Thom, clearly reveal the remains of a people deeply concerned with measuring time. Megalithic art, with its sundials and calendars, is a reflection of that pre-occupation.

Time is invisible and its images are necessarily abstract. The sun and moon appear as schematic symbols, frequently integrated with representations of days, months or years. In a sundial space is divided by the geometric projections of rays of light or shadows, and often concepts of time and space are struck on the same rock.

Astronomy and sundialling were the starting points of geometrical figures which made possible the accurate measurement of time. This leads to the idea of infinity and consideration of the universe as an ordered whole, which is the basis of any cosmology. Many of the elements found in the art are cosmograms or graphic models of the structure of time and space. On the stone from satellite Z a radiant sunburst in the picture field is only part of a composition wherein opposing clockwise and anti-clockwise spirals express the idea of reciprocal forces in the universe, and lines whose ends are their beginnings and whose beginnings are their ends suggest the concept of time as infinity.

The circle

The circle represents that which has no shape and that which contains all shapes. It is the simplest and most fundamental primary, describing both the shape of celestial objects and their movement. The circle of the horizon surrounded by the circular dome of the sky gives rise to a model of the universe as a system of concentric shells.

Concentric circles start to form spirals, as on the stone from King's Mountain near Loughcrew and another at Cairn I. On Knockmany 4, two sets of 6 concentric circles are aligned vertically. On Ballinvally I, a complex labyrinth of 12 groups of circles and arcs transform and revolve in a pattern.

BALLINVALLY 3

LOUGHCREW,
KING'S MOUNTAIN

CLOVERHILL,
CO. SLIGO

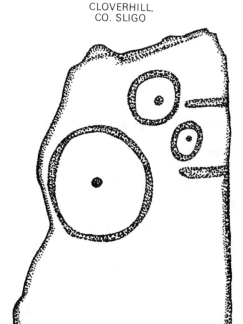

BALLINVALLY 1

LOUGHCREW, CAIRN I, STONE 4

KNOCKMANY, STONE 4

The quadrangle

As symbols of totality, the quadrangle and the circle are very similar, but express different aspects of primary forces that shape and structure existence. The quadrangle is closely related to the most important of bi-axial designs, the cross, and it carries the same value and meaning. This equivalence can be seen in the cross-within-the-triangle shapes engraved across the top of stone 22 at Cairn L, and also in the incised cross which begins to form a quadrangle in the centre of the Tournant stone. The concept of the cross in the circle, one of the most fundamental symbols in both the art and the architecture of megalithic solar constructs, is beautifully engraved on Knockmany 2.

Inherent in the structure of the quadrangle are the concepts of the centre and the unification or reconciliation of opposites. It is basically composed of two opposing triangles. Both equilateral and isosceles triangles appear in megalithic art, but they are superseded by the all-encompassing form of the quadrangle. Linking the opposing cardinal directions it becomes emblematic of the four corners of the earth. Thus, sunrise, sunset, midday and midnight, the equinoxes and the solstices, and the four cross-quarter days marking the seasons are all bound together in the unity of symbol.

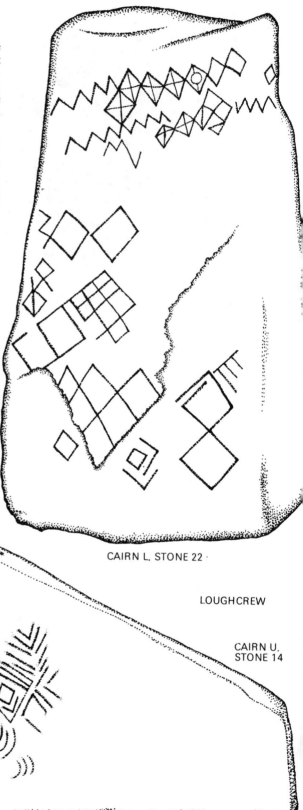

CAIRN L, STONE 22

LOUGHCREW

CAIRN U, STONE 14

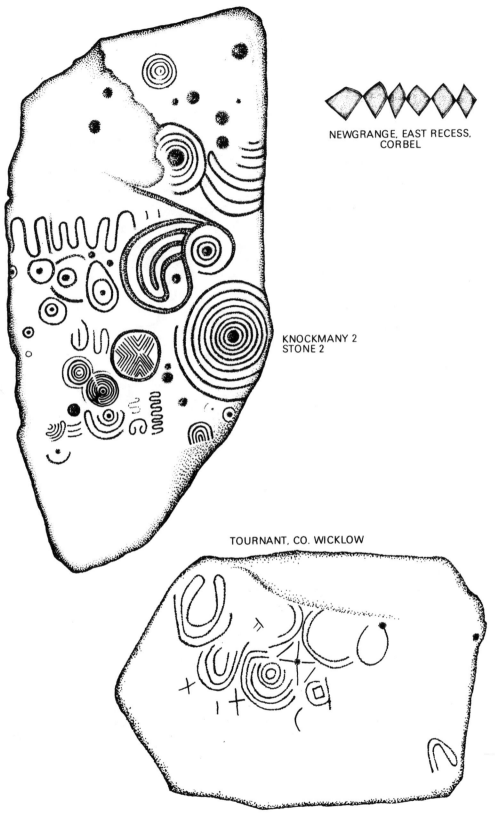

NEWGRANGE, EAST RECESS,
CORBEL

KNOCKMANY 2
STONE 2

TOURNANT, CO. WICKLOW

183

FOURKNOCKS

There are three constructs containing megalithic art which are not orientated towards the sun. Baltinglass is aligned due north in the direction of the polestar. The passages of Fourknocks and Seefin are skewed clockwise 17 degrees east of north, and the quadrangle provides the main imagery in both. The chamber of Seefin is orientated on the cardinal directions and the only two engraved stones are in the passage. Fourknocks is regarded as unique because its exceptionally large chamber could only have been roofed with wooden beams. In the illustration (before reconstruction) the rising sun at its most northerly position at summer solstice is depicted on the right, far out of alignment with the passage.

As Lockyer pointed out, the heliacal rising of certain stars was used by early astronomers to determine the occurrence of key calendrical events. In ancient Mesoamerican astronomy similar strategies have been detected, the largest group being known as the '17-degree family of orientations'. At Fourknocks quadrangles that become zigzags could be images of star fields. The constellations are considered to have been the starting point for geometrical figures, giving rise to the idea of a point and triangles and quadrangles. The entrance lintel (now placed to the left of the entrance), the former lintel of the exterior entrance, and the lintel of the central recess, are aligned to the stars. The associ-

ation of quadrangular patterns and stars is common to many cultures. The 'star blankets' of the Sioux Indians, for example, are covered in diamond-shaped patterns which can be compared to megalithic sky imagery.

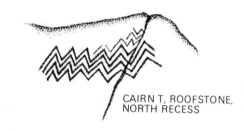

CAIRN T, ROOFSTONE,
NORTH RECESS

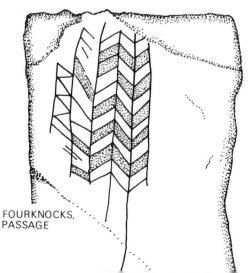

FOURKNOCKS,
PASSAGE

FOURKNOCKS, CENTRAL RECESS LINTEL

FOURKNOCKS, WEST RECESS LINTEL

FOURKNOCKS, ENTRANCE LINTEL

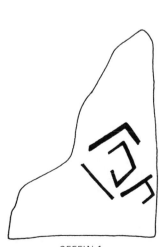

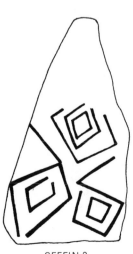

SEEFIN 1   SEEFIN 2   FOURKNOCKS, CHAMBER

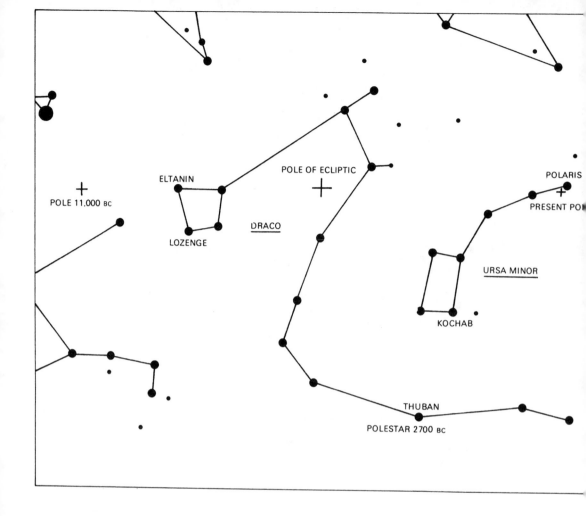

POLE OF ECLIPTIC

ELTANIN

POLE 11,000 BC

DRACO

LOZENGE

POLARIS

PRESENT PO[

URSA MINOR

KOCHAB

THUBAN

POLESTAR 2700 BC

The quadrangle appears very early in prehistoric art and could have originated as a sky symbol when the celestial pole was near the rectangular formation of stars in the constellation Draco. The pole is always the centre around which the stars appear to revolve, regardless of the slow shift in its position as a result of the wobble in the earth's polar axis. It is always north and directly opposed to the sun at its highest point in the sky to the south. Early observers of the sky were aware of this relationship between the sun and the stars, and they knew that the yearly cycle of the stars (366 days) was closely correlated to the yearly cycle of the sun (365 days). This reinforced the concept of a universe that was primarily ordered by the sun. On the stone from satellite Z at the beginning of this section a solar image emanates rays which form into triangles and quadrangles. This composition contains all the primary elements in megalithic art, and its main themes are derived from astronomy.

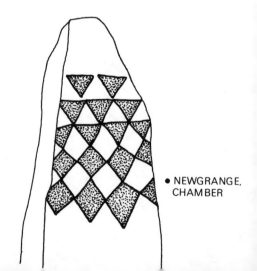

● NEWGRANGE,
CHAMBER

● NEWGRANGE, CORBEL IN CHAMBER

Patterns which begin to emerge at Loughcrew are more fully worked out in the Boyne Valley. Above, a pattern of 29 units surmounts zigzags which indicate 22 and could represent the days during which light enters the chamber. Another pattern in the chamber is composed of 9 triangles and 8 quadrangles arranged to form a large inner quad-rangle of 12 positive and negative units. It is curious that the chamber and passage of New-grange is composed of 60 stones and the kerbstones, excluding the entrance stone (which is actually not a kerbstone) total 96. The chamber and passage of Gavrinis is constructed of 30 stones.

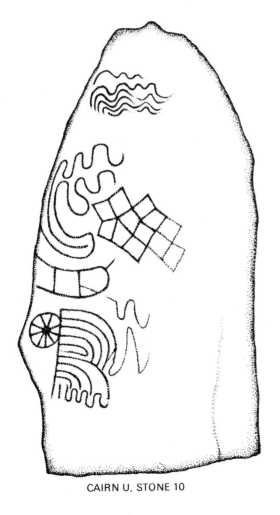

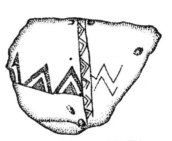

KILLIN HILL, CO. LOUTH

CAIRN U, STONE 10

CAIRN F, STONE 5

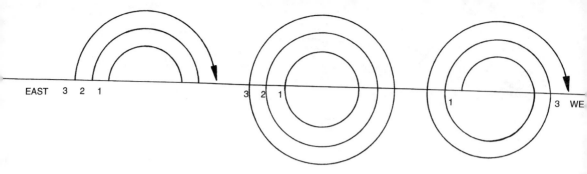

EAST 3 2 1   3 2 1   1   3 WE

The primary apparent motion of the sun is from east to west. The diagram represents the sun's motion in the sky at winter solstice (*1*), equinox (*2*) and summer solstice (*3*). The sun's reappearance on the horizon suggests that its path forms circles. In order to account for movement from a smaller circle to a larger circle a spiral motion is required. Hence, from earliest times the spiral represented the rotation of the sun and expressed its power.

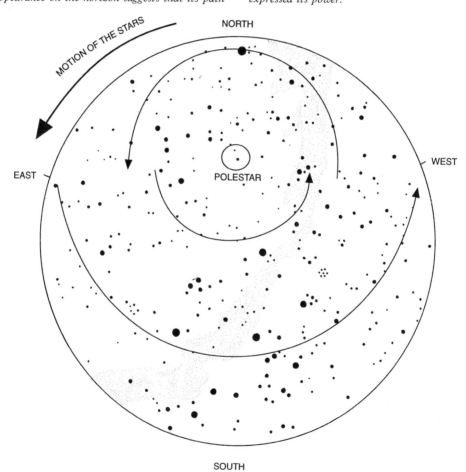

By watching the stars at night it was observed that they too displayed geometric characteristics that could be expressed in the same visual terms. Because of the earth's rotation all celestial objects appear to rise in the east and set in the west. However, if one views the stars in the direction of the polestar they appear to move anti-clockwise, or from right to left in an opposite motion to that of the sun.

The spiral

In archaic astronomy the heavens were usually viewed as spiralling. As Ptolemy states, 'I search with my mind into the multitudinous revolving spirals of the stars.' The spiral appears early in an astronomical context in megalithic art and gains prominence in the Boyne Valley solar constructs. The sun moves in a clockwise spiral and the stars revolve anti-clockwise. The moon's path is not a true circle but a spiral whose successive loops cross the ecliptic in a westward, anti-clockwise motion opposed to the direction of the sun and planets.

On SW18 left-handed spirals are organized in a geometric pattern. Right-handed spirals on Sw7 are balanced by a single anti-clockwise spiral to which a circle and crescent is attached.

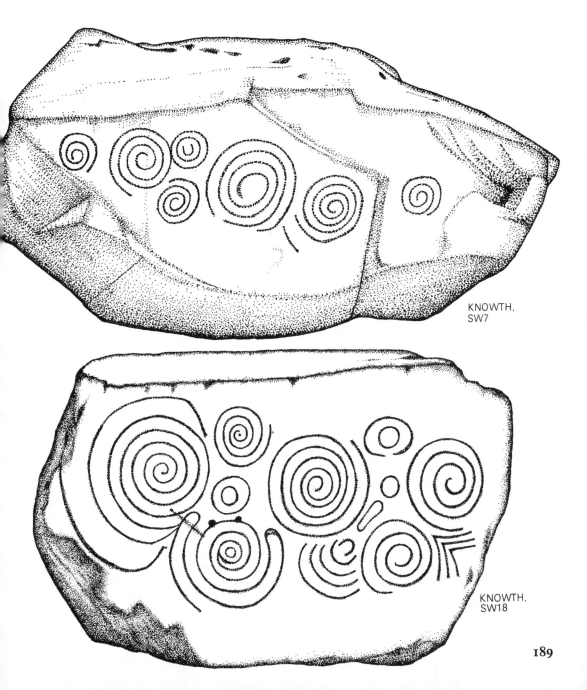

KNOWTH,
SW7

KNOWTH,
SW18

SUMMER SOLSTICE

EQUINOX

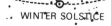
WINTER SOLSTICE

The sun's apparent path through the stars brings it to its furthest points above and below the celestial equator at the solstices and on the equator at equinox. The changing length and arc of the sun's shadow varies each day, corresponding to its changing position in the sky.

SUMMER SOLSTICE — GNOMON

EQUINOX

WINTER SOLSTICE

N

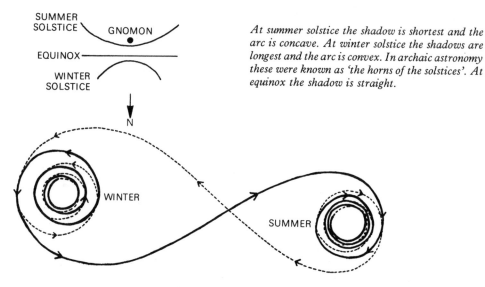

WINTER

SUMMER

At summer solstice the shadow is shortest and the arc is concave. At winter solstice the shadows are longest and the arc is convex. In archaic astronomy these were known as 'the horns of the solstices'. At equinox the shadow is straight.

If the shadows of the sun are correlated over a period of one year in chronological order following their curvature they form a double spiral. In winter the spiral is counter-clockwise and the coils are wide. The shadows begin to straighten as equinox approaches, and after equinox they begin to wind into a clockwise spiral and tighten. They contract until the summer solstice and the right-hand spiral begins to expand after the solstice, straighten again at equinox and return to a left-handed spiral again in winter to continue the process perpetually.

The Boyne Valley artists developed the double spiral and displayed it prominently (overleaf). Recently, an American artist, Charles Ross, arrived at a double spiral in a controlled experiment documenting the sun's path through the year. Using a stationary focused magnifying glass, he placed wooden planks in a fixed position for 366 consecutive days. The sun's rays burned a pattern in the planks which when graphed showed a precisely executed double spiral.

The sun's motion is conceived of spirally in the sundial imagery on SE4. The extreme annual positions of the sun's shadows cast from the upper gnomon are shown in diagram 1. Diagram 2 shows the positions at midday. The sun casts its shadow on the spiral indicating the beginning and end of a solar year at winter solstice. The left-handed winding of the spiral is matched to the anti-clockwise double-spiral year shape at winter. The shadow continually returns to the spiral and emerges from it at the turning of the year. Units of the radial emanate from the spiral in much the same way that lunar crescents emerge from the spiral on SW22.

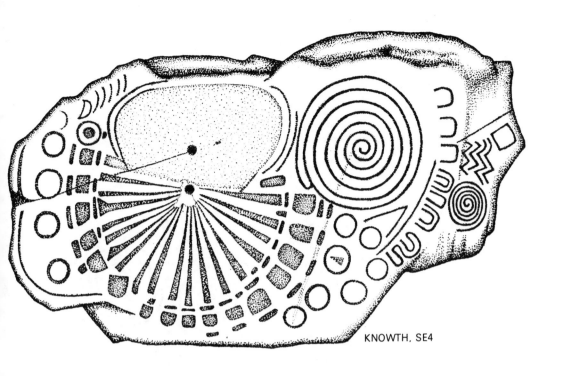

KNOWTH, SE4

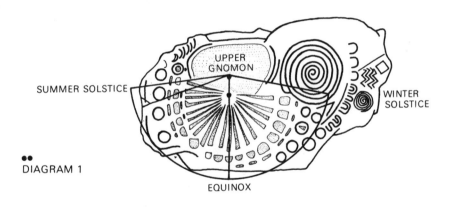

SUMMER SOLSTICE

UPPER
GNOMON

WINTER
SOLSTICE

EQUINOX

●●
DIAGRAM 1

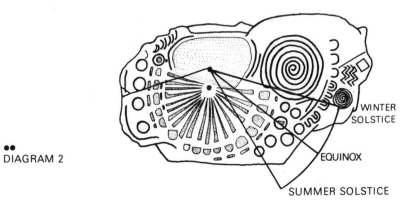

WINTER
SOLSTICE

EQUINOX

●●
DIAGRAM 2

SUMMER SOLSTICE

The major compositions on the kerbstones of New-grange are aligned with reference to the solstices. In principle, the rising and setting positions of the sun at the solstices are equidistant from the cardinal directions which form a cross dividing space into four quarters. The sun also generates time and the four quarters of the year. The cross and the circle represent the sun as a circle which generates the cross of the quarters of time. Newgrange is an elaborate expression of this basic concept.

The quadrangle and the spiral are evolved variants of the cross and circle. The circle of the sun develops into the more complex double spiral and the four quarters of the cross develop into the quadrangle. Both are prominently displayed at Newgrange, linked with astronomical alignments.

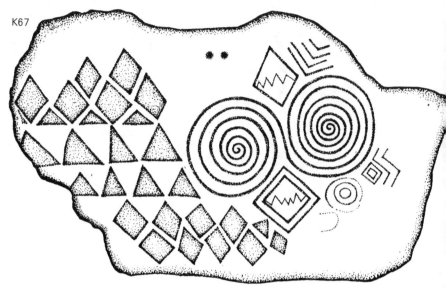

K67

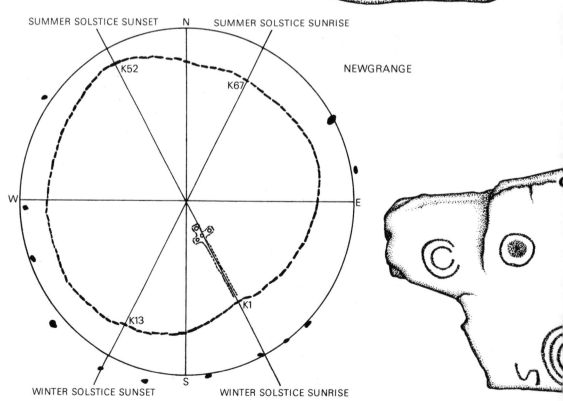

SUMMER SOLSTICE SUNSET   N   SUMMER SOLSTICE SUNRISE

K52

K67

NEWGRANGE

W

E

K1

K13

WINTER SOLSTICE SUNSET   S   WINTER SOLSTICE SUNRISE

The double spiral on K67 tightens on the right and expands on the left, matching the year shape of the sun's shadows. Out of the spiral emerges two quadrangles. This is an image of the universe in its totality and a true cosmogram. A further series of 27 triangles and quadrangles are generated to complete a set of 29 units. A 30th quadrangle is on the right. This is the conventional cyclical format shown on SW22 at Knowth. Its use seems consistent and is surely an intentional, pre-determined arrangement.

K1, 30 stones to the left of K67, is an even more elaborate variation of the quadrangle and the spiral theme. Anti-clockwise spirals on the left form a triple spiral, and the vertical line indicating the sun's position transforms into right-handed spirals creating a cosmic swirl out of which quadrangles are formed. A minimum of intelligent participation is required to see in this ancient fixed horizon marker a celebration of the winter solstice sunrise as a symbol of creation and the power of light over darkness.

The impressive monumental display of imagery on K1 is contrasted by the hidden imagery on K13. The images are occulted and sealed in the mound. It seems that the symbols, as expressions of universal totality, were regarded as having applications on both visible and invisible levels.

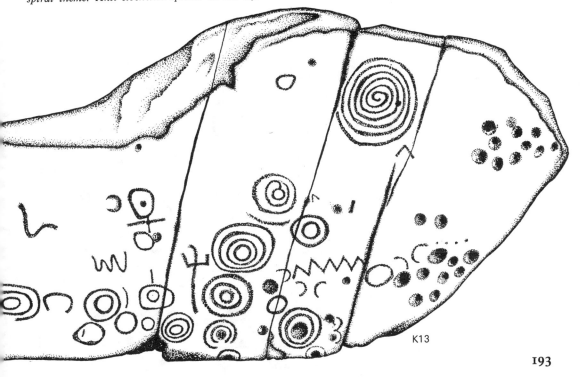

K13

• NEWGRANGE,
CHAMBER,
CENTRAL RECESS

WEST RAY,
ORKNEY,
BRITAIN

NEWGRANGE,
K52, LEFT SIDE

BARCLODIAD Y GAWRES,
ANGLESEY, BRITAIN

CAPE CLEAR,
CO. CORK

EDAY MANSE,
ORKNEY,
BRITAIN

On K67 at Newgrange a double spiral generates 30 units of triangles and quadrangles. The left side of K52 is a variation using a triple spiral and 24 units in a pattern that includes a zigzag indicating 8. Like the right side (see p. 177), on which a representation of the number 9 clearly shows multiplication of 3, these are number symbols expressing abstract numerical concepts which have cosmological significance. The numbers used in calendrical compositions, in which schematic years or months are represented by units which are tied to the objects numbered, are bijections or one-to-one correspondences that count time.

The stones above show the widespread distribution of variations on a fundamental theme. The separation of a formless unity into two reciprocal principles which generate a third and form the multiplicity of creation is a universal and archaic cosmological idea. In sky imagery the sun and moon represent the two opposite principles and the stars represent multiplicity. Together they make up time and space and the entire universe. The megalithic artist apparently viewed the multiplicity of the stars and the multiplicity of the 'world' below as originating from the same source, and both are seen to conform to basic geometrical structures.

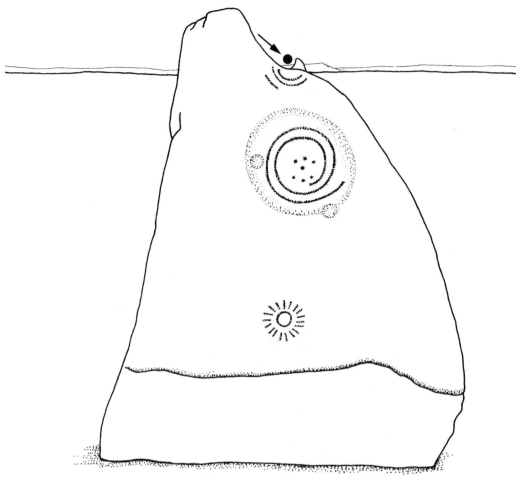

CAIRN N, STANDING STONE

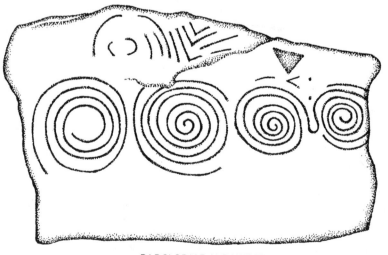

BARCLODIAD Y GAWRES,
ANGLESEY BRITAIN

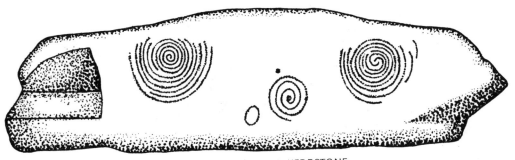

KNOWTH, SATELLITE 12, KERBSTONE

A standing stone near the remains of Cairn N is aligned to the unusually shaped Hill of Fore and the winter solstice sunset indicated by the arrow. The left-handed spiral describes the turning of the year and a rayed disc hovering above a horizontal line makes a pictographic representation of the event. Barclodiad y Gawres, a cruciform passage mound believed to be aligned to summer solstice sunset, and the kerbstones of the Knowth satellites, echo the recurring cosmological themes in unique ways, but within the canons of a traditional system.

The anti-clockwise spiral is associated with the sun's winter solstice and also with the moon in luni-solar spiral compositions. The association comes from the anti-clockwise motion that the moon exhibits in its motion and the prominence of the full moon in the winter sky. At satellite mound 2, a crescent is attached to the anti-clockwise spiral.

KNOWTH, SATELLITE 2, KERBSTONE

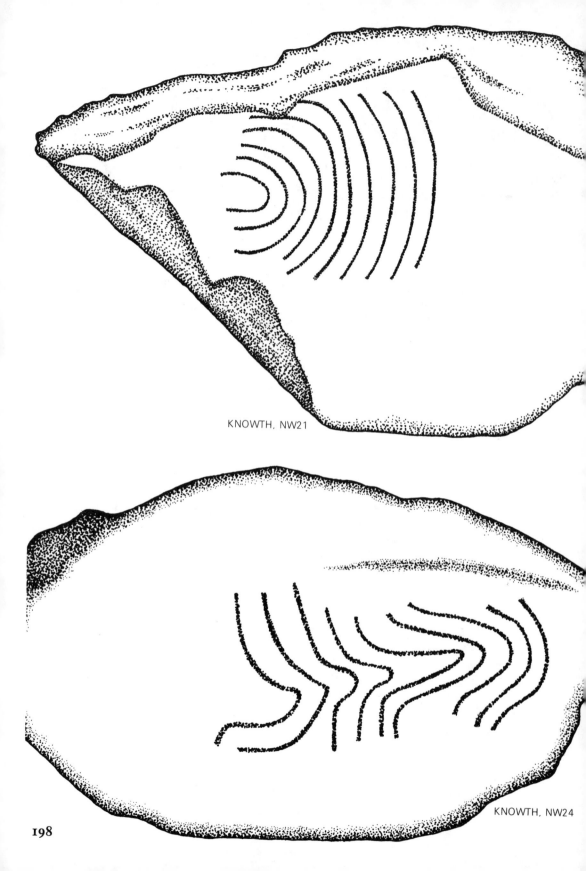

KNOWTH, NW21

KNOWTH, NW24

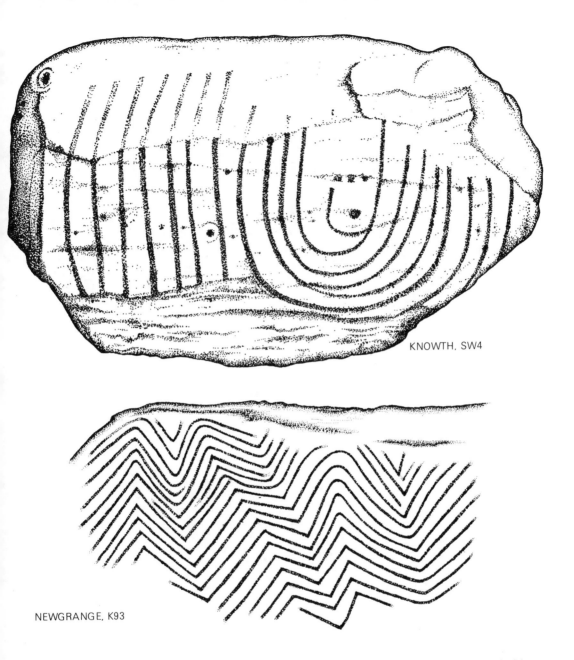

KNOWTH, SW4

NEWGRANGE, K93

Some of the highly abstracted imagery in megalithic art may be representations of light. Panels of fluctuating wave patterns occur frequently and often with direct reference to projected light beams. SW4 is positioned opposite the SE4 sundial composition. Straight lines could easily represent the straight shadows of equinox and the arcs may refer to the curved shadows of the solstices, so that the composition is simply a very abstract year sign. The spiral on the entrance stone of the nearby passage (see p. 103) has a vertical line and the spiral is executed in straight lines making a fret, in contrast to the curved spirals of the Newgrange entrance stone. Patterns on kerbstone 93 are matched to the shadow of standing stone 12 of Newgrange at sunrise, winter solstice (p. 101). A characteristic of the panels and the art in general are lines which build up wave fields immediately suggesting light and energy.

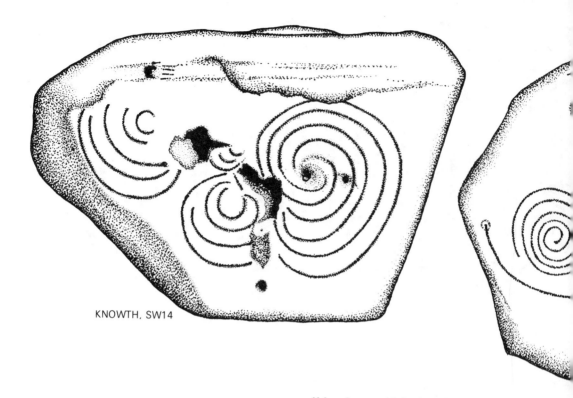

KNOWTH, SW14

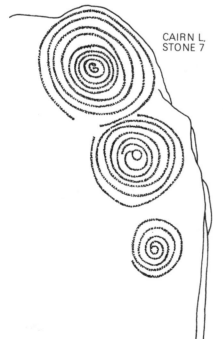

CAIRN L,
STONE 7

Although traceable back to Loughcrew the triple spiral is only fully developed at Newgrange. Elsewhere in the Boyne Valley, single spirals appear at Dowth, double spirals at Knowth. It is interesting that this development relates to the sequence of mound construction, Dowth having been followed by Knowth and Newgrange.

The right edge of stone 8 at Cairn T models the projected beam of light in the chamber. SW2 at Knowth is on the path of the shadows of summer solstice cast from the standing stones outside the passage entrance. The symbolic significance of the number 8 is reflected in the number of spirals, and this theme seems to be carried over from SW1. Positioned opposite SW2 on the other side of the mound, SE2 (next page) seems to elaborate on the number symbolism in a way that recalls imagery at Cairn H.

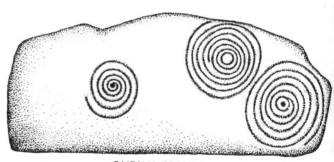

CAIRN H, STONE 1

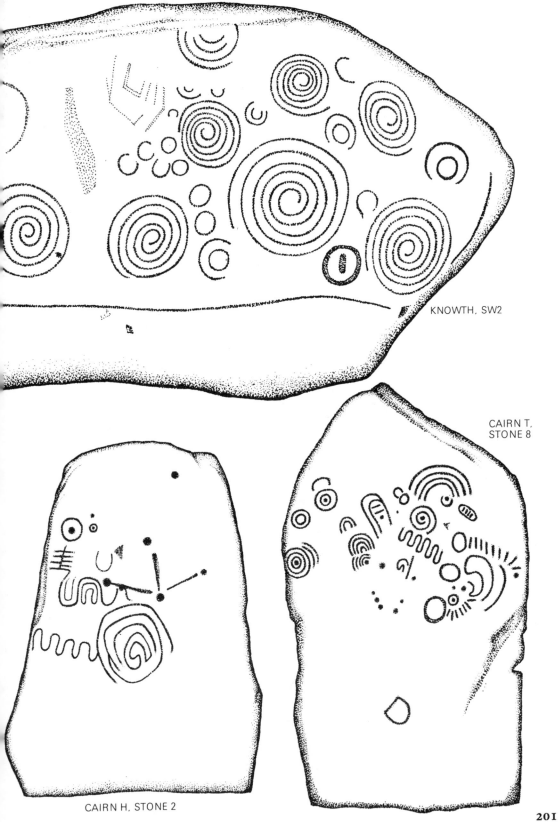

KNOWTH, SW2

CAIRN T,
STONE 8

CAIRN H, STONE 2

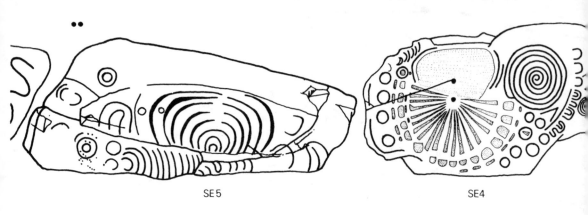

SE 5

SE 4

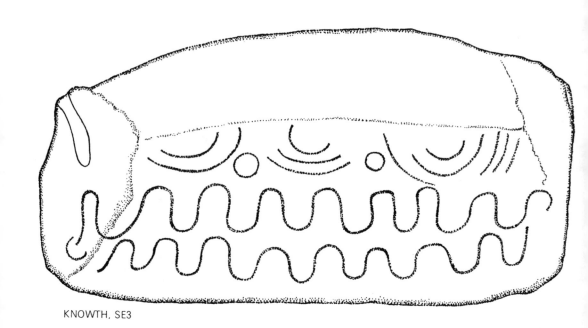

KNOWTH, SE3

CAIRN W,
STONE 2

SE3

SE2

SE1

VI

KNOWTH, SE2

The two wavy lines on SE3 have 17 and 16 turnings respectively, totalling 33. The top row has a left crescent which determines the beginning of the count. The stone is orientated towards the east, facing the appearance of the last crescent in the eastern sky near dawn. A count of 33 lunations brings the wavy line development back to the starting position and the reappearance of the last crescent. This is an alternative method of reckoning a month by the method of bijection. The imagery and positioning of the stone next to the sundial demonstrates that time is being measured. But precisely what is being measured is altogether less certain.

If SE3 represents a day count a similar set of repeat units with the same count may represent a month count on SE2. A wavy line of 16 turnings

emerges from a quadrangle on SE2, paralleling the lower line of SE3. A series of what seems to be 17 crescents is connected to the wavy line and the entire series totals 33. The count of 17 relies on a reconstruction of the damaged part of the stone based on the spacing of the intact units. The count can never be determined with absolute certainty. More than likely it is a calendrical computation based on 33 months and an allusion is made to the 33 day count. The 33-month count could be a more compact representation of its multiple, the 99-month count, which is the formula for a convenient calendrical fitting into 8 years (see Dowth K51, p. 166). Some of the most interesting geometrical numbers and year signs are well preserved. Subsets are attached to the main wavy line and sometimes relate closely to the numerical sequence.

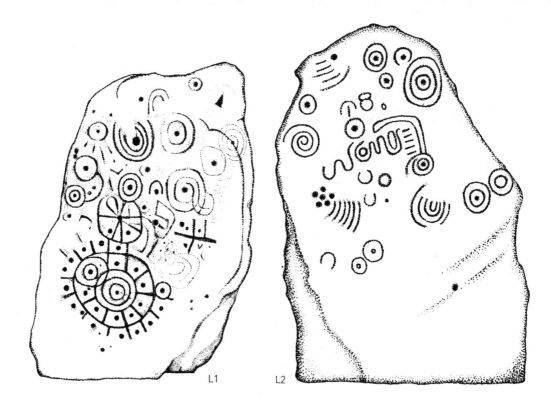

L1   L2

CAIRN T.
PASSAGE STONES

Conclusions

The art and cosmology expressed in the Boyne Valley are a refinement of an already ancient and evolved system that flourished at Loughcrew and had its focal point in Cairn T. Each mound in each complex is synchronized to the beacons of the sun, and each displays numerous variations of the same sky imagery which relates astronomical observations to cosmic models of rotating spheres and shells and the criss-cross patterns they generate. In the final analysis the light itself emerges as the primary symbol of the mound builders.

The human mind tends to associate rayed circles with the sun, crescents with the moon and stars with points. Although essentially correct, these associations are not completely convincing because they are subjective and observer imposed. The beam of light, however, is not posed; it is a real projection contrived by the builders themselves, directly confirming the link between the light and the images.

The art at Cairn T can be viewed at any time, but it is best experienced in the light of the rising sun as it illuminates stones L1, L2 and L3 before flashing into the back recess. The greatest recognizable achievement of the megalith builders was to create functioning structures that would operate indefinitely, conveying their leading ideas through light and symbol. Intentionally or not, they provided the mounds with a built-in self-decoding device that places the art in context and reinforces the communicative power of symbols to the extent that they become universal and timeless imprints of mankind's fascination with the sun, the moon and the stars.

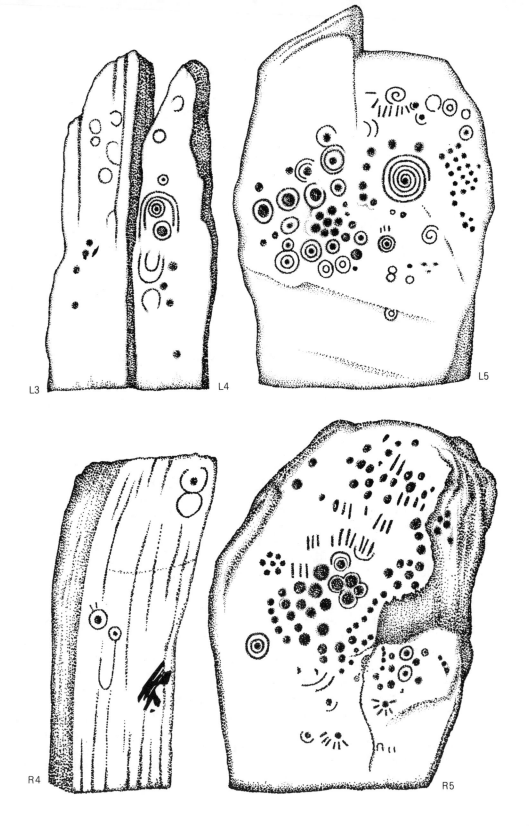

L3

L4

L5

R4

R5

Part IV

EPILOGUE

Aligning stone structures with the sun to create effects of light and shadow is a widespread phenomenon that seems to reflect an inclination inherent in human consciousness. When viewed in the context of other alignments, the megalithic mounds of Ireland are of paramount importance: Not only are they older than any other solar constructs presently known but they are more numerous and in general, built on a larger scale. Newgrange represents only the tip of the iceberg. If these are stones of time, Newgrange is the alarm clock; it serves to awaken us to a grand scheme representing a tradition extending back hundreds, perhaps thousands of years.

In Europe the fascination with light and shadow did not cease with the advent of Christianity, it merely changed focus. Christmas, originally a solstice celebration, was moved four days later to avoid its original pagan associations. As we have seen in this book, in ancient Ireland the equinox was the major celebration and thus Saint Patrick's Day was moved four days earlier to March 17, removing the feast day from its pagan origins. Rather than aligning to equinoxes and solstices medieval churches tended to be aligned toward the rising sun on the feast day of the saint it was dedicated to. Some cathedrals retained solstice and equinox light and shadow effects. Inscribed on the clock on the church tower of Durham Cathedral in England is the statement "Time is a sacred thing." In the cloister a meridian line is engraved partly on the south wall and partly on the pavement. Ten feet from the floor a piece of stone with a circular aperture one inch in diameter is inserted. At noon on summer solstice the projected beam of light strikes the meridian line on the pavement. At noon on winter solstice it strikes the opposite extreme of the meridian line engraved on the wall.

The use of light and shadow techniques in architecture became prevalent in Italian Baroque styles from the late sixteenth to the late seventeenth centuries. Of those who played with the dramatic effects of lighting, Francesco Borromini (1599-1667) is perhaps the most remarkable. He was a passionate student of antiquity and his designs were always based on a rigorous geometrical system. His masterpiece was Sant Ivo della Sapienza, the church of the University of Rome. For this Borromini used a centralized plan based on two interlocking equilateral triangles, forming a six-pointed Star of David. The church is full of symbolism alluding to the Temple of Solomon, the seat of wisdom. He designed a unique statue of a patron in a grotto: a toe on the foot of the statue is kissed by the sun on a certain day of the year. His most haunting image in light is the design of his own tomb, which he never occupied. In a crypt underneath the altar of the tiny church of San Carlino, a cross-shaped basement window casts a cruciform beam of light upon the heart of the entombed, at dawn on Borromini's birthday.

In ancient Egypt, the emergence of the sun at midwinter morning was thought to be a reenactment of the supreme creative moment of the first morning. The Egyptian *Book of Caverns* describes the journey of the sun as it passes through a succession of caves between sunrise and sunset. The same theme is found in *The Book of the Making of the Sun's Disc,* painted on the walls of Ramesside temples. The idea of observing the sun's movement throughout the entire day of the solstice closely parallels what I found in the Boyne Valley wherein Newgrange is the beginning of a series of mounds illuminated by the sun in a succession that culminates at sunset in Dowth.

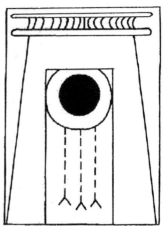

These were not the only parallels. Modern researchers have for quite some time known that the ancient Egyptians were adept at aligning their

The Egyptian hieroglyph, "sun in gate"

monuments to the rising and setting of the sun at significant times during the yearly cycle. It is well known that at Abu Simbel, twice a year the sun shines directly on the sculpted faces of Rameses II, Amon-Re, the Sun God, and Re Harakhty.

An Egyptian hieroglyph of the sighting of the sun through astronomical gates bore a strong resemblance to much of the phenomena I was witnessing during fieldwork in Ireland. The hieroglyph, from a New Kingdom papyrus, clearly depicted the sun framed in a architectural structure.

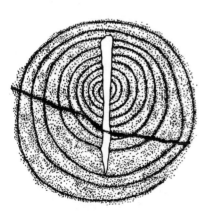

Chaco Canyon light beam, noon of midsummer solstice, 1978

Another interesting parallel occurred in 1978, while I was in the midst of fieldwork in Ireland. A spectacular discovery was made in Chaco Canyon, New Mexico, by Anna Sofaer, an artist engaged in recording native rock engravings. In 1977 she had climbed a high sandstone formation, the Fajada Butte, and to her delight came across two spirals carved on a rock face. These were sheltered by three great stone slabs. She noticed something peculiar. It was around noon on June 29. As the sun was near its highest point in the skies, a thin dagger of light was projected through a crack in the slabs falling just to the right of the largest spiral.

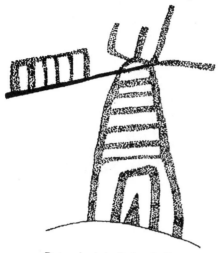

Petroglyph in Baja, California

Sofaer reasoned that this could be an indication of the summer solstice. The area had been inhabited up to about A.D. 1200 by a mysterious people whom the modern Pueblo Indians call the Anasazi or "the ancient folk." American students of native astronomy had been interested in evidence of astronomical orientation in their native monuments and buildings and their systems of perfectly straight long roads. This civilization would be quite capable of constructing a solar device to measure the year. Actually the spiral was found to accurately record both the equinoxes and solstices. At equinox the dagger of light broke into two beams that neatly framed the spiral. On the next summer solstice the ray of light was observed passing exactly through the center of the spiral precisely at noon. Since then several other groups of rock engravings have been recognized as indicators of astronomical events.

In his book published in 1991 called *Beyond the Blue Horizon,* E. C. Krupp, an astronomer and director of Griffith Observatory in Los Angeles called attention to similar light phenomena on a cliff face at San Carlos Mesa in Baja, California.

The engraving resembles the type of houses constructed by the Tipai Indians who inhabit the area. At midmorning during the summer solstice, a triangular chunk of light forms to the left of the carving. The light seeps into the house and after eleven minutes it sinks into the triangular shape framed by the doorway before disappearing. Here is a literal depiction of the house of the sun. This kind of imagery closely reflects the traditions of many tribes in the southwestern United States. As explained by Hopi Don Talayesva in his book *Sun Chief,* it was necessary to keep close watch on the sun's movements to regulate tribal activities. The sunwatcher kept track of planting and harvesting seasons by observing where the sun appeared and disappeared on the horizon throughout the year. Ceremonial events and hunting times were also determined in this way. The point of sunrise on the shortest day of the year was called "sun's winter home." On the longest day of the year the sun was said to occupy his "summer home."

In the 1970s, scholars of Native American cultures began to accept the idea that the knowledge of astronomical events figured significantly in pre-Columbian architecture and planning, and as a consequence, many new discoveries are coming to light, especially in Mesoamerican cultures. The history of noting astronomical alignments in the Americas goes back to at least 1609 with the publication of Garcilaso De la Vega's *The Royal Commentaries of the Incas.* He informs us of the legend of the founder of the Inca dynasty, Manco Capac, first son of the Sun, who descends from the heavens and comes to the valley of Cuzco in Peru. He marks the center of the "Land of Four Quarters" by building the Coricancha, the "Enclosure of Gold," the "Center of the World," now known as the Temple of the Sun.

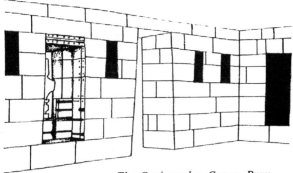

The Coricancha, Cuzco, Peru

De la Vega relates that the emperor takes a seat in the "tabernacle" during solstice celebration ceremonies. This niche can be seen to the left of the door in the illustration above. It was covered with gold plates and settings of gems. Pedro de Cieza de Léon said that the niche is situated so that when the sun rose on the solstice a beam of light would illuminate this "tabernacle" bathing the emperor in golden light. It is here that fact and legend seem to coincide: the emperor was regarded as the living incarnation of the sun, such alignments would not be beyond great architects such as the Inca, and it appears that the series of holes and grooves that can now be seen in the "tabernacle" were used to secure the plates of gold and gems.

Like the Inca, Mayan rulers were also considered incarnations of the sun. Recent decodings of the inscriptions in the Temple of the Sun at Palenque reveal that in his accession texts Chan-Bahlum declares himself a living incarnation of the sun in A.D. 690. The Maya were always regarded as being highly proficient in astronomy. New decipherments are unveiling an even deeper concern with the heavens than previously thought. The Maya hardly distinguish between religious and astronomical matters and even in historical events the position of Venus and the times of the equinoxes and solstices are of fundamental importance.

One result of the recent work of ancient Mayan sites is an awakening of interest in contemporary Mayan people and their rituals. Previously it was not realized that there is a close relationship between the ceremonies of the living Maya and those of their ancestors. A book by Rafael Girard, *Los Mayas: su civilizacion, su historia, sus vinculaciones continentales* published in 1966 in Mexico is only now beginning to be translated. It gives us a unique view of the place of solstices and equinoxes in ancient rituals as practiced by a contemporary people. Girard describes a ceremony at the start of the solar year (in the spring) in which five stones are obtained representing five magical positions in an ideogram of the cosmos. The ritual is a reenactment of the creation replicating the way the gods fashioned the world at the beginning of time. The act of placing the stones not only reenacts the creation of the world but it starts the new calendar by resetting the world in motion. The first stone is placed in the northeast and corresponds to the sun in the rising position of the summer solstice. The second stone is placed in the northwest, the setting position of the sun in the same solstice. The third stone, corresponding to the setting position of the sun at winter solstice, is placed in the southwest. The fourth stone is placed in the southeast and corresponds to the sun in the rising position of the winter solstice. Lastly in the middle is placed the stone representing the God of the Center of the World thus reproducing the schematic of the universe. Other modern rituals such as "the Raising of the Sky" performed by priests representing the gods of the four corners of the world closely relate to creation mythology now being revealed in ancient Mayan texts. Apparently the modern rituals echo with stones what their ancestors did on a larger scale with their temples.

Throughout Mesoamerica known pyramid alignments to the rising sun at equinoxes and solstices are numerous although I do not believe a complete and systematic study of this has yet been made. There will be many more revelations to be uncovered in this rich field. One alignment of light and shadow in particular seems to have captured the imagination of people to a large extent. At the spring equinox each year, up to fourteen thousand visitors gather at Chichén Itzá in the Yucatan to observe a symbolic seasonal display of light. The main temple, El Castillo, shows a strong Toltec influence but was built in the tenth century A.D. by a Mayan group that moved to Chichén Itzá from the Gulf Coast.

The pattern of light and shadow develops on the west balustrade of the north stairway about two hours before the sun sets. First a flash of light creates a triangle at the top of the staircase. Slowly and dramatically, one

El Castillo at equinox sunset

at a time, a series of seven triangles descend the staircase to unite with a serpent's head at the bottom. The writhing snake produced by light effects appears to descend from the sky. As this temple is dedicated to Kùkulcàn, the plumed serpent-god, whose motif is used throughout the temple, we are apparently witnessing a symbolic seasonal descent of the serpent god from the heavens, which is quite appropriate as this god is associated with the equinox, death, rebirth, Venus as the morning star, wind, rain and fertility.

As spectacular as they are, the solar alignments of the megalithic mounds of Ireland are not really surprising when such structuring is considered as a universal human tendency rather than a unique innovation. The alignments are completely within the range of the technical capabilities of Neolithic civilization as we presently conceive it, although we may be awed at the number, the size, and the degree of sophistication attained. They provide us with a key stepping-stone to the understanding that the origins of astronomy, mankind's oldest and most widely practiced science, can be traced back to the ritual observation of the sun and moon. However, they do not radically and dramatically change our basic perceptions regarding the earliest developments in astronomy. It is the stone engravings which do that and the information they contain is what is truly surprising.

It is the presence of sophisticated calendars and sundials that completely changes our view of the history of science. Previously such developments were perceived as having first begun in the Middle East, with the earliest known sundials being Egyptian, dating from 1200 B.C. But the fully worked out, correctly aligned dials I describe at Knowth predate the Egyptian devices by thousands of years, making the area of major breakthroughs in sundialling Neolithic Western Europe. Regardless of any ritual considerations the Calendar Stone (page 144) represents the establishment of a reliable calendar, the basic prerequisite for formulating the beginnings of true astronomy, regardless of how elementary. It is a formidable demonstration of the vigor of prehistoric creativity and imagination in confronting the fundamental problems inherent in any serious calendar making.

In looking at kerbstone NE7, a minimal amount of participation is required in order to realize that the artist is grappling with the problem of the unfolding of time as perceived through the motions of the moon. Two separate time-series displays are ingeniously linked to provide visual access to the presentation of information.

Kerbstone NE7 at Knowth. A diagram of this stone in context appears on page 139.

The time-series display on top is a numerical representation of the lunar cycle. The graphical element that plots the data is a wavy line with thirty oscillations counting the days in a month. The same period of time is represented below in terms of a graphic design incorporating visual aspects of the moon's appearance in various phases. The artist explores the unfolding of time by cleverly integrating the two separate data sets. The result is that the viewer is given the advantage of conceptualizing a month in both form and number in an integrated visual display. On a single stone we are witnessing not only some of the earliest recorded attempts at astronomy but the earliest known records of mankind's use of number as a tool in representing time.

The engravings are capable of transmitting other kinds of information.

My very first insight into the meaning of a rock inscription came from the recognition that the vertical line on the entrance stone at Newgrange indicates an entrance to a passage (page 72) and that vertical lines on the entrance stones at Knowth have the same function (page 103). Newgrange, Knowth, and Dowth form a triad, they dominate the landscape and are built exactly on the same scale. Both Knowth and Dowth contain two passages whereas only one had been discovered at Newgrange. During the excavations at Newgrange workers in the interior chamber heard rocks falling further on in the interior of the mound. This would indicate the presence of a chamber. Professor O'Kelly thought this was highly likely and he searched unsuccessfully around the rear of the mound looking for the entrance. I think it is very probable that there is a second passage. I would venture to say that if it does exist it would be found by probing behind stone K52 (page 73) which has a very pronounced vertical line. This would indicate a passage that would align to the setting sun at summer solstice and together the three mounds would align to extreme rising and setting positions of the sun throughout the year.

The Calendar Stone (Page 144) is a luni-solar time-measuring device that provides a frame of reference by which the lunar cycle can be compared to the solar cycle. It uses the same technique employed by the Coligny Calendar discovered in Europe and attributed to Celtic Druids dating from the first century A.D. John Phelps felt that the origins of the Coligny Calendar had roots extending far back in antiquity. In his book, *The Prehistoric Solar Calendar* (1955), he wrote: "The natural conclusion was that there had been a prehistoric solar calendar of a very remote origin, and of a type wholly unknown to the modern world and the ancient classical world; and which, except in Celtic regions had become extinct nearly 2400 years ago." I believe that the Calendar Stone at Knowth provides clear evidence for this assertion.

I had for long held that not only the Celtic calendar but Celtic art had its origins in Irish Neolithic Culture. Outside of some of the more ornate engravings at Newgrange I lacked strong evidence for this idea. In September of 1982, Professor Eoghan's excavation at Knowth provided a missing link.

The illustrations on the previous page are two views of a small stone just over three inches long in size but gigantic in their implications. It is a ritual object in the form of a flint mace-head. Carbon dating places it at about 5,000 years old. Apparently it was attached to a stick by means of a hole drilled through its center. Professor Eoghan described it as "the only one of its kind and of particular significance in its early context." He added that its craftwork made it a forerunner of the much later Tara Brooch, using spirals and delta-shaped whirls in ridges. The single discovery shattered the long-held and widespread view that Celtic art in Ireland was imported from abroad.

Controversies regarding the astronomical alignments at Stonehenge have raged for centuries. The new discipline of archaeoastronomy has been immensely successful in resolving many controversies in a relatively short period of time. Today almost any history of astronomy will feature a photograph of Stonehenge, with practically everyone agreeing that the formation is at least aligned to the summer solstice.

Recently while in Vermont I visited an old friend, Sig Lonegren. Among other things Sig is a writer, a dowser and an expert on labyrinths. We had lectured together in England but I had not seen him for many years. He related an interesting story about a recent excursion he had made to the Loughcrew Mountains in Ireland accompanied by Jack Roberts and Toby Hall, members of the original team I had organized to explore solar alignments, and the English writers and researchers John Mitchell and Jamie George. They intended to view the entry of light into Cairn T during the spring equinox. To their surprise, upon reaching the entrance of the passage they were met by a group of researchers from the archaeological department of Cork University equipped with clipboards, cameras, and stopwatches. Jack was told that they could not be admitted as scientific research was in progress. Jack was justifiably vexed as he and I had been the very first to have witnessed the phenomena and had for years tried our best to bring it to the attention of archaeologists. Sig smiled at the irony of the situation as he listened to exclamations of awe from the researchers inside the chamber.

I am reminded of a Gaelic poem about Newgrange written by the ancient Irish poet, MacNia, son of Oenn:

> Behold the *sidh* before your eyes,
> It is manifest to you that it is a king's mansion,
> Which was built by the firm Dagda,
> It was a wonder, a court, a wonder hill.

December 21, 1993
Great Barrington, Massachusetts

Select bibliography

Abbreviations

JRSAI   *Journal of the Royal Society of Antiquaries of Ireland*
PRIA   *Proceedings of the Royal Irish Academy*
PSAS   *Proceedings of the Society of Antiquaries of Scotland*
TRIA   *Transactions of the Royal Irish Academy*
UJA   *Ulster Journal of Archaeology*

ARNHEIM, R. *Visual Thinking*, London 1970.
BEAUFORT, L. C. 'An Essay upon the state of Architecture and Antiquities, previous to the landing of the Anglo-Normans in Ireland', *TRIA* 15 (1828), 101–242.
BRENNAN, M. *The Boyne Valley Vision*, Dublin 1980.
BURENHULT, G. *The Archaeological Excavation at Carrowmore, Co. Sligo, Ireland*, Stockholm 1980.
COFFEY, G. 'On the Tumuli and Inscribed Stones at New Grange, Dowth and Knowth', *TRIA* 30 (1892–96), 1–96.
—— 'Notes on the Prehistoric Cemetery of Loughcrew with a Fasciculus of Photographic Illustrations of the Sepulchral Cairns', *TRIA* 31 (1896–1901), 23–38.
—— 'Knockmany', *JRSAI* (1898), 93–111.
—— 'Prehistoric Grave at Seskilgreen', *JRSAI* 41 (1911), 175–79.
—— *Newgrange and Other incised Tumuli in Ireland*, Dublin 1912, reissued Poole 1977.
COLLINS, A. E. P. and WATERMAN, D. M. 'Knockmany Chambered Grave, Co. Tyrone', *UJA* series 3, 15 (1952), 26–30.
CONWELL, E. A. 'On Ancient Sepulchral Cairns on the Loughcrew Hills', *PRIA* 9 (1864–66), 355–79.
—— *The Discovery of the Tomb of Ollamh Fodhla*, Dublin 1873.
EOGAN, G. 'The Knowth (County Meath) Excavations', *Antiquity* 41 (1967), 203–4.
—— 'Excavations at Knowth, Co. Meath, 1962–1965', *PRIA* 66C (1967–68), 299–400.
—— 'Excavations at Knowth, Co. Meath, 1968', *Antiquity* 43 (1969), 8–14.
FRAZER, W. 'Incised Sculpturings on stones in County Meath', *PSAS* 27 (1892–93), 294–340.
GATTY, A. *The Book of Sundials*, London 1900.
HARTNETT, P. J. 'Excavations of a Passage Grave at Fourknocks, Co. Meath', *PRIA* 58C (1956–57), 197–277.
HERITY, M. *Irish Passage Graves*, Dublin 1974.
KRUPP, E. C. *In Search of Ancient Astronomies*, New York 1977, London 1979.
LEASK, H. 'Inscribed Stones Recently Discovered at Dowth Tumulus, Co. Meath', *PRIA* 41C (1932–34), 162–67.
LOCKYER, N. J. *The Dawn of Astronomy*, London 1894, reissued Cambridge, Mass. 1964.
—— *Stonehenge and other British Stone Monuments Astronomically Considered*, London 1909.
MACALISTER, R. A. S. *Ireland in Pre-Celtic Times*, Dublin 1921.

—— *The Archaeology of Ireland*, London 1928.
—— 'A Burial Cairn on Seefin Mountain, Co. Wicklow', *JRSAI* 62 (1932), 153–57.
—— 'Two Carved Stones in the Seefin Cairn', *JRSAI* 67 (1937), 312–13.
—— 'Preliminary report on the excavation of Knowth', *PRIA* 49C (1943–44), 131–66.
MARSHACK, A. 'Lunar Notation on Upper Paleolithic remains', *Science* 146 (1964), 743–45.
—— *The Roots of Civilization*, New York 1972.
—— 'Upper Paleolithic Notation and Symbol', *Science* 178 (1972), 817–28.
—— 'Cognitive Aspects of Upper Paleolithic Engraving, *Current Anthropology* 13, no. 3–4 (1972).
—— 'Exploring the Mind of Ice Age Man', *National Geographic* 147, 4 (1975), 62–89.
MICHELL, J. *The Old Stones of Land's End*, London 1974.
—— *Megalithomania: Artists, antiquarians, and archaeologists at the old stone monuments*, London and New York 1982.
NEUGEBAUER, O. *The Exact Sciences in Antiquity*, 2nd edn, New York 1962.
O'KELLY, C. *Illustrated Guide to New Grange*, revised edn, Cork 1978.
—— *Passage-grave Art in the Boyne Valley*, Cork 1978.
O'KELLY, M. J. *Newgrange*, London 1982, New York 1983.
Ó RÍORDÁIN, S. P. and DANIEL, G. E. *New Grange and The Bend of the Boyne*, London and New York 1964.
PATRICK, J. 'Midwinter Sunrise at Newgrange', *Nature* 249 (1974), 517–19.
POWER, M. *An Irish Astronomical Tract*, Irish Texts Society, vol. XIV, London 1914.
RENFREW, C. *Before Civilization*, London 1973.
ROTHERHAM, E. 'On the Excavation of a Cairn on Shieve-na-Caillighe, Loughcrew', *JRSAID* 25 (1895), 311–16.
SHEE, E. 'Techniques of Irish Passage Grave Art', in Daniel, G. E. and Kjaerum, P. (eds.) *Megalithic Graves and Ritual*, Jutland Archaeological Society 1973, 163–72.
SHEE-TWOHIG, E. *The Megalithic Art of Western Europe*, Oxford 1981.
SMITH, S. 'An Account of some Characters found on Stones on the Tops of Knockmany Hill, County Tyrone', *PRIA* 2 (1840–44), 190–91.
STUKELEY, W. *Abury Described*, London 1743.
VALLANCEY, C. *Collectanea de rebus Hibernicis*, Dublin 1770–1804.
WAKEMAN, W. F. 'The Megalithic Sepulchral Chamber of Knockmany, Co. Tyrone', *JRSAI* 14 (1876–78), 95–106.
—— 'On Several Sepulchral Scribings and Rock Markings, Found in the North-West of Ireland', *JRSAI* 15 (1879–82), 538–60.
WAUGH, A. *Sundials, Their Theory and Construction*, New York 1973.
WILDE, W. *The Beauties of the Boyne and its Tributary, the Blackwater*, Dublin 1849.
WILKINSON, G. *Practical Geology and Ancient Architecture of Ireland*, London 1845.

Index of sites and stones

Page numbers in italic indicate illustrations

ATHGREANY *161*

BALLINVALLY *69*; loose stones found at 62, *63*, 132,
133, *180*, *181*
Baltinglass 8; astronomical alignments 64, 122, *123*
Barclodiad y Gawres 140, *141*, *196*

CARNANMORE 8, *140*
Cairn F, astronomical alignments 55, 69, 108, 109,
114, *115*; missing stone *165*; stone 2 *115*, *151*;
stone 3 114, *115*, *151*; stone 5 *115*, *187*
Cairn H, astronomical alignments 63, *64*, 108, 109,
114; stone 1 *114*, *200*; stone 2 *114*, *200*
Cairn I, astronomical alignments 55, 63, 69, 98, *108*,
109, 114; stone 2 *109*, *165*; stone 4 *109*, *181*; stone 5
109, *173*; stone 6 *109*, *173*; stone 6a *109*, *165*
Cairn L, astronomical alignments 45, 48, 50, 51, 53,
63, 69, 108, *110*, *111*, *112*, 121, *175*; standing stone
48, 105, *110*, *111*; stone basin *110*, *111*, 175; stone
3 *111*, *112*, 113; stone 4 *111*, *112*, 113; stone 7 *111*,
200; stone 8 *111*, *156*; stone 13 *111*, *112*, *113*; stone
19 *111*, *175*; stone 20 *110*, *111*; stone 22 *111*, *182*
Cairn N 69; astronomical alignments *196*, 197
Cairn S, astronomical alignments 55, 69, 87, 108,
114, *116*, 117, 121; stone 2 *116*, *117*; stone 3 *116*,
156
Cairn T, astronomical alignments 45, 46, 47, 48, *49*,
50, 52, 62, 63, 69, 87, *90–100*, 108, 109, 114, 123,
169, 200, *201*; roofstones *169*, *184*; stone L1 *91*,
96, *204*; stone L2 *91*, *96*, *204*; stone L3 48, *91*, *96*;
stone L4 *91*, *96*, 204, *205*: stone L5 *91*, *96*, 204,
205; stone R4 *91*, *205*; stone R5 *91*, *205*; stone 1 *91*,
96, *99*, *162*; stone 2 *91*, *96*; stone 4 *91*, *97*; stone 5
91, *96*, *97*, *158*; stone 6 52, *94*, 98, *99*; stone 8 *91*,
96, *99*, 200, *201*; stone 10 *91*, *160*; stone 11 *91*, *96*;
stone 12 *91*, *96*; stone 14 47, *92*, *93*, *94*, *95*, *96*, *97*,
100, *165*, 169; stone 15 *91*, *97*, *151*; stone 20 *91*, *148*
Cairn U, astronomical alignments 53, 63, 69, 87,
89, *110*, *116*, *117*, 121; stone fragment 140; stone 8
87, *89*, *117*, *177*; stone 10 *117*, *187*; stone 14 *117*,
182
Cairn V 69; astronomical alignments *86*, 87
Cairn W 69; astronomical alignments 87, *124*, *125*;
stone 2 *124*, *202*
Cairn X1 31, 69, *161*
Cape Clear 8, *195*
Carapito *162*, *163*
Carrowmore 8; mound 7 *61*
Cloverhill 8; *180*

DISSIGNAC, astronomical alignments 62
Dowth, astronomical alignments 9, 13, 51, 53, 63, 64,
65, 70, 71, *82–84*, 121, 123, *127*; entrance stone *82*;
chamber stone *160*; stone K50 *166*; stone K51 *166*,
167, 203; stone K52 *166*, *167*; stone 5 *83–85*; stone
6 *83–85*; stone 13 *83*, 123, *127*, *160*, *161*; wavy line
at *141*

EDAY MANSE *195*

FOURKNOCKS *8*; lintel stones *168*, *185*; stone in
chamber *185*; stones in passage *184*

GAVRINIS, astronomical alignments 33, 54, *168*

JEREZ DE LOS CABALLEROS *164*

KILLIN HILL 8, *177*, *187*
Killtierney 8, 140, *141*
King's Mountain *180*
Knockmany, astronomical alignments *123*, *124*, *125*;
stone 1 *123*, *125*; stone 2 *123*, 125, *183*; stone 3 *123*,
125; stone 4 *123*, 125, *180*, *181*; stone 5 *123*, *125*;
stone 6 *123*, *124*
Knowth, astronomical alignments 52, 57, 58, 59, 65,
70, 82, *101–105*, ·123; eastern passage *102*, *103*,
107, *172*, *174*; entrance stone of eastern passage
102, *103*, 107, 155; entrance stone western passage
58, 65, *101*, *102*, 107, *128*, *176*; standing stones 58,
65, *101*, *102*, *104*, *105*, 200; stone basins 107, 132,
133, *174*; stones in satellites of *128*, *130*, *162*, *197*;
stone NE1 *102*, *103*; stone NE4 *102*, *158*, *159*, 161;
stone NE6 *102*, *136*, *137*, *138*, *139*; stone NE7 *102*,
139; stone NE23 *102*, *148*; stone NE28 *102*, *155*;
stone NW1 *102*, *103*, *128*, 155; stone NW4 *102*,
146, *147*; stone NW5 *102*, *172*, *173*; stone NW6
102, *138*; stone NW7 *102*, 148, *149*; stone NW8
102, *140*; stone NW9 *102*, *153*; stone NW10 *102*,
156; stone NW12 *102*, *154*, 155; stone NW15 *102*,
156, *157*, 172; stone NW16 *102*, *172*; stone NW17 *102*,
151, *152*, *153*, *172*; stone NW18 *102*, *151*, *152*,
172; stone NW19 *148*, *149*, *150*; stone NW20 *102*,
150; stone NW21 *102*, *198*; stone NW 23 *102*, *143*;
stone NW24 *102*, *198*; stone SE1 *102*, *103*, *203*;
stone SE2 *102*, 200, *203*; stone SE3 *202*, *203*; stone
SE4 *102*, *190*, *191*, *199*, *202*, *203*; stone SE5 *172*,
202, *203*; stone SE6 *102*, *172*; stone SE28 *102*, *132*;
stone SE29 *102*, *139*; stone SE31 *102*, 147; stone
SE34 *102*, *142*; stone SW1 *101–103*, *128*, *129*, *176*;
stone SW2 *102*, *129*, *170*, *176*, 200, *201*; stone
SW3 *102*, *129*, *156*, *157*, *170*; stone SW4 *102*, *170*,
199; stone SW5 *102*, *171*; stone SW6 *102*, *170*,
171; stone SW7 *102*, *189*; stone SW9 *102*, *138*;
stone SW10 *102*, *142*; stone SW14 *102*, *200*; stone
SW17 *102*, *137*; stone SW18 *102*, *189*; stone SW22
144, *145*, *146*, *148*, *190*, *193*; stone SW23 *102*, *144*,
145: stone South 0 *102*, *154*, 155; western passage
in *102*, *103*, 107, *172*, *174*

LE PETIT MONT *166*
Lia Fal 14, *120*, *121*

MOUND G 70, *71*, *140*
Mound K 70; astronomical alignments *122*, 123,
141; engravings *170*, *171*, 174
Mound L 70; astronomical alignments 123
Mound Z 70; astronomical alignments 123; stone
basin *174*; stone from *178*, *179*, *186*
NEWGRANGE, astronomical alignments 7, 9, *11*, *12*,
18, *19*, *20*, *21*, 22, *29*, *30*, *32*, *33*, *34*, *36*, *37*, 45, 50,
53, 58, 64, 65, 67, *70–77*, 82, *101*, *118*, *119*, 123,
126, *192*; entrance stone 18, 58, 65, *72*, *76*, *79*, *101*,
192, *193*; corbel stones *75*, *76*, *143*, *159*, *183*, *187*;
lintel of roofbox *74*, *75*, *168*; roofbox *74*, *75*, *76*, *79*,

80; standing stone 1 58, 65, 67, 72, 74, 77, 101; standing stone 2 77, 126; standing stone 5 118, 119; standing stone 10 118, 119; standing stone 11 77; standing stone 12 77, 101, 199; stone basins 78, 81; stone C10 79, 194; stone C22 79, 80; stone K4 126; stone K13 192, 193; stone K18 118; stone K52 72, 73, 166, 177, 192, 194, 195; stone K67 192, 193, 195; stone K82 118, 119; stone K91 175; stone K93 101, 199; stone L18 79, 80; stone L19 79, 80; stone R12 76, 79; stone R21 76, 79, 118, 119, 126

POLA DE ALANDE 145

SATELLITE K see Mound K

Satellite 2 see Mound Z
Seefin, astronomical alignments 184; stones in 185
Sess Kilgreen, astronomical alignments 55, 88, 89; roofing slab 35; stone 5 88; stone 6 88, 89

TAL QADI 152
Tara, astronomical alignments 14, 15, 53, 54, 63, 120, 121, 175; engraved stone 120, 175
Tournant 182, 183

VALE DE RODRIGO 141

WEST RAY 194

2103